OUR LOVE IS OUR POWER:

Working With the Net
of Light that Holds the Earth

—————◆•◉•◆—————

By

Sharon McErlane

Net of Light Press
www.grandmothersspeak.com

Published by Net of Light Press, 9/1/09
www.grandmothersspeak.com

ISBN: 978-0-9788468-1-7

Cover Art: *Mother and Daughter*, 1981.
© Meinrad Craighead.
Photograph courtesy of Pomegranate Communications, Inc.

Cover Design: Timothy W. Brittain

Printed in the United States of America by Net Pub Press

Copies of this book are available through Net of Light Press at
www.grandmothersspeak.com

"When the wisdom of the Grandmothers
is heard, the world will heal."
—*Native American prophecy*

CONTENTS

INTRODUCTION
Return of God the Mother

The time of earth changes, foretold by ancient teachings is upon us. At such moments in history, the Divine comes to Earth to intervene. In the ancient Vedic text, the Bhagavad Gita, Lord Krishna says that when unrighteousness holds sway and darkness covers the Earth, then God will come to restore the path of righteousness. This moment in history has been referred to in many cultures as the time when God the Mother will return to earth. We are living at a moment when the energies of yin, the feminine principle, and the energies of yang, the masculine principle, on our planet are shifting.

We inhabit a sacred universe. Earth, water, trees, animals and people hum with the presence of the Divine. It just takes a little 'something' to call that presence forth. That little something appeared to me one day while I was walking my dog, in the form of the Great Council of the Grandmothers. Shortly after that life-altering visitation I began to call women together to share their message and receive their empowerment into the energy of yin.

An aspect of the Divine Feminine has come to Earth in the form of the Grandmothers. These wise elders invite us to join in partnership with them to hold the earth steady. **"We will infuse the energy of yin back into your planet whether or not you work with us,"** they say. **"But if you choose to participate, you will have the joy of being along on the ride with us."** I have had this joy now since 1996 and working with the Council has blessed my life.

Women began to meet at my home in early 1997 to hear the Grandmothers' message, and as we worked with these wise elders and they entered our lives, each of us experienced the power of the Feminine Principle of creation. This connection radically changed us. The Grandmothers' mission (and ours) is to restore the Feminine Principle of energy back to our beloved planet, which at this time suffers from a depletion of the energy of yin and an over supply of the energy of yang.

The Empowerment the Grandmothers bring fills a woman with a steadiness and grace she has never before known as they ignite the flame of sacred Yin within the heart of each woman. The Grandmothers give the Cloak of Comfort to men, letting them know what it's like to be held and comforted by the Mother—something most men in our culture have never experienced.

We who have been drawn to these wise teachers have seen our lives change in the most wonderful and practical ways and this of course inspires us to share their message with others who in turn pass it on to their sisters and brothers. Now, each month, all over the world Grandmothers' groups gather to pass their message and gift of empowerment to others, and because the Grandmothers' work is selfless, we gladly do this as service.

Watching this message spread over the world is enormously gratifying, but the most moving evidence of the Grandmothers' power lies in how they effect change in the lives of those they call. Early on they said, **"The greatest use you can make of our message is to live it."** This dictum has become our goal.

Now and then something happens that makes me aware of what a different woman I am today from the one who first encountered the Grandmothers. Yesterday I spoke with a friend I hadn't seen in a long while and she asked if working with the Grandmothers had changed me. Her question gave me pause but after I thought about it I said, "I'm calm now. I don't have anxiety hanging over me the way I used to. I'm relaxed and confident and I know I'm on the right track. This may sound strange to you," I said, "when you remember how anxious I always was, but the truth is, it's rare these days for me to doubt myself. This," I said, "has to be the Grandmothers."

I don't know why I'm still surprised by stories I hear of the Grandmothers' miracles. I should be used to them by now. People from across the world write, telling me how the Grandmothers have blessed their lives, saved them from harm, drawn their families together, and averted accidents, illnesses and calamities of all sorts. Take Sophie for instance, a beautiful woman in her 80s who went shopping with her daughter about a year after she received the Grandmothers Empowerment and had a stroke in Nordstrom's sportswear department. Knowing her mother relied on the Grandmothers, as soon as she saw Sophie fall, her daughter screamed, "Grandmothers, help my mother!"

It turned out there was a hospital next door, so paramedics were there in a flash. And no sooner did they get Sophie to the E.R. than a visiting specialist who'd come that day to train the staff in a new, life-saving stroke treatment jumped into action. Within thirty minutes Sophie was sitting up, her recovery so rapid that the staff couldn't stop talking about it, and when she went home, she suffered few ill effects. Today she walks, drives and carries on conversations just as she always did. When she tells the story of what happened to her that day she gives full credit for her recovery to the Grandmothers. And her story is only one of many.

The Grandmothers give purpose to seemingly meaningless lives and joy to grieving hearts but their universal gift is that of confidence. Everyone they touch fills with it. Women who initially describe themselves as shy begin to speak out. Some go on to teach classes or offer seminars. I love to see the looks of wonder on their faces when they share what has happened to them. They can't stop being surprised either.

They break into new careers, stand up to dominating husbands, mothers and bosses and take control of their finances. They leave vertigo, phobias, bad habits and relationships behind. Once they feel the Grandmothers love, they automatically love themselves, and others. Most amazing is, this happens with what the Grandmothers call, "effortless effort." They are delighted to discover that both loving others and accepting love becomes easy—natural. **"When a woman awakens to the beauty/power within her,"** the Grandmothers say, **"she will bloom as the flower she has always been and always will be."** One after another I have seen women and now men too come into bloom.

As I was finishing this paragraph, one of the women in the Grandmothers' group called to tell me that she no longer allows herself to get out of bed in the morning until she has first spent time with the Grandmothers. "If I forget about it and just get up," she said, "the day doesn't go right. It's a dud. So I make myself lie there until I've talked to them. Then everything flows."

The Grandmothers are loving, joyful and funny. They are compassionate, approachable and will help anyone who calls on them. They have come to help humanity, to save life on earth and say they have no time to waste. **"The time is now,"** they say, and when they say "now," they don't mean some indeterminate moment in the future. **"The present imbalance of energy on earth has placed all life in danger,"** they say. **"It is time to return to balance, and for this, women must lead. Women must take the first step. It can be no other way."** The Grandmothers mean what they say, say what they mean, and they don't mess around.

Many people have asked, "Why did the Grandmothers come to

you? What was it that made them choose you?" To these questions I always answer, "I don't know," because honestly, I don't. Before they showed up I had been praying hard to be of service, to work with everything I had, to cook on all my burners, so-to-speak. This may have had some bearing on their coming, but I don't really know. When I began to work with the Grandmothers, I put this question to them too, but all they would ever say in response was, **"Why not you?"** After hearing this a few times, I finally came to accept that they had needed someone to do this job, and why shouldn't it have been me?

The Grandmothers are on a mission to bring the energies of yin and yang back into balance—and before I met them, I too was on a mission. Mine was to live my life one hundred percent, in service to God. I was serious about this. I had reached my mid-fifties by this point and had for many years meditated, studied spiritual pathways and made several trips to India. By the time the Grandmothers showed up, I was a woman obsessed, so focused on serving with everything I had, I could think of little else. They had to have known of this one-pointed dedication.

When I set my intention to serve the Divine, the Grandmothers were not what I had in mind. Before they entered my life I had thought of "God" as the Force, the Source, or the One. Never did I dream that God could and would show Himself/Herself in the form of a bunch of charming old women. The Divine was awe-inspiring, that I was sure of, and a fun-loving group of old ladies did not inspire awe in me—at least not at first.

Over the years these wise women taught me so much, and it was humbling as well as refreshing to over and over again be shown that I knew so little. Perhaps the Grandmothers came to me because they knew they did not fit my image of "God." Had they picked a more relaxed woman, someone more open-minded, maybe they wouldn't have been able to help her grow as much as they helped me. Perhaps they liked a challenge. Perhaps, perhaps.... Because my mind likes to try to figure things out, I wrestled with "Why did the Grandmothers come to me?" until I finally lost interest in the question. The truth is, the Grandmothers came because they did. And I am sure I'm not the only one who has met them in one of their glorious forms, not the only one who has gone on to work with them. The Grandmothers after all are divine, unlimited, and with the universal message they have come to bring, I'm sure they are working through many of us.

It is now more than twelve years since they first appeared as I walked the dog that September day. Much has changed since then—certainly me, but other things too. Soon after the Grandmothers showed up, I was led to a shaman who taught me how to 'journey' to other levels of reality so I might find them again. Until recently I faithfully followed this method, learning in this way, not only from the Grandmothers, but also from the helping animal spirits of the lower world. I always spoke these sessions into a recorder so as to lose none of their information and the Grandmothers' first book, *A Call to Power: the Grandmothers Speak*, is a record of this method of learning.

The energy on earth is shifting now and as this occurs, the Grandmothers come forward and give us the Net of Light. Early on, they asked that each time we meet, we work with this Net that holds and upholds the life on our planet. **"We ask you to do this,"** they said, **"because the Net of Light will hold the earth steady during the times of change that are upon you.** This is the Net of Light," they say, "that will hold the earth as the energies of yin and yang come back into balance." Like an endlessly lighted fishnet, the Net spreads farther than the eye can see. It covers and cradles the earth, blankets and permeates it, while it holds it steady. This is the Net that will hold the earth while the energies of yin and yang swoop, shake, rock and roll back into balance.

"There will be destruction during this time of shifting energy," the Grandmothers say, **"but the earth itself will not be destroyed."** They are offering us the opportunity to become part of the Net of Light, asking us to take our place on this radiant network of support for our planet. The Net of Light is lit by the hearts of those who hold it, lit by the sacred places on earth, by the saints, sages and avatars who have come to uphold our planet at this time and by all those who love life and gladly serve.

A Call to Power: the Grandmothers Speak tells the story of how the Grandmothers came, why they came, and gives the reader basic tools for working with them. A few months after they showed up I began to hold meetings in my home to pass on their message and empowerment into the energy of yin. After more than 2000 women received the Grandmothers' Empowerment and men started coming forward to receive the Cloak of Comfort I stopped counting. Grandmothers' groups were springing up everywhere. It had become a grassroots movement. People would hear about the Grandmothers from a friend or read *A Call to Power: the Grandmothers Speak*, form a group in their community and pass the empowerment on to others. Before long, there were gatherings all over the world with the Grandmothers' book being translated into other languages.

The Grandmothers' lessons are meant to be shared and since their work is ongoing, so too is the job of recording it. Nearly every word the Grandmothers speak to the author is also meant for the reader. *Our Love is Our Power: Working with the Net of Light that Holds the Earth* continues where *A Call to Power* left off.

Our love is Our Power teaches us how to work with the Net of Light in order to become part of it. Building on the foundation set by *A Call to Power: the Grandmothers Speak,* this book anchors the presence of the Net of Light so the Net can more easily support the earth during these turbulent times. It also offers new lessons from the Grandmothers, each one designed to help us live their message.

Happily, there are more of us holding the Net of Light today than one would imagine. It is to these people whose numbers are growing each moment and to the Divine in all its radiant forms, working with and through us, that this book is dedicated.

In Gratitude

The following people have played a large part in the Grandmothers' work, including this book. Many thanks to Pat O'Brien and Suzanne Stein for editing *Our Love is Our Power: Working With the Net of Light that Holds the Earth* and to Christan Hummel for her patience in guiding me into the world of self-publishing and helping with a hundred other things. To Jenneken Berends, Babs Rentjes, Seersha O'Sullivan, Ruth Frei, Nellie Perneel and Helena Enq'a who have done much to spread the Grandmothers' message throughout Europe. To Lillian Reiter, J. D. Peterson, Karen Fernside, Anne Cressy, Jane Henderson, Lin Evanko, and Pamela Falciani for supporting me, the hundred-plus Grandmothers' group leaders around the world, and the new women who come forward to lead groups. To Meinrad Craighead for her guidance, inspiration, and the beautiful cover of this book, and to Mahri Kintz my beloved friend who unfailingly supported this work, believing in it even during the roughest of times. Her love lies at the heart of *Our Love is Our Power: Working with the Net of Light that Holds the Earth.* And last of all, to my dear husband, Roger, who may not always have understood what I was doing, but never stopped encouraging me to move forward with the Grandmothers, follow my guidance and my heart.

There are others who have been part of bringing this work to fruition—too many to name here, but they know who they are and I am grateful to each one of them. I have been blessed to share this work with a dedicated team, and I treasure every one of them.

CHAPTER 1

Who is the Doer?

*"Each time you come together there is
more power in the wings."*

One September morning in 1996 my life changed forever. I was minding my own business, just walking the dog beside the beach the way I did every day, when suddenly I found myself surrounded by a group of old women of different races, wearing native costumes—waving at me and singing. **"We are the Great Council of the Grandmothers,"** they said, and added, **"We have come because earth has suffered too long from an excess of *yang* and insufficient *yin*. It is time to return to balance,"** they said, **"and for this women must lead."**

Two days after they appeared, a golden eagle landed in my garden and shortly after that I was led to a shaman who taught me how to journey to the Grandmothers. This is how my adventure with these wise teachers began. In a short time, I became the Grandmothers' student, recording and passing on what they taught me and then transcribing these early teachings and experiences into their book, *A Call to Power: the Grandmothers Speak.*

After the Grandmothers entered my life, shocking me into action with their message and surprising teaching methods, I began to hold gatherings in my home, sharing their teachings and passing on their Empowerment into the Feminine Principle of creation with anyone who wanted to come.

The gatherings went on for several years. Women brought their friends, daughters, mothers, sisters and as time went on, some began to bring their husbands or boyfriends too. Every month there was a combination of returning people and new people, and after each meeting, many of them told me what a difference these wise women had made in their lives and how much happier and more confident they were now than they had been before they met the Grandmothers. One after another, women told their stories of how receiving the empowerment had made them more courageous, more loving, calmer and more at ease in a stress-filled world.

They were grateful that I had stepped forward with this message and so was I, but preparing for and running these meetings was taking up a lot of time and energy. I didn't feel right charging money for this work and was aware that I also needed to pay attention to my private psychotherapy practice. Sometimes it felt like there wasn't enough of me to go around, and whenever I began to feel that way, I got confused about my priorities. How was I supposed to handle this new 'job' with the Grandmothers? As months and then years rolled by, I began to question if holding the monthly meetings was worth the effort I was putting out. How long did I want to keep it up? After fussing about this for some time, one day it dawned on me to go to the Grandmothers and ask them.

By this time I was comfortable with what the Grandmothers refer to as inter-dimensional travel and many call shamanic journeying. A shaman taught me how to do this shortly after the Grandmothers first appeared, and though I was initially frightened by this strange way of seeking wisdom, in time I learned to trust my teachers in non-ordinary reality and enjoy the process. The Grandmothers, the shaman said, were to be found in what she called 'the upper world.' She taught me how to enter this realm, letting me know that though I might enter here, I would only be able to find the Grandmothers if they wanted me to. I had never experienced anything like this before and knew I was clearly out of my depth. But because this method of learning and exploration was something my mind couldn't grasp, venturing into these heretofore-unexplored realms served me well. The method was not 'rational,' and because it wasn't, I was forced to learn, not by theory, but by direct experience.

Because I was so shocked by 'not being in control,' my mind still tried to figure the method out. But although it labored hard, I could never anticipate or 'figure out' what might happen on a journey to these other levels of reality. So after innumerable struggles with my ego about 'who had control here,' I eventually gave up and let the spirits lead me where they would. Almost everything between the covers of *A Call to Power: The Grandmothers Speak* came from these early experiences with the Grandmothers and the helping animal spirits.

My 'travels' as my husband calls them were surprising to me. The helping spirits of the upper and lower worlds are consummate teachers and quickly showed me that their reach extended beyond the limitations of my mind. They would teach me through experience. What

I saw, tasted, smelled, felt and heard would be my truth. I had always thought of myself as a creative person, but not in my wildest imaginings could I have come up with the lessons they gave. And because each voyage was a surprise, it was clear I hadn't dreamed up these events. I was now traveling beyond the confines of my mind and found that I *liked* it.

Following the pattern I had learned, I began my next journey to the Grandmothers as I had first been taught—I thought of climbing to the top of a tree I loved, felt and saw myself doing it, and then willed myself to leap from its uppermost branches. But as soon as I began to rise into the air I noticed something was amiss. I was accustomed to soaring like a bird, but today it felt like I had a little motor inside my chest and it was this that was propelling me. This motor-driven flight was hard work. My chest was buzzing like mad, and instead of gliding like an eagle, now I was flying like a bee. I didn't know why this was happening, but figured there must be a purpose for it. By this time I had learned that *everything* that occurred in non-ordinary reality had a purpose. I would simply have to wait to find out what it was.

With my tiny wings a blur, I whirred through the first level of the upper world, but when I reached the top of it, I wasn't sure how to get through the membrane that separated it from the next level. I had done this hundreds of times before, but today it felt like I had never done it. No matter how I racked my brain, I couldn't remember how to break through.

Before I could solve this strange dilemma, I was blasted through the membrane to a point high above it. Suspended in midair, I paused long enough to recognize the Grandmothers' valley lying below me, and then gasped as I plummeted earthward, my bee body shooting toward the ground. Before I hit, I squeezed my eyes shut and when at last the sensation of falling stopped and all was quiet again, I opened them to find myself lying flat on my back. The force of impact had stamped my wings and body into the earth and now only my toes were visible.

When I got over the shock of landing I hauled myself up, amazed to discover that I wasn't injured. This had been a spectacular crash; the panic that had gripped me as I hurtled toward earth was so vivid I had forgotten that I was journeying. Even now I could hardly believe it. What had happened? Had this crash taken place on earth I would have been killed, but because it occurred in non-ordinary reality, I didn't have even a scratch.

"What an entrance," I marveled, as I stepped before the Grandmothers who today stood before me in eagle form. Shoulder to shoulder, twelve enormous birds regarded me with unsmiling eyes. Sometimes they appeared in human form and sometimes they looked like this, and although they had appeared like eagles many times, those raptor eyes always gave me pause. But because I had learned while traveling to other dimensions to stick with my original question, I didn't allow myself to be distracted. Instead, I swallowed hard and said, "Grandmothers, about the up-coming gathering...are these meetings something you want me to continue?"

Their wings rose in unison while their majestic heads tilted back and then rocked forward. "Yes," they said, seeming to glare at me over the tops of their beaks. "The gatherings bring in power. Each time you come together there is more power in the wings." "Okay," I replied, though I wasn't sure what "power in the wings" meant. Whose wings were they talking about anyway? I peered at them quizzically, but they only beetled their brows and fixed me with a look even fiercer. "Oh h h h," I whispered as understanding finally dawned, "They mean THE WINGS. The meetings give power to the collective wings, the ones that support life. The meetings support the earth." I glanced up at them as this thought came, hoping for a response, and they nodded, "Yes."

"Grandmothers," I continued, "Is there anything you want me to pass on at these gatherings?" and seeing their look, I quickly added, "besides your empowerment, that is?" Dark feathers flashed, and as the air crackled with power, I shivered. "Maybe I said the wrong thing," I thought as again they leveled me with that look. "Is there anything else you want me to pass on?" I repeated, my voice a croak.

"Power," they said, and pierced me with their eyes. "You want *me* to pass on power?" I squeaked, dumbfounded that they would expect me to do this. But the great eagles said nothing, only continued to stare, until I finally stammered, "Ummmm, uh...how do I do that, Grandmothers?"

"Drum for the gathering," they said. "Drum, and as you do, ask everyone there to hold the intention of taking on more power. Let that be their prayer—to be given power—power for their good and for the good of the world."

They pointed to the ground at my feet and as I followed their eyes, I saw that spread before us and twinkling far into the distance floated the Net of Light. Here was the great Net the Grandmothers had said would hold the earth steady while the energies of yin and yang shifted. Shortly after I began to work with them, they had taught me how to work with the Net of Light and over the years I had seen this radiant web or net grow thicker and more brilliant as more and more people accessed it.

I gazed at its sparkling expanse now and as I did, someone whispered, "Net of Light, Net of Light, Net of Light." "Ah!" I said, and the Grandmothers watched me as understanding came again. "In this meeting, first you want us to meditate on the Net of Light, and then you want me to drum while they ask for more power. Is that right?" I asked.

"If you do these things in this order," they said, "the power each one receives will fill not only them, but the Net of Light as well. It will magnify the Net, infuse more yin energy into each person, and infuse yin into the earth as well.

"As they ask for power, they must be open to how it is being given to them," they said. "Remind them of this. *Where* in their bodies are they taking it in?" they asked, their great heads bobbing. "As power enters them, healing will also take place. *Where* is healing taking place?" they asked. "Where is there a breakthrough? Where an awakening? Where are there openings and releases?" they asked. "They must be aware of the responses within their body," they said, giving me a firm nod.

"The spirit of Eagle will come into the room," they said and I glanced up in surprise, but before I could ask what this meant, I saw Eagle flying in my living room. His massive talons lightly touched a woman's head while his wings brushed a man and then he rose higher and circled the entire group. Fascinated, I kept my eyes on him and as I watched, the Grandmothers spoke. "Eagle will fly to each one and bring whatever she or he needs. As they open to receive," they said, "each of them will become a vortex of light. After this session," they said, "Wherever they find themselves, power will radiate from that place. Wherever they stand—power will be there. As more and more force enters into them, it will change and charge them. Each of them will become a walking prayer, a blessing for everything and everyone they meet.

"This is the potential for this work," they said, tossing back their heads. "Greatness! Its potential is far more than you can imagine. And what we have described will take place within each person who comes to this gathering," they said, eyeing me. I nodded back, my mouth open as I tried to take in what they had said. "The more these people are in alignment with the state of the walking prayer *before* they come to this meeting, the more power they will have to help others; some will have more and some will have less."

I realized that as I hung on their words I had been holding my breath. They began to touch and lightly probe me with the tips of their feathers then, and squinting while they watched me, they said, "Talk about...," and paused, seeming to search for the right words. "Speaking only good," they said at last. **"Talk about the wisdom of thinking only good thoughts and tell everyone at the meeting how important it is for them to open their hearts and banish all negative states of consciousness. Speaking and thinking only good will bring their behavior into alignment with the consciousness of the walking prayer,"** they explained.

"The walking prayer is already alive within them," they explained, **"so as soon as they open to it, they will recognize it and realize they have come home."** The Grandmothers were teaching us how to move into this state, how to become this 'walking prayer' they were talking about. I listened intently.

Twelve Grandmother eagles fluffed their wings then and stood even taller, their posture telegraphing the import of their words. **"No matter to what level a person's, speech, thoughts and feelings have evolved,"** they shook their heads as they spoke, **"the consciousness of the walking prayer lies waiting in their heart. Don't be fooled by anyone's behavior, no matter how bizarre it may seem,"** they said. **"What we are calling the walking prayer is latent within *every* human being."**

When I heard this, I began to feel a bit uncomfortable. "*Every* human being?" I asked. Then I began to wonder. How aligned was I with what they were describing? I didn't feel like a walking prayer. Pretty far from it. How could I expect to pass this teaching on to others when I myself wasn't living it? "I don't know," I said to myself, not realizing I'd spoken out loud, and twelve serious Grandmother birds interrupted my line of thought when they loudly chorused, **"There must be no unnecessary time spent in criticizing oneself. None at all,"** they scolded, and held their gazes on me until I whispered, "Yes, Grandmothers."

"Coming into alignment with 'the Higher' has already begun," they assured me and patted me with their wings, **"and by desiring this alignment, it will simply happen faster."** Stroking me slowly, they said, **"Begin to spend your time thinking about where it is you want to go, not about how far from the goal you are. This is a better way,"** they said, smiling and nodding. I saw their smiles of understanding then, felt their compassion, and sighed. I would do as they were suggesting.

"Each person who is drawn to these gatherings is needed for this work," they said. "Yes, Grandmothers," I answered. It was quiet for a moment and then they turned their heads to gaze questioningly into my eyes. "Why are they staring at me?" I wondered, but they held my gaze, and as they did, I realized I hadn't really been paying attention to them. I also noticed I was holding my breath. My mind had been busy worrying about who might show up for this next Grandmothers' meeting. What they were saying was pretty potent stuff— **"Be a walking prayer, banish negative thoughts, speak only good."** What if the people who showed up for the next meeting weren't ready for it?

"Uh, Grandmothers," I said, "this walking prayer business," I struggled on; "um, I don't think everyone who comes to these meetings has this degree of commitment. What if the people...." Unaffected by what I was saying, twelve Grandmother eagles gazed calmly at me over the tops of their beaks; **"Only those whom we call will come,"** they said.

I pondered this. They had said it before, and as I reflected on past Grandmothers' gatherings, I had to admit that each time we held a meeting they *did* draw the right people. The mixture of humanity they called to this work never failed to amaze me. Business people, housewives, career women, 'new age' types, Christians, Jews, Hindus, Buddhists, teen-agers, street people, nuns, priests, even a few Muslims—all sorts came through my door to learn about the Grandmothers. **"You have grown in strength,"** they said, interrupting my train of thought, and when I looked up in surprise, they added, **"others are growing also."**

As their words sank in, I stopped holding my breath. They were telling me I wasn't alone in this work any more; now there were others with a commitment as strong as mine. Their message was spreading and they were forming a team to carry it forward. As these thoughts came, twelve no longer fierce-looking eagles nodded their approval.

"Grandmothers, I can feel all the ways I can move my wings now," I said. As my body had relaxed, I had again become aware of my bee self. "When these wings move up and down," I said, demonstrating this bee movement, "I feel a pulling in my chest," I announced. Thrilled by my discovery, I waited for their response, but they only smiled politely. They looked a bit bored. **"Each person who comes to our meetings has a part to play in this work,"** they said. **"Tell them this."** They were changing the subject. I might find the evolution of my wings fascinating, but we weren't going to talk about that today.

"Ask those who come to this meeting to pray for every person they see," they said, **"to look for the light within each one, to bless and pray for them. This is what the Net of Light does,"** they said. **"This is how it upholds the earth and lifts each one.**

"And if you find someone you cannot bring yourself to pray

for," they said, "ask *us* to help that one and then quickly turn your thoughts to something good. *Do not dwell where there is pain and negativity,*" they beetled their brows. "Instead, pray for those you *can* pray for, turn everyone else over to us or to any form of the Divine you love, and then move your thoughts to something good. These sorts of prayers vitalize the strands of the Net of Light," they said. "Each time you turn away from negativity toward good, you strengthen and mend the Net of Light that holds the earth. "Wow!" I muttered, "Even our thoughts affect the Net of Light."

"It is not necessary to feel personal love for everyone," the Grandmothers said, giving me a meaningful look, and I glanced up questioningly. "Often there are too many blockages in your memory banks for you to be able to do that," they explained. "But if you ask us to love through you, we will. There is a great need for this love now, so ask," they said. "Okay, Grandmothers," I agreed, "Yes, I see what you mean. If I can't bring myself to feel love for someone, I can ask you to love them." "And whenever you ask, we will send this love *through* you," they added, "even in the most difficult of cases.

"Each time you choose to love both that which is easy and that which is difficult, you say 'yes' to life," they said, feathered heads bobbing happily. "And each time you do this, you strengthen the energy of yin on your planet. This is what is needed now," they said. "*This,*" each Grandmother lifted a wing in emphasis, "is your work."

Again I saw my living room and again it was full of people. But now each person was connected to the Net of Light and as I looked on, I saw the Net glowing more brilliantly than it had before; it looked like its wattage had doubled.

"After you finish drumming," the Grandmothers said, "ask everyone to reflect on the light they sent forth into the Net of Light. Then ask them to observe as this light comes rushing back to them. They will notice," they said, "that more light returns to them than they originally sent forth." Smiling knowingly, they swept their wings wide and said, "The moment of giving is always the moment of receiving." "Grandmothers," I said, "each time we connect to the Net of Light there is an increase in power, in us and in the Net, isn't there?" Then I asked, "Is the Net of Light a visual picture of the power of prayer?" "Yes," they said.

Puffing out their chests, the Grandmothers stretched their necks, lifted their heads high and said, "Breathe in our energy as we breathe in yours. When we inhale, we take in your energy, and when you inhale, you take in ours." I synchronized my breath with theirs and instantly I swelled with radiance. "This is what it's like to fold my energy into one with the Grandmothers," I whispered, awestruck. After breathing like this for a minute or two, the drumbeat on my recorder signaled me to return to ordinary reality so I turned to the Grandmothers and bowed to them in gratitude. And when I lifted off the ground to return to ordinary reality, I was so energized that even though I was still flying as a bee, this time my flight was effortless.

When I replayed this visit to the Grandmothers it came to me that this time my flight to the upper world had felt like work because I had been holding the thought of the Grandmothers' meetings as "work." With my tiny wings abuzz this *busy little bee,* had considered the meetings "her" job. My mind had convinced me that *I* was the doer, and this false sense of responsibility had turned even these joyful events into labor. I chucked at how my ego had fooled me into thinking everything was *my* responsibility. Then I recalled my crash landing. The Grandmothers had demonstrated exactly where this sort of thinking would take me.

After they showed me the potential for the monthly meetings—infusing more power into the Net of Light that supports the earth—all sense of effort left me. This stuff wasn't work; it was what I *wanted* to do. Once again I marveled at their teaching skills and laughed out loud at my yang fixation on "doing" and "work." The Grandmothers hadn't once addressed my busy bee persona. They hadn't lectured me on my attitude or how I'd misunderstood my role in their mission either, but I got their point all the same.

CHAPTER 2

The Power of Yin

"We breathe you; God breathes you."

The topic of yin and yang was something the Grandmothers returned to again and again. This shouldn't have been a mystery to me, as after all, these are the primary building blocks of the cosmos. Yet my comprehension of these energies was so minimal that their lessons continued to surprise me. Initially I had no understanding at all of yin and yang and now, after working with the Grandmothers for over twelve years, I still struggled to comprehend how they fit together.

When I next encountered the Grandmothers I posed a question about the relationship between men and women. Each time I journeyed, I aimed for something with implications beyond just my personal life. Because I'd been married a long time, I knew how difficult it could be to understand the opposite sex, but I didn't just want to better understand my husband and myself, I wanted to understand the whole female/male play. Here was a place where yin and yang could be grossly out of balance.

Recently I'd seen this imbalance acted out in my psychotherapy practice. In fact I was now seeing several couples that were quite estranged from one another. The Grandmothers said this sort of pain was connected to the imbalance of yin and yang on our planet and because these primal energies were so out of harmony today, misunderstandings between the sexes had reached a critical level. This was what I was seeing.

Wives screamed their pain, berated their husbands, and sobbed their feelings of helplessness while their husbands sat stoically by—shocked, bewildered and emotionally shut down. The couples were miserable, their children were acting out, and their marriages were floundering. From my years as a therapist, I knew how to 'treat' cases like these with standard psychological tools, but this time I wanted something more. How to correct the imbalance of yin and yang within human relationships? How could we apply the Grandmothers' lessons to our personal lives? For this I needed guidance from these wise women.

When I next went to the upper world I rose from my tree, held my concentration on the Grandmothers, and asked them to teach me. Today I was coming with a question reflecting the anguish of many. The imbalance of yin and yang was not just a theory. It was creating a great deal of misery.

At last their valley appeared below and there they were. Today they appeared as women, and stood in a circle waiting for me. "Grandmothers," I said as I stepped before them, "I am concerned about the relationships between men and women today." **"So are we,"** they said. "What would you have me say about this?" I asked, and noticed that as soon as I spoke, my hands had opened and formed the position of a receptive mudra.

"Let us fill you," they said and motioned me to sit down on the ground with them. **"Let your body drink in what we are giving you,"** they said. "Oh!" I replied, "This must be why I'm holding my hands like little cups." **"Yes,"** they nodded, **"Your body is wise; it understands what is happening long before your mind does. In time your mind will also absorb what we are giving you, but for now it is more than it can hold."** Wrinkling their brows, they gave me a serious look and said, **"Trust your body.**

"Receive," they said and motioned me to lie down; **"an empty vessel can give nothing. First allow yourself to fill,"** they said. **"Let your back, buttocks, legs, heart, arms, and hands fill,"** they said, and I lay flat on my back with my palms open at my sides, willing myself to do just that. **"As you receive through your body, your vibration will change. Feel the change beginning."** And when I turned my focus inward, I felt it. I was larger and more solid, while at the same time, I felt lighter. "What a combination!" I marveled, "how can I be more solid and at the same time lighter?"

After a pause the Grandmothers spoke again. **"Receiving through the body slows down your mind enough so you can absorb what we are giving,"** they said. **"And,"** they added, **"from the act of receiving comes more receiving."** They smiled then and stretched their arms wide and as they pantomimed receiving, I felt my body expanding and harmonizing with theirs. Suddenly I too was filled with joy, and with each second that passed, I grew softer and softer, larger and larger. Later, when I played back the recording, at this point I heard myself humming.

I floated in this state of happiness for what seemed a long time but was really only a minute or two until I heard them say, **"You cannot help men."** This snapped me to attention and I looked up with total concentration. Shaking their heads sadly, they said, **"You cannot relate to men in a healing way until you *yourself* are filled with the energy of yin."** "Ah," I sighed, "I understand. This is why I feel so soft and expanded. This is what the energy of yin feels like."

They nodded and said, "Breathe with us. Breathe in, and when you exhale, notice how everything within you that's ready to leave, simply goes. Old thoughts, ideas, memories and stress will leave," they said, flicking their hands in dismissal. "That's all there is to it. Breathe in and breathe out," they said, their chests rising and falling in rhythm with mine, "and synchronize your breath with ours. We breathe you. God breathes you," they said and watched to be sure I was in rhythm with them. "Inhale, and release," they said and I patterned my breath with theirs, reminding myself that whenever I exhaled, everything old inside me was leaving. "Let your breathing be effortless," they said, and it was.

This breathing exercise was a bit different from the previous one. The first had as its purpose developing a deeper, more trusting relationship with the Divine, i.e. surrendering everything to the Grandmothers. With the second exercise I followed the breath, knowing that with each exhalation old states of consciousness were being expelled. This one was more a psychic house cleaning.

"Now turn your attention to us," they said, and quickly I glanced up again. **"We are in this room with you,"** they said, **"and at the same time we are hovering over this room. We are here!"** they cried, pointing to themselves, **"and we are everywhere! We stand behind you and in front of you, we stand to the left and to the right,"** they laughed at the look of surprise on my face. **"We surround you.**

"You," they pointed at me, **"are part of the Great Mother."** My eyes widened and I must have looked shocked because they began to laugh. **"The Mother is with you always,"** they nodded. **"Let yourself fill with the energy of the Great Mother, and each time you think of filling, as you breathe in, you will enliven Her presence within you. We, the Grand Mothers are at one with the Mother,"** they said, chuckling, **"and we are always with you."** Placing hands on their hips then, they swayed back and forth together and sang, **"Always we are with you. Behind you,"** they chorused, dipping their heads back and forth. **"Around you, and in front of you. Everywhere!"** they exclaimed, **"We are everywhere."** Then smiling coyly, these lovable, playful Grandmothers said, **"We wait for your call."**

I closed my eyes and prayed to know this truth—to know that the Grandmothers and the Great Mother were always with me, and instantly I felt the presence of the Mother inside my body. I was huge. And full. I was astounded by my own enormity. "I am love," I said to myself, my voice surprisingly confident; "that's what it is, I am love."

I was also powerful—quietly and relentlessly powerful. My body thrummed with a force, potent and full. I was surprised by the naturalness of it, as if I had always been this way. "The Grandmothers are right," I said to myself and to them, "the Mother *is* inside me. In fact," I marveled, "I can't tell where She lets off and I begin." I was merging with the Feminine Principle of creation, helpless to stop it and not wanting to stop it.

"**Let the walls of your small self begin to soften,**" the Grandmothers said as they watched me, their voices full of love. "**Let it soften and expand into the great Self that you are. *This* is who you are,**" they said and I could hardly breathe, I was so amazed by the feeling inside. "**This magnificent Self, the expanded one that exists beyond the limits of your skin, beyond the limits of your mind and experience—*this* is who you are.**"

This, I realized, as the beating of my heart slowed and my breathing returned to normal, was what I had recognized as the Great Mother. And this was what the Grandmothers had wanted me to feel when they told me to fill with the energy of the Mother—more, much more, than my 'self.' "**When the bustle of life again captures your attention, you may forget this,**" they said, regarding me fondly, "**but this *is* who you are.**" I listened and trembled with joy. I had never, *ever*, felt so large, so limitless. I was deep; I was full—and all of it at once.

When they saw the state I was in, they quickly said, "**Return your focus to your body,**" and I willed myself to do it. "Breathe and feel," I said to myself, "breathe and feel," and soon I became aware of the weight of my buttocks on the floor, the position of my feet, and of my head as it rested on the ground.

"**You may sense a different vibration inside,**" the Grandmothers said, "**the vibration of awakening and expansion. This is *you*,**" they joyfully laughed. "This *is* me," I said, my voice filled with wonder, and as I spoke, a wave-like movement began inside. Everything was humming and flowing. "**This experience belongs to you,**" they said, nodding approval. "**Own it and occupy your big Self.**

"**You are great,**" they said, ignoring the look of astonishment on my face. "**Magnificent!**" they continued, "**much more than you have ever known. Your nature is joy and full-heartedness.**" I listened, nodding as if I understood, but I didn't. I couldn't take it all in. What I was experiencing far surpassed my wildest expectations. "Becoming one with the Great Mother," I whispered, "how can this be possible?" But the Grandmothers paid no attention to my star struck state.

I stared uncomprehendingly and when they saw the stunned look on my face, they said, **"Rest now. This is enough for one day. Come back to us tomorrow and we will teach you more."** "Okay, Grandmothers," I said, so tired I could barely get the words out. "I will return." And with that I thanked them, turned away and began to make my way to ordinary reality. As soon as I returned I went straight to bed. I think I slept the entire afternoon.

"This is who you are. The great container."

The next day I returned. "Grandmothers," I said, as I stepped before them, " I'm back. Please teach me more." They eyed me carefully, looking me over to assure themselves that I was indeed ready for more. Then they nodded, **"It is time to experience the container that you are,"** they said, launching into their next teaching. **"You are the container that holds love,"** they explained, **"that holds life, and supports everything that lives. Your capacity is enormous."** "What," I asked, "does this mean, Grandmothers? I don't get it," I stammered, but they held my eyes with theirs and replied, **"Feel it! Become aware of yourself."** "Oh," I said as a glimmer of understanding came. Okay, Grandmothers, okay," I said, "I'll do it," and taking a breath, I focused in my body and in no time at all I began to swell again, this time expanding to such a size that there seemed no end to 'me.'

"*This* is who you are!" they said, their faces lit with joy. Clearly they had been looking forward to giving me this experience. **"Your mind keeps you so busy!"** they laughed, **"running here and there, all the while chattering and worrying. Reaching and grabbing,"** they said, **"hiding and wanting—these are all tricks of the mind! Your thoughts keep you so busy,"** they threw their heads back, and with a great belly laugh, shouted, **"you've forgotten who you are! "*This* is who you are! Feel it! The great container,"** they said, nodding to emphasize their words. **"She who holds and is held."**

"Own it!" they commanded, **"and take this experience in so thoroughly that as you go about your days it will be easy to recall."** Then they drew themselves to their full height and twelve regal Grandmothers intoned, **"She who holds. She who accepts what lies before her, holds it and is at the same time held. Whenever you open and allow**

yourself to embody the container, you ARE the state of Holding," they said. "When you bring to life the consciousness of the one who holds, you become one with the Great Mother." And crossing their arms across their chests, they seemed to dare me to disagree with them.

"*This* will take a while to absorb," I said, but the Grandmothers simply smiled and nodded their understanding. "Now take a moment to invite in anyone or anything that comes to mind. Your husband," they said, "your son or daughter, a parent, a friend, an enemy, an idea, a memory—whatever and whoever comes. Quietly hold what comes to you. In the vastness of your being, you can do this. You are great enough to hold everything!"

I did as they said; thought of holding, willed myself to open, to invite in whomever came. It didn't take long. In fact, it quickly became quite busy in there and I watched as a succession of people, problems, and stories paraded through my mind. On they came, one after another, each one vying for attention but from where I sat with the Grandmothers, I was strangely immune to their charms. It was like being at the movies. Usually these stories from the past fascinated me, but in this position, I simply watched, accepted and "held" them as they came up, and one after another, not one of them captured my attention.

"As you go through life," the Grandmothers said, "stay within the awareness of the container and hold whatever comes. Hold it as a basin holds water or as a planter holds earth. Water does not change the shape or color of a basin; earth does not alter the size or shape of a pot. A container *is*," they said. "It holds. *You* hold," they stated. "You will find that there is nothing to resist or fight against in this world because you encompass it all!" Then they swept their arms wide and said, "*It is your nature to be the container. This* is Yin."

I felt the truth in what they were saying. "Yes, Grandmothers," I said, but no sooner was this out of my mouth than a weaving object appeared in front of us. It looked like a figure eight. Energy seemed to weave in and out of the two sides —in and around, out and around, following the curves of the eight. It lay on its side like a rounded infinity symbol, while energy flowed through it. "What you are seeing," the Grandmothers said, "is the feminine and masculine principles of energy harmonized together. The infinity movement originates in the holding state you just experienced. It is the power inherent within the container that allows this rhythmic dance to take place. "This is interesting, Grandmothers," I mused. I've never thought of the act of holding the way you're describing it. To me a container is just a thing, an inert object that sits. But that's *not* what is happening here."

I watched as the Grandmothers filled the container, one moment with earth and the next with water. "**The container that *you* are is filled with life, and whenever you choose to 'hold,' you create an important vibration.**" As they spoke, energy shimmered up the sides of the container, at last filling it to the rim. And as soon as this happened, the infinity symbol appeared again. "It's the vibration of holding that creates this rolling infinity movement," I said, repeating the Grandmothers' words. This time I had seen it happen.

"**Yes,**" they answered, smiling broadly. "**What you are seeing occurs *always and only* when yin is in full supply. Then the energies of yin and yang flow and dance together in an endless looping pattern. This movement is what you are calling the infinity symbol.**" They folded their arms then, rocked back on their heals and beamed happiness at me. Their joy must have been contagious, because as I watched the liquid-like rhythm of the figure eight I felt it too and smiled along with them.

Now the two halves of the eight began to weave and dance toward and then away from each other. I glanced over to the Grandmothers to ask what this meant, but they had their eyes locked on the figure, and when I turned my head to look back at it, it was no longer just the figure eight, but my husband and I who were dancing. He formed one half of the eight and I the other. Happiness lit his face as he moved toward me and when he came closer, I felt my heart lifting. Then we began to roll and circle around each other. Back and forth we rocked, until at last we washed over one another in a series of waves.

"This infinity dance is propelled by light," I said, my voice full of surprise as rays of light wove and shot from one end of the figure to the other. The eight was lit and so was I. As I watched I felt such intense happiness that tears welled up, turning all the lights to a glorious blur and when the dancing finally stopped, I gazed across at the Grandmothers and saw that they were glowing too. Their happiness was a great as mine. "**We bless you,**" they said and I bowed and kissed their hands.

I stood with them for a moment or two and watched the figure eight as it receded into the distance. "**We bless you,**" they repeated. "**We bless all of you who do this sacred work. You are purifying your hearts and your lives will be blessed.**" Then they paused a moment, and added, "**This work is only for certain ones.**" Again they were telling me not to worry about who came or did not come to a Grandmothers' meeting. My job was simple. I was to share their information and then relax, knowing *they* would draw the right people to hear it.

I bowed a long, slow bow and nodded my understanding. From now on I would trust that they, not I, would call the right people to this work. If their message was only for certain ones, *they* must be the ones to choose them. With my head bent I stood quietly before them and as I waited, blessings poured down on me. It felt like a warm rain showering my body. I felt so safe and comforted that I could have stayed in that position forever, but once again the drumbeat intervened, signaling me to return to ordinary reality. And as I drifted down toward the earth, I heard the Grandmothers say, **"Now you carry this consciousness with you."**

"Being the container"

The concept of woman being *the container* had a huge effect on me. Little by little, as I grew to understand what 'being the container' meant, it infiltrated my life and as it did, I began to live it. Right away I noticed I was looking at men differently. I seemed to understand them better than I had before. Instead of falling into opposition with them and getting involved in power struggles as I had so often done in the past, arguing over who was right and who was wrong, I found I actually *liked* men, respected them, enjoyed them, and even loved them. This happened right after this trip to the Grandmothers, and, believe me, no one was more amazed at my change of viewpoint than I. Not only did I like men; I liked everyone. The position of the container was so potent that now I was ready to embrace them all.

In my years with the Grandmothers I developed a great deal of inner strength. However, after this journey I zoomed up the chart. Now I understood what it felt like to be a queen. The confidence, the understanding of 'who you are,' that one of royal birth carries. After this experience I *knew* what it was to feel one's own greatness. The quality of queenliness was one I carried too.

As I opened myself to 'holding,' to being the container, and then shared this teaching, I was able to help others live from the position of the container too. I shared the message with some of the women in the Grandmothers' group and for those who weren't open to an idea this foreign, I shared it in subtle ways. But whether I spoke this truth, or practiced living it, the wonderful feeling that came from "holding" grew and grew until my capacity to give and receive love took a quantum leap.

"Effortless effort"

From the very first the Grandmothers' work had a calming, steadying effect on me. They eliminated my frantic rushing through life by moving me from the belief that I was responsible for everything, to a position of simple observation. As I became more a watcher than a "doer," I began to appreciate what life brought me instead of trying to engineer what it "should" bring. And strangely, while my tendency to worry about and anticipate events dropped, my ability to get things done shot up. Although now I actually "did" less, more got accomplished. I had read about this phenomenon, but now I was living it. **"Effortless effort,"** the Grandmothers called it. **"Trust in the rhythm of life,"** they said, **"and *dance* with life!"** At last I was learning a few steps.

Practicing what the Grandmothers called "being the container" let me know what it was like to *be* them. The power and steadiness that filled me whenever I sat quietly, thought of myself in this way, and consciously "held," was immense. Whenever I did this, I became one with the Grandmothers, one with the foundation of life. When I moved into "holding," there was nothing I couldn't do and no one I couldn't love. I felt more understanding and less angry judgment. This shift in attitude amazed me, but I was even more surprised to discover that I carried an understanding of the archetype of the container inside myself. What the Grandmothers called "The one who holds" was already anchored in the cell beds of my body.

The container also gave me an understanding of the Great Mother. Shortly after the Grandmothers came to my life I began to search for information on the feminine aspect of the Divine because until I met the Grandmothers, I had no knowledge of, nor really any interest in the feminine divine. Although this admission appalls me today, at that time I knew nothing of the feminine aspect of creation and my ignorance was just fine with me. I had been raised with God the Father and as far as I knew that was all there was.

The first person I met who had an understanding of the Great Mother was Meinrad Craighead, a feminist artist, living in the Southwest. When I traveled to New Mexico to take an art class from her, she opened my eyes to the feminine principle. Gingerly I explored what Meinrad called, "the feminine divine," and after a while I got up the courage to pray to Her. On several early journeys to the Grandmothers, the Mother actually appeared. I saw Her, talked with Her, and little by little grew to love and revere this heretofore-unknown (to me) aspect of divinity.

"We have come for all"

As soon as the Grandmothers gave me this meditation, I began to practice sitting quietly, thinking of myself as the container and 'holding' the way they had taught me. Imagine my surprise while in the midst of 'holding,' I found myself merging with the Great Mother. And this occurred not once, but *every time* I meditated like this. I was thrilled by how simple it was. Mergence occurred. Each time I made the decision to 'hold' and become a vessel for whatever the universe wanted to give, my consciousness shifted and I felt Her presence. Little by little I came to understand that we were one and the same.

The effect this had on me was profound. My personality quirks and those of my family, friends, and associates immediately became less important. "Eh?" I'd say to myself. "Who cares?" and anger would fade. Fear faded. So did hurt. My level of stress dropped. I am a psychotherapist by profession and not only had analyzing my own and other people's behavior been my chosen work; it had been my private fixation. "What was it that made my son react that way?" I'd ask myself. "Why was I *really* that hurt by my friend last night?" I had spent most of my adult life pondering questions like these, believing if I thought hard enough, examined long enough, *Truth* would reveal itself.

Now I no longer cared. None of this stuff held my interest the way it once had. I found it impossible to hold onto wounds from the past when I was at one with the Mother. They wouldn't stick. Where once upon a time I had hashed and re-hashed perceived slights, now most of the time they crossed the screen of my mind once and then were gone. I don't want to give the impression that I lived uninterrupted in this state. I didn't. Now and then I still got sucked into one of life's dramas, but whenever I remembered to meditate on holding, sat quietly and opened to the consciousness of the container, drama paled. And as this happened, life became more pleasant. I'm sure I also became more pleasant.

The women who came to our monthly meetings and ceremonies also reported changes in their lives. As we studied *A Call to Power: the Grandmothers Speak*, shared with one another, and put the Grandmothers' lessons into practice, we deepened our connection with these wise elders. Marriages and friendships bloomed, old wounds healed, and *Self-confidence* reigned supreme.

One person who illustrated this was Kathy, part of the Grandmothers' group in Laguna Beach for over 10 years. She is married to a hot-headed man who loves to argue, and since her nature is sweet and submissive, her husband had gotten into the habit of verbally abusing her. But after receiving the Grandmothers' Empowerment she began to change. Whenever he lectured or berated her, instead of shrinking down inside herself, the way she'd done before, now she stood back and observed his behavior. She didn't react to him; she simply 'held' him and whatever he was dishing out—the way a container holds water. Not affected, just watching and "holding." She was astounded by the strength this gave her. "I don't care now whether he gets angry or not," she told us. "I can see that it has nothing to do with me. I just watch, let the Grandmothers hold me and him," she says, "and you know what? Now he seldom does it. I think that as he saw me get stronger, he calmed down."

Another example is Christine, a beautiful young woman who works in banking management and has many times shared the challenges she faces in her 'yang' work environment. She laughs at how whenever she sits in on high-powered meetings she calls on the Grandmothers and the Net of Light. "I feel like I'm leading a double life," she says. "I put on my suit, walk in with my briefcase and no one at the bank has any idea that I'm working with the Grandmothers." She mentors young women at work, teaching them by example and a few well-chosen words the reality of Beauty/Power. Last spring, in the middle of a Grandmothers' retreat, her boss called to let her know that she had been promoted. "A BIG promotion," she said, her eyes wide. "I guess they like what I'm doing." Then, giving a secret smile, she said, "It's the Grandmothers."

In the last few years, men also started coming to our meetings. At first this surprised me because I had thought this work was only for women. But when I asked the Grandmothers, they said, **"We have come for all,"** and showed us how to pass the Cloak of Comfort on to men. This simple ceremony affirms a man while blessing and holding him steady within the embrace of yin. Only a few men attend our meetings, but what a difference their presence makes! Women remark on how much more power they feel when we perform the Empowerment ceremony with men present, supporting us. The Grandmothers say, **"Yang held and reinforced by yin will always reach out in support of life."** This is what we feel when men stand with and behind us.

"Because a woman in this state of consciousness is compelling, everything comes to her."

After I had taught the container meditation to several groups, I began to wonder if the dancing infinity symbol could help women and men better relate to one another. I would go to the Grandmothers and find out. "Grandmothers," I said as I stood in front of them, "if the infinity symbol is something others can benefit from, please teach me. We need a way for men and women to connect."

"We will teach you," they said. I bowed, and when I looked up I saw that they were wearing long gowns that trailed along the ground as they walked. I followed close behind them and couldn't help but notice the graceful way they swayed in their long-skirts. It came to me then that in these gowns they resembled their feathered bird selves—both were elegant, elongated forms. They might vary their appearance from journey to journey, sometimes appearing as human beings, sometimes like great birds, but however they showed themselves, they had a dignity and natural grace I seldom saw in modern life. "The Grandmothers are classically feminine," I said to myself.

No sooner were the words out of my mouth than they turned, and pointed to a figure standing behind me. "Oh," I said as I turned around. The figure was 'me', but this me was sitting in a chair, with her palms up and her feet planted on the ground. As I examined 'myself', I noticed how open and relaxed my body looked. **"Yes,"** the Grandmothers said, **"what you see here is *yourself* as a container."**

I wanted to ask what they meant, but before I could, I *became* the figure. The first thing I noticed as I slipped into this posture was my cupped palms. Then I realized that not only my hands, but my entire body, was cupped. I was forming a 'C' shape and strangely, being in this curved position somehow gave me a feeling of strength and stability. In fact, the longer I sat like this, the more calm and contented I became. "Grandmothers," I said, "I just love this bowl-like posture. Now I can feel what it is to be a container. Even my feet and toes are full."

As I continued, serene and still, I began to hum until even my organs were singing. I closed my eyes to enjoy the vibration inside and when I opened them again there was the figure eight again, lying on its side. Except this time my own body formed one side of it. When I glanced at the other side, I saw a vague male figure that seemed to be moving toward me. "What is this?" I wondered, and then I realized that by being at one with the container and the state of holding, I was drawing the male figure toward myself. I was a magnet. With perfect equanimity, as if this sort of thing happened to me every day, I watched the power of attraction draw the male figure forward. I was irresistible. That was just how it was. When I realized what was happening, I remember thinking, "This is like one of my childhood fantasies, being irresistible and all. This should be funny," I told myself, but I wasn't laughing. I was too relaxed to laugh.

Now the magnetic pull inside surged and began to pull *everything* to itself! Not just men, but everything. It wasn't that I was trying to draw anything to myself; I wasn't. I was simply open. And because I was open, and in a way, empty, everything *wanted* to come to me.

Suddenly I recalled something the Grandmothers had said earlier, **"The infinity movement originates in the holding state. It is created by the holding energy of the container."** "Oh!" I exclaimed as I realized that *I* had created this and turned to the Grandmothers with my mouth hanging open. **"Yes,"** they said as they rubbed my back to reassure me. **"Because a woman in this state of consciousness is compelling,"** they spoke slowly, choosing their words, **"everything comes to her."** "W-o-w," I whispered, drawing the word out. "She doesn't have to '*do*' anything. Everything comes to her." And as I spoke my body was so calm and loose I could hardly get the words out.

After several minutes of silence I heard myself speak again. "Yes," I said, and this time my voice sounded strong. "When a woman takes the position of holding, energy weaves back and forth between women and men. It happens effortlessly," I said as I watched it take place. "But it's not just men and women who are affected by this holding," I said, my voice rising in surprise as animals, people, rocks—all sorts of things— began to draw close to me. "The position of reception is so magnetic that it draws *everything to itself. Really* draws!" I exclaimed. "Everyone and everything wants to be in this place of being held."

"The container is the Great Feminine," they said, **"so of course everything wants to be with Her."** Then they laughed good-naturedly and embraced me. "Everything wants *me* to hold it now," I said, taken aback by this position of oneness with the Great Mother. "She is irresistible," I said, and after a pause while the Grandmothers fixed me with their eyes, I corrected myself. "I am irresistible," I said, hardly able to get the words out. The Grandmothers only smiled and looked on.

"This position of the container…." I said at last, "fills a woman to completion. And, Grandmothers," I said, "it heals men too. It makes them whole." As I spoke I wondered where these words were coming from. "A man's energy is drawn to the infinity symbol," I continued, "where it circles around behind the woman and gets recharged. Then masculine energy moves outward and makes the second loop by itself, but it always does so in rhythm with the energy of the feminine. Men are able to do this only *because* they are held," I said, incredulous at the complexity of my explanation. "Yin is the Mother ship," I went on. "Smaller boats go out on forays from the Mother and then gratefully return home to Her." I stopped then and stared in wonder at the Grandmothers who beamed me their gentlest smiles.

"This is so, so…completing?" I said, searching for the right expression. I didn't know if completing was a real word or not, but it was *the* word for what I was experiencing. "There is nothing more I need or want now, Grandmothers," I said. "This is everything." I was aware that at this moment I was whole, replete. I was ready to return to ordinary reality; this experience was all I could ask.

After I said, "this is everything," there was a brief pause and in a minute or so I heard myself whisper, "Wow!" the word nearly inaudible. I had attempted to lift my hand to wave good-bye to the Grandmothers and found I couldn't. I couldn't move any part of myself. It wasn't within my power to return to ordinary reality—not yet, not until the deep holding energy of yin had run its course. "Gosh," I muttered, "I can't budge. I have to stay here, Grandmothers," I said, looking at them in wonder, "until this energy grounds itself in me." They nodded, and gestured for me to wait so I stilled my thoughts and did just that. And they waited with me—smiling all the while.

"I'm anchored," I announced at last as I felt a fundamental connection between the earth and myself take place. "In fact," I said, "I'm inset." I watched, and in the distance saw pylons being pounded deep into the earth. "I am those pylons," I said to myself, and "Oh," I marveled, "how strong I am. Totally grounded," I announced. **"This is the power of completion,"** the Grandmothers said.

I closed my eyes and rested for a moment, hoping to digest what I had just experienced and as each moment passed I felt larger, deeper, and more fully anchored to the earth. At last I gave up. Far too much had happened for me to be able to grasp it all now. "Grandmothers," I said, shaking my head in wonder, "that was really something." **"Yes,"** they said, **"you have to be willing to become a woman to do this work."** "Yes," I nodded in understanding. Opening to the consciousness of the container is not a job for a girl. This is work of courage and deep commitment—work for a woman, a Great Woman. The kind the Grandmothers were calling us to be.

On this journey the Grandmothers shared a potent secret with me– the primal energy of Woman. Not the yang-based power that is nearly worshiped in our world, but *real* power. Woman as the container; the one who sets the tone and makes things move. Woman, the hub of the wheel, the Mother ship, She who holds. These ideas are foreign in our culture, foreign in our world. For thousands of years woman has been treated as the 'second sex' the 'also ran' of the human family, told to 'stand behind' men and know her place. Woman as shakti, the Feminine Principle, the elemental power of the universe, is not something our culture understands.

The might the Grandmothers allowed me to experience on this journey changed my worldview. After I felt the drawing power of the magnet I became when I opened to being 'a container,' I realized that when I was aligned with the Great Feminine what a force I became. Woman is an untapped and undiscovered power, a force of and for good. Women hold this energy naturally; it is our birthright. It doesn't matter that for eons of time it has been hidden from us, causing the power of shakti to lie dormant. After this journey, I truly understood what the Grandmothers mean when they say, **"The energies of yin and yang are shifting now. It is time to return to balance, and for this, women must lead. It can be no other way."**

CHAPTER 3

The Net of Light Amplified

"Single point of focus"

When I look back over the years I am amazed to see how the Grandmothers' teachings address the needs of both personal and planetary conditions. They work equally effectively in the microcosm of my life and in the macrocosm of the planet. With them the adage, "As above, so below; as below, so above," is always operative. After the tragedy of September 11, they worked to calm me and at the same time, taught me how to be a force for peace in a terribly shaken world. After the twin towers fell, I went to them many times, often asking the same question: what could we do to help heal the trauma to our nation and the world?

On one such visit, no sooner did I rise through the membrane that separated ordinary reality from the first level of the upper world than Eagle swooped in and grabbed me by a harness at my upper back. This had happened when I was first learning about the Grandmothers, and now, once again Eagle held me suspended beneath him. This time I was there to learn to fly as he flew.

I spread my wings beneath his and a gust of wind rushed through my feathers. "What velocity!" I cried, thrilled by the speed, but he only gave me a moment to enjoy the sensation before he dropped me and down I plunged, pitching head over heals, until I was finally able to right myself again. With my heart hammering in my chest, I shakily managed to maneuver my wings enough to stay air borne and for a few seconds I maintained my course, but even though I was now far below Eagle I couldn't hold even this altitude and soon drifted even lower. At last I dropped so far beneath the great bird that I could no longer see him. But before I could cry out for help there was a flash of darkness and on my left there he was. With a penetrating look, he assessed my situation. "**Align with me,**" he said. "**Focus! Focus hard!**"

I held my breath, stiffened my spine and concentrated on moving as he moved, on feeling what he felt, willing myself to fly as he flew and realized just how hard I was trying when I started to get a headache. "Focus," I muttered to myself, "focus," and soon I could again see him, his wings beating above me. The harness was gone and surprisingly now I was gaining altitude, rising, rather than falling behind. Something inside me had shifted. **"Single point of focus,"** Eagle called, and this time I understood what he meant. I was to hold a single point, not just now, but always. This lesson was about more than flying.

"Okay," I called back and then began to chant, "The Grandmothers, the Grandmothers, I want the Grandmothers." A force was building inside me and now there was no casualness about my intention. I was focused all right, entirely focused. Suddenly I heard myself shout, "It's coming, I feel it! The power to stay air born is coming!" At the top of my lungs I announced to the universe, "I want alignment with God. Full alignment! Yes!" I shouted, and in my determination, the force of that 'yes' lifted me still higher.

Eagle was my teacher, a master of intensity. For a moment I hovered in the air beside him and felt what he felt. Fearless confidence. Single point of focus. He nodded to me and then glanced downward. My eyes followed his and in the valley far below, I saw the Grandmothers standing together, forming a circle. **"Dive!"** he cried and tilting his wings, plummeted earthward. Before I could consider what I was doing, I plunged after him, abandoning myself to the fall as chills ran over me.

I sped in close behind him as he sailed in above the Grandmothers and with my great talons barely touching ground skidded to a stop in the midst of them. Bowing low, I spread my wings in greeting and said, "Thank you for Eagle, Grandmothers. Thank you for this teacher."

They smiled and nodded their understanding, and quickly I shifted back to the purpose of my visit. "Grandmothers," I said, "people are coming soon for your meeting. This is a *very* important time for us," I said, tearing up. "There is so much suffering, and every person who comes to this meeting will hold in her heart the desire to serve. Use us, please," I said. "Please use us. How can we be of service?"

Again they nodded and stepped toward me, so close, their faces were all I could see. But I felt their hands on my head, my neck, shoulders and down my wings, all the way to my wrists and talons. They were placing a blessing on my eagle body. **"Remember who you are,"** they said as they held me close, **remember this."** "I am the eagle," I whispered, "I am Eagle." Then they moved into eagle form themselves, and as their mighty wings rose, mine followed suite. My feathers lifted and my talons gripped the earth as again chills ran over me.

They showed me how to flex my talons, how to spread and grasp with them when necessary. I was to hold my ground as I spoke to those who would be coming to the next meeting—my prodigious feet spreading and anchoring. "Grandmothers," I asked, "what do you want me to say at this meeting?" "**Remind them of who they are,**" they said. "**Eagle will sweep the room and intensify power. With every beat of the drum we want them to feel anchored and aware of the power coursing through them. The strength each of them holds is tremendous,**" they said. "**They anchor the Net of Light for the entire planet.**" Giving me a fierce look, they added, "**Say this.**"

My mind reeled. "Whoa, Grandmothers," I muttered, but they were almost savage in their intensity. "**Feel power coming into your shoulders now. Pounding into your head,**" they said, their words ringing with urgency. "**It is pouring from us into you, pouring all the way through your feet. This force will anchor you so you can do our work.**" They nodded then, and squinting their eyes, seemed to size me up. "**From this place of power within, from** *this place*," they emphasized and I felt a rhythmic movement beginning in my chest, "*We* **will cast the Net of Light. As soon as you think the thought of casting the Net,** *We* **will do it.**"

"Hum," I murmured, "when I started here today I was told to come into alignment with Eagle and now you are telling me to come into alignment with you. Everything is lining me up with the Divine." I looked at them questioningly and they nodded. "**Yes,**" they said, "**this is correct.**

"**Think of yourself as that pitcher we showed you long ago,**" they said. "**The cream colored pitcher that sits on a table in front of a window.**" (They were referring to the Pitcher and Cup meditation in *A Call to Power: the Grandmothers Speak.*) "**We remind you that this pitcher is filled to the rim with goodness. And next to the pitcher sits a cup. You** *are* **that pitcher,**" they said. "**We will fill you, and from you we will pour out our goodness to everyone and everything.**

"**Watch the pitcher now as it fills the cup,**" they said, and I watched. "**Now look inside the pitcher. It is entirely full! This pitcher can** *never* **be emptied. We fill it,**" they said, "**and we will keep it ever filled.**" They looked at me as if to say, 'Do you dare doubt us?' and I replied, "Yes, Grandmothers, I see." "**Let us fill you,**" they said. "**Take this stance in life: you are the pitcher that cannot be emptied. You are the container.**

"**After you have taken this stance, do everything you are drawn to do from this place. Don't go off on your own, trying to figure life** out and do things all by yourself," they shook their heads. "There is no need for that," they said, lifting their heads and drawing themselves to their full height. "That, after all, is how you become depleted, and you need never become depleted again. We will fill you, we will always fill you.

"From this place of fullness," they said, "cast the Net of Light to those who desperately need it. The Net of Light will remind them they are loved and held in light. Whenever you cast the Net, you remind people that they are precious members of the human family. You allow them to become part of the Net of Light that holds the earth.

"When you cast the Net of Light to the terrorists," they said, "work delicately so you don't become affected by their pain and confusion. When you work with them you must remain aware of how deeply anchored you are and how firmly held in light. You will be able to do this work effectively and you will be protected. Through you, we will send the Net of Light to everyone who needs it," they said. "It will uplift even these tortured souls and remind them of who they are.

"Let power fill you," they said, "more and more power." I sat quietly and thought of receiving what was coming to me and when I was so full I couldn't take in any more, I exhaled deeply. "Experience the center of your chest now," they said.

"Oh!" I exclaimed, and then cried, "Oh, my God!" No sooner had my awareness moved to my chest than I saw that my heart *had become a rose*. A deep pink bloom with a heavenly scent. Petal folded over petal, over and over again until this massive rose spilled over the horizon. *I* was this rose that now covered the world and as I saw and felt it, my heart swelled in gratitude. Then I burst into sobs.

My body began to shake as waves of love overwhelmed me. "We will expand this tender love," they said, patting my back to reassure me, "so you can allow yourself to be carried along with the rose as it grows. Take in as much of this expansion as you want. But only go as far as feels right to you. And remember," they wagged their fingers before my face, "We are the ones who perform this work. There is nothing for you to do but experience it."

When I later listened to this part of the recording all I could hear was my deep breathing and an occasional sob or groan of ecstasy. "We will give you only as much expansion as is right for you," the Grandmothers said, "no more. The increase is tremendous. And whenever you begin to swell like this, keep yourself anchored by thinking of your feet. As we extend the rose farther and farther, keep coming back to check on your feet," they reminded me. "**If you do this, you won't become overwhelmed, but will be able to ride the waves of expansion and still stay grounded. Always remember to let us do the work. This is the right way,**" they nodded, looking pleased with themselves. "**And when you have had enough, return your awareness to your heart, the center of sweetness and joy within you.**

"**This is how you will become a conduit for us,**" they said, "**a plug in the wall.**" Again they looked pleased with themselves, pleased with me as well. "**Always anchored, always firm, steady and grounded— right here and now, so we can work with and through you—right here and now. If you become too caught up in the sensations of expansion, you will become airy and will dwell too much in your mind. When that happens, you lose grounding and we cannot work through you.**" Then motioning me to lie down, they said, "**We will teach you how to do this.**"

I was so enthralled by what it had felt like to be that massive rose, that all I could do was mumble, "Thank you, Grandmothers." Patting me gently while they massaged my back, they said, "**Breathe slowly and settle into yourself now. We are aligned with you. We stand behind you, around you and in front of you. We cover you with our love and light. You are our own,**" they whispered as they rocked me in their arms. I closed my eyes as they had directed and I rested. I had just begun to stammer my thanks to them when the drumbeat signaled me to return to ordinary reality.

I came back feeling unusually quiet, more full of peace than I could remember. I couldn't get my mind off that rose and every time I thought of it I was washed with contentment. My question for the Grandmothers had been, 'how can we serve at this time,' and they had responded by pushing me into expansion and then more expansion. First Eagle dropped me midair, forcing me to focus harder than I ever had. Next the Grandmothers encouraged me to take on more power and in the process expanded my heart far beyond its previous capacity. I had been given the answer to my question all right, but I wasn't ready yet to explain it to others. The answer to 'How can we help?' was expansion, but it would take time to integrate all they had given me. At this point, my energy was turned within myself, to the reservoir of strength and stillness building inside.

Each time I visited the Grandmothers they stretched and challenged me to go beyond where I had gone before. As I looked back on this journey, it reminded me of something a friend had once shared with me. We had been telling our stories, marveling over the way we had each survived an especially difficult period in life when he turned to me and quoted a saying from long ago. "Go!" he said. "Go beyond. Go beyond the beyond. Hail the go!" This too was the answer to my question.

"We will cast the Net of Light from each of you to different places on the earth"

Two years later, on the anniversary of September 11, I returned to the Grandmothers with a similar question. The world situation was, if anything, more perilous than before, and I was feeling truly desperate. When at last I came to their valley, the Great Council regarded me seriously and as they appraised me, I became conscious of my eagle self. The Grandmothers were also in eagle form, and as they eyed me, their wings began to beat. Quickly mine fell into rhythm with theirs, and as the rhythm grew more definite, familiar chills flooded my body. When at last they lifted their wings and shook their feathers, mine shook too. Waves of cold washed me and I began to tremble, becoming so chilled it was hard to concentrate. Still I held to my question like a lifeline.

"Grandmothers," I asked, "what do you want us to do at this difficult time? How can we be of service?" **"Open,"** they replied and the top of my head twitched. **"Open,"** they repeated and stared at me. "Grandmothers, show me how," I pleaded. "How do I do this?" **"Open to us,"** they answered, locking fierce gazes onto mine.

Now, not only the top of my head but all my chakras began to twitch, opening both at the front and the back. I was still shaking with cold, but clung to my question nevertheless. "Show me how we can help," I said, and again they replied, **"Open to us."** This time I felt a small shock in my heart. "Oh!" I exclaimed and jumped, "my heart is being re-wired." Such a strange sensation: one I'd never imagined. The Grandmothers were connecting me with them and with the Net of Light. Again I had no idea how I knew this but I did, and by this time I didn't care. I was freezing, I was tired and everything that was happening to me was way beyond my comprehension.

For a moment I dropped my eyes from their gaze and when I did, I glimpsed the Net of Light spread out before us. As I observed it, a corner of the Net lifted and lightly touched each of my chakras, connecting my body to itself. In fascination I peered at it as it rose high into the air, finally looping itself to the Grandmothers who stood above me. They were holding its strands in their hands and from where I stood it looked like the Net of Light was more thickly crosshatched than it had been before. It seemed to have more heft and appeared to be multidimensional, both horizontal and vertical. Now more like a grid than a fishing net.

I watched as they cast the Net and when it flew outward, my observations were confirmed. There were new layers that both strengthened and enlarged it. Next they began to stake the Net into the ground, hammering and anchoring it to various points on earth. I watched as over and over again they cast, and then staked. **"We will cast the Net of Light from each of you to different places on the earth,"** they said as I watched it fly outward. "Look at that," I said, surprised as it moved from me to the country of Turkey.

The Net fanned out in all directions while point-by-point, the Grandmothers hammered it into the earth. They seemed to be connecting *everything* to the Net of Light. "This is new," I said. "Before this, the Net had seemed horizontal, more like a fishing net, but now," I marveled, "it's vertical *and* horizontal, it's diagonal and it's everywhere." As the Grandmothers worked, the Net of Light criss-crossed more and more of the planet as it cradled the earth from above and from below.

Now it began to connect groups of people to one another, touching individuals, families, cities and whole countries. **"Each of you have specific jobs to carry out,"** the Grandmothers explained, **"and we will work through you so these are fulfilled. You are connected through the Net of Light in a sacred way to different areas and cultures. And through you, we will work with these peoples and places."**

I listened and wondered how this worked. I had always assumed if I were to work with a people, it would be my ancestral group. My family had originated in Poland so I had assumed if I were to work with a particular nationality, it would be the Poles. But Turkey? "Turkey?" I asked. "Grandmothers, why Turkey? I'm not Turkish. I don't know anything about that part of the world, so why am I working there?" They shook their heads, chuckled, and said, **"Enjoy exploring your special connection to this place, enjoy the specific work you are being given."**

Before I could ask more, they said, **"Our mission is being stepped up now. There is no time to waste. No time will be wasted,"** they added, giving me a meaningful look. **"You have a chance to do important work,"** they said, nodding as they pointed fingers at me, **"to be part of something that makes a difference in this world. You can participate in holding the earth and cradling life."** "Thank you, Grandmothers," I said. "They know what they're doing, even if I don't. Turkey may not make sense to me, but it makes sense to them. And that's all I need to know."

I watched the Net of Light construct a web of support underneath every place on the planet. "This is amazing," I marveled, but the Grandmothers interrupted my reverie and said, **"More is happening now than you are aware of. More than you need to be aware of,"** they added, **"but by making yourself available for this work, you will serve the good. You will serve all beings."** Then quietly, but firmly they stated, **"You are not the one choosing to whom to send the Net of Light. We are. The work we are doing together is quickening now and must become more selfless."** "Yes, Grandmothers," I replied, "you know what must be done. Use me however you see fit."

They nodded, watching me with faint smiles on their faces. **"Experience your inner authority,"** they said. **"It is time."** I looked up questioningly. "What does *this* mean?" I thought. **"Whenever you hold and uphold the Net of Light, a deepening takes place within you and within the Net, a deepening and an expansion,"** they added, then regarded me seriously and said, *"The sound of OM is resounding throughout your being, resounding throughout the universe."* And as soon as they spoke the word "OM" I felt its vibration pulse in the surrounding air and inside me too. The echo was so strong it began to vibrate the cells of my body.

"Your connection to the Net of Light is sending you deeper into yourself," the Grandmothers said, **"rooting you to the source of life. Today the Net of Light has become a multi-layered, multi-faceted, multi-dimensional web of light,"** they announced.

Their words sent me further inward and my breathing became slower as I dived into myself. Although I was still conscious of my body, I was also aware that I was much more than this body. I could feel the vastness of my being and as I hummed with the OM and floated in the endless sea within, the Grandmothers said, **"The Net of Light will hold the earth steady and prevent its destruction. We thank you for doing this work today. It is service selflessly given and we thank you for it."**

I was so moved by their words I didn't know what to say. "Why are they thanking me?" I asked, "I'm the one who's grateful." And as I stumbled around, trying to find the right way to express my feelings of gratitude to *them*, the Grandmothers said, **"Feel light gushing from your heart now. Feel it flooding from your throat and pouring out your arms, hands, and head."** "Oh!" I exclaimed as I felt it all. I had become a fountain. Light had taken over my body and was rushing through me, bubbling up and pouring outward.

"Light is pouring out your third eye," they said, "out the top of your head, through your solar plexus, and the back, front, and sides of each of your energy systems. Light is pulsing beneath your naval, your root chakra, your pubic bone, and anus, flowing through your feet and knees." They were right. I was awash in light, flooded with a rushing, flushing radiance. Speechless by the suddenness and force of the flood, I stood where I was and stared.

"You are a grid of light," they laughed, enjoying my look of amazement. "Light is pouring outward from your major energy centers and the minor ones as well. Today we have formed a web of light to hold the earth, and safe and steady we will hold it." Then gazing at me tenderly, they added, "Safe and steady we will hold you."

"Grandmothers," I said, "this is too much. I'm overcome by all this light. It's flowing inside me, flowing through me, around me and I'm nothing but light," I said, amazed. They smiled as they watched me but said nothing; they seemed to be waiting for something. "Grandmothers," I finally said, "even though I understand so little of what you're doing, still I have to ask you something." I had a question, an important one, for myself and for everyone. "I know the Net of Light is here to support us and to support the earth, but we have been told that there will be great destruction as the earth goes through these long predicted changes. "Grandmothers," I said, "will it be very bad?"

"There will be destruction," they said. "There will be shock and loss, but the earth itself will not be destroyed." Shaking their heads, they let me know they would say no more about this now. Then they repeated, "We thank you for doing this work today," and again I was so overwhelmed by them thanking *me*, that I could only murmur, "Oh, Grandmothers."

They walked forward then, encircled me and spread their wings over me, saying, "Rest. You have labored hard. The Net of Light will hold you now. Let it hold you, rock you and uphold you." Their words comforted me and when they wrapped me in their wings, it was truly bliss. As they embraced me, a few of them began to push in lightly on my third eye—to align me more with themselves. As I felt the pressure, I understood that at the up-coming Grandmothers' meeting, they would do the same with each person who came, aligning these people with them too. The Grandmothers would select only those who were up to the task of working with them, and everyone who came would move closer to these wise teachers.

"We are finished for now," they said and rocked me in their embrace. "Rest in our love." "Thank you, Grandmothers," I murmured sleepily and I must have dozed for a moment or two because I woke to the change of the drumbeat, the signal for me to return to ordinary reality. As I bowed good-bye, again they softly touched my third eye. I knew this touch was a blessing and with a heart full of happiness I rose from it and began my journey back.

This lesson began a shift in my understanding of the Net of Light. Up to this point other than feeling a connection with the Net whenever I thought of casting it to others, I hadn't felt the Net of Light inside my own body. At most what I had experienced was a warm spot in the center of my chest. I had seen the Net of Light as a construct that supported the planet and supported me, but I had no inkling of its power and reach. After this lesson I understood the Net of Light was foundational, providing a structure for the entire planet as well as for every form of life on it. And though it connected all parts of our planet, it was also present in my energy systems. The Grandmothers had demonstrated some of the Net's reach and potential, but it was too much for me to take in at this time. I finally had to let it go and leave the subject in their capable hands. It would be years before I really "got" it.

"On this day, the broad band of humanity is particularly flexible."

A few days later, while sitting quietly, meditating and communing with the Grandmothers, for no particular reason, my mind returned to the subject of September 11. The date just popped to mind. My most recent visit to them had been on the anniversary of that date. It had been my worry about the fate of the world that had propelled me to go to them and they had used my worry as a springboard to teach me of the increased power and reach of the Net of Light. "Humm," I mused, "I wonder why I'm thinking about September 11 again."

The Grandmothers came onto the screen of my mind then, smiled knowingly and said, **"Let us teach you about the significance of that date."** "Oh!" I exclaimed, surprised by their sudden appearance. Then as they waited for my response, I remembered my manners. "Okay, Grandmothers," I said. " Thank you."

Instantly they lifted what looked like an unusually wide rubber band and held it out before them. **"On this day, on September 11,"** they explained, **"a broad band is activated for humanity."** I looked up expectantly. **"Over time, the patterns that people live in become hardened and stratified. Inflexible,"** they explained, **"but on this day**

it is different." As I watched and listened, it came to me that 'the broad band' they were talking about was our connection to one another, the connection that underlies our varied cultural conditionings. And it is this bedrock connection that is capable of allowing us to surmount the inflexibility that many times keeps us stuck in a particular 'way of life.'

"**Because the events of September 11 were so shocking and the loss of life so indiscriminate,**" they said, "**the pain and horror of that day were shared by people all over the world. The broad band of humanity was accessed that day. After that human beings were able to make connections with one another that breached all cultures and continents on earth,**" they said and alternately stretched and relaxed the band as I thought about what they were sharing. "**On this day, September 11,**" they said, "**the broad band of humanity is particularly flexible.**

"**Practically speaking, this band allows you closer contact with one another at the core level of being. On this day you can more easily move past superficial relating into the sinews and ligaments that connect and bind you one to another. Not bound by habits or expectations,**" they said, "**but as souls joined together for the purpose of evolving into greatness. This is an elemental connection,**" they explained, "**and brings with it an opportunity for evolution, true evolution.**" Then they smiled and shook their heads at the questioning look on my face, letting me know that for now they would speak no more of this.

As I mulled over their words, I remembered the Net of Light and the way it had looked the last time I'd seen it. It had been thicker and more expanded in all directions—outward as well as inward. More flexible and omnipresent than when I'd first seen it. The 'broad band of humanity' that the Grandmothers were talking about was undoubtedly connected to this expansion in the Net of Light.

Ever since I began to work with them, the Grandmothers had many times reminded me to "Cast the Net," and for all those years I, and thousands of others had done that. What they had just shared reminded me again of how important the Net of Light was. And after today, whether I was with a group or by myself, I would go out of my way to cast the Net of Light every September 11. The Net of Light and this 'broad band of humanity' was awakening to its elemental connection, had a great deal to do with each other.

CHAPTER 4
Cover the World

"Each one seeking position, probing for advantage, jealously guarding and at the same time tentatively exploring."

As the Grandmothers led on, they pushed and stretched me in many ways. I knew now that the Net of Light was 'real' and knew also that the small dramas that occurred in my life were for the most part insignificant. But now and then one of them would catch me unaware, and whenever that happened I had to pull myself back again to what was 'real.' The Grandmothers were my true north, and I tried to stay ever mindful of the direction I was heading.

For years I worked steadily on *A Call to Power: the Grandmothers Speak,* sharing their messages and teachings with anyone who was interested and putting them into manuscript form. This, plus running monthly meetings became my life's focus. I continued my psychotherapy practice, my painting, sculpture, and my family life, but no matter what I did, my heart was always with the Grandmothers. And because of my bond with them, my therapy work went deeper and so did my art.

Although this period of life was exciting, it was at the same time lonely and frustrating. There was no one who truly understood what I was learning so I didn't have anyone to talk to about it. I was also surprised by the many difficulties I had to face as I followed the Grandmothers. I had assumed that with a message as pure and powerful as theirs, the universe would go out of its way to support it. This, however, was not the case.

I couldn't find anyone to publish their book, and the more I pursued agents and publishers, the more rejections I got. At last I was faced with either finding a way to publish *A Call to Power: the Grandmothers Speak* myself or putting it away and forgetting about it. I couldn't do that.

I also began to encounter jealousy. A few women began to belittle my motives, criticize what I was doing and tease me for being "special" because of this work. Again I was taken by surprise. I had expected everyone, but especially women, to feel the love in the Grandmothers' message and automatically open to them and to me, their messenger. When instead some of them sought to undermine me, I was shocked. After this happened a few times I began to question whether or not I should continue with this work. Then I had a dream.

In it I stood alone in front of our local movie theater where I was to be a speaker. Several men were scheduled to speak before me and as I waited my turn I listened to them go on at length, expounding on their theories, pushing hard to sell their ideas and products, so hard that people began to walk out of the theater. I had placed pamphlets describing the universality of the Grandmothers' message in the lobby, and now another group of men—ministers, rabbis and Muslim clerics, all dressed in dark suits, critically eyed them, and me. In the dream I felt courage seeping out of my body through the soles of my feet, and when I turned away from the theater to start for home, I saw the familiar holy man, the one in the orange robe who had for years taught me in my dreams. He stood alone, beside the entrance to the theater and seemed to be studying me. "I don't know what to do," I said to him, wringing my hands in despair. "These are important men and they don't approve of me speaking."

He gave me a severe look and replied, **"What are you going to do? Cry?"** His words shocked me so that I woke with a start. "Cry?" I repeated. "Is that what I'm going to do? "No," I said to him and to myself, "I'm not going to do that." I didn't know how I would find the courage to continue the Grandmothers' work, but I was determined I would.

Soon after this, Wolf—one of the helping spirits who had appeared in my journeys to the Lower World—began to also show up in my dreams. Sometimes I'd see him off in the distance, and at other times he would simply stand quietly beside me. Often he scared me. He was fierce and wild and sometimes snapped. When he kept returning, I realized I would have to go to the world of the animal spirits to find out why. What did he want?

At the same time I learned how to work with the Grandmothers, I also began to work with the helping animal spirits of what shamans call 'the lower world.' I quickly found that the wisdom of the animal spirits, although different from that of the Grandmothers, was just as valuable. In my forays to the world of the animal spirits I had met Wolf only once or twice, and always when I was accompanied by Bear, my main animal teacher. But now it that seemed that I had business with Wolf alone. Once that became clear, I decided to journey to him to find out what he wanted.

"Wolf, Wolf!" I called, as I dove through my opening into the earth, and downward I plunged until I entered the familiar territory of the lower world. At last I pushed my way through thick foliage and cried, "Wolf! Please come." I didn't see him at first, but started when I felt warm breath on me. Surprised, I turned my head, and there he was. "Wolf, I don't know you well," I said, stepping back a pace and eying his intelligent face, "but you've been coming in my dreams. Is there something you want?"

Like a playful dog, he jumped up, placed his paws on my shoulders and looked me in the eyes. "Teach me, Wolf," I said, "show me what you want." **"I am a teacher,"** he said, **"trust me."** I began to stroke the thick ruff of his neck and as he relaxed his body into mine, I nuzzled his ears. Then, paws and arms around each other, we embraced, his head on my chest and mine on his. "Wolf!" I laughed as we fell to the ground, rolled over and lay in each other's arms/paws. It felt so natural to lie folded into him like this that suddenly I felt I knew him very well.

"I am your guardian," he said. **"Call me."** How massive he is, I thought, and how elegant. "Wolf," I said as he licked my face, "I thought this might be why you began to appear in my dreams. I thought maybe you wanted to work with me. When the attack came from D," I said, "and you started appearing, I thought you might be coming to protect me." **"Yes,"** he said, **"and there are others too. You are the target of jealousy."**

We sat up and, leaning into each other, gazed out over what appeared to be a southwestern landscape and because we were seated high on a mesa we could see far into the distance. **"Look!"** he said and I did, but his vision was keener than mine and it took me a while to make out what he had seen immediately. Packs of animals were running off in the distance. They seemed to be everywhere. I watched as masses of them shifted, ran as a unit and then shifted again. "Packs!" I said, stunned by their numbers and by the way they traveled, never as individuals, but always together. Then I noticed that some of them looked too upright to be animals. Were they human?

"The veil between this reality and ordinary reality is thinning for you," Wolf said. **"That is why your visions are not as dramatic as they were earlier. You are no longer always outside inter-dimensional contact,"** he said, **"you are in it all the time."** I wasn't sure what this meant, but I wanted to learn whatever I could from him so I said, "Teach me, Wolf, teach me!" **"I am teacher,"** he repeated. **"Watch."**

The packs approached one another, sniffed, circled warily and checked each other out. **"This is how it is,"** Wolf said. **"Each one seeking position, probing for advantage, jealously guarding and at** the same time tentatively exploring. They seek approval from one another but they are not trusting." As I listened I began to wonder if this was how I was supposed to be. Maybe I was too trusting. Maybe I was supposed to be alert and protect myself more. Was this what he was showing me? **"No,"** he growled, answering my unspoken question. **"Do not worry about protecting yourself. I will do that. Just watch."**

He motioned me to walk forward and then, positioning himself at my left shoulder, he stalked, rather than walked, beside me. As I registered his movements, the familiar chill of recognition ran over my body. "Wolf knows how to guard," I said, "he knows this realm and way of being well and will watch out for me." With bright eyes and lolling tongue, Wolf smiled his lupine smile. **"I want you to call on me,"** he said, **"because without me it is too dangerous for you, and with me, everything will be taken care of.** *He* **sent me,"** he said, referring to the holy man. **"You are to keep me with you all the time."**

He pointed out the massing, sneaking packs in the distance and as I watched, I became aware of the energy of wariness that lay over them. "This state of wariness is what we on earth call 'looking out for number one,'" I said. "It's common here, something many live by." **"But you do not have to live like that,"** Wolf replied. **"You can observe this way of being, in fact it is good for you to be aware of it,"** he added, **"but you can remain apart from it."** "Thank you, Wolf," I said, full of gratitude for his gift of guardianship. "Because he knows this part of life so well, with him at my side I will be protected," I sighed in relief.

"Is there more you want me to learn now?" I asked him. **"No,"** he said, and leaped into the air, began to jump about and race back and forth. As he cavorted, chased his tail and turned summersaults he was so charming, so utterly hilarious that I roared with laughter. "I love your fur, Wolf," I said, "I love your angular body and your lupine, foxy sort of face. Much bigger than a fox face though," I corrected myself, "you have a deeper and more powerful look. "Oh," I exclaimed, "I see what it is. I identify with you. I have the same longing that I see in your face, Wolf. You're wise; you know there is more to life than meets the eye and you want that 'more.' And my body is long too, just like yours." **"We fit,"** he said.

I leaned against him and rested. Wolf is majestic; he is also menacing when need be. When he first appeared in my dreams, he knew just how to get my attention—he scared me. In both dreams, Wolf in the first one, and wolf pups in the second, bit at my hands—not hard, but hard enough to startle me and make sure I remembered the sensation when I awoke.

"Thank you for coming to me," I said. "I'm not always aware of my need for protection. It's not clear to me yet and I guess I don't like to think about it." **"Watch,"** was all he would say. Again I felt him behind my left shoulder, installing himself behind my heart. He would watch from here. "Um m m," I mused. "I see how it will be." He was now so close that we were nearly merged, but whenever he needed to, he would separate himself out a bit—just enough so that he could see and be seen. "Thank you, Wolf," I said. "Thank you very much."

"Poison comes from many lifetimes"

The animal spirits are entirely compassionate and give to us in ways that are far beyond our understanding. And, unlike human beings, they are selfless as well as powerful. Once Wolf assured me of his protection, I lost my hesitancy, knowing he would guard me in both ordinary and non-ordinary reality.

For a short period after this encounter, I began to spend more time with the compassionate animal spirits than with the Grandmothers. This was a change, as in the months before Wolf's appearance I had been so eager to learn what the Grandmothers had to teach me that I had begun going to the lower world less and less. I was too eager to learn, it turned out, because in ignoring the help of the compassionate animal spirits and instead, pushing myself to learn more and more, my health began to suffer and before I knew it I was once again tolerating headaches, back pain, insomnia and fatigue. All of this so I could learn at a faster rate. As my friend, Katy would have said, "I was too dang yang."

Right from the start the Grandmothers told me, **"Go to the helping animal spirits of the lower world three times for healing for every time you come to us for learning."** Because I had suffered from physical pain for many years, when they told me this, I followed their guidance—that is, until my health improved. Once I felt somewhat better, I 'forgot' about the importance of the lower world and might have gone on like this for a long while, ignoring the animal world, except for Wolf and also for Bear who began appearing in my dreams around the same time. Night after night Bear came, and when at last he appeared twice in one night I could put it off no longer. He wouldn't relent until I came to see him.

As I dove through my opening to the lower world, I called to him all the way down the tunnel and when I reached the place where he always showed himself, I said, "Bear, I'm here. You called and so I came." I looked up and there he was. He swayed on two feet and as he lurched forward, he towered over me. I had forgotten about his great size and as I gazed up at his massive form, I said, "At least I think that was you calling me, Bear." The more I looked at him the more I wondered if maybe I had been wrong. Maybe that nocturnal visitor hadn't been *my* Bear. Maybe it was just a figure in a dream. "Was that you who…" I began, but before I could finish, he grabbed me by the nape of the neck, and growling to himself, trotted through the forest, carrying me dangling from his mouth like a cub.

When we came to a clearing in the trees, I turned my head a little so I could see where we were when "Whoa!" I shouted, as unceremoniously he dropped me into a pool of hot water. "**Stay there!**" he grunted and shambled away. The steaming water felt so good that I floated in it, playing with the muddy sides as Bear paced back and forth, casting worried looks at me and rumbling with each step he took.

At last I realized his growling and pacing were coming from his concern for me and I felt ashamed of myself. "I have been so stupid not to come here," I said as the relief of again being in his presence washed over me. "Why am I always in such a hurry to work? in such a hurry to learn?" I asked myself. "Why am I always hurrying?"

"**You have forgotten to come to me,**" Bear said as he tilted me forward and slapped mud on my spine. It felt wonderful and I could tell by the way Bear did this that he was not so much angry with me for neglecting my commitment to the animal world as he was hurrying to help me. Whatever it was, I was so relieved to have those huge paws on me again that I cried in relief. "I had no idea," I said, "no idea how much I needed to come. "**Umph,**" he grunted and with a claw he slit open the skin of my spine and packed mud into it. "**I must do this,**" he said and I wondered, "What does he mean? Where are the helpers who usually work with him here?" "*I must do this,*" he emphasized and I understood that for some reason he was the one who had to perform this work.

"Oh, thank you, Bear," I said, "Thank you so much." He didn't say a word, nor did he waste a moment, but slit open the back of my legs too and piled on a steaming poultice of leaves and mud until I could feel the minerals and herbs seeping into my body. Next he sliced the bottoms of my feet, opened up my hips and packed mud onto my stomach. I was now entirely blanketed with leaves and earth, and the heat and weight of it soothed everything in me. "**Much poisons,**" Bear said, "**much poisons here.**"

He worked on, relentlessly piling mud onto my heart and mounding more of it beneath my back. He slit open my temples, jaw line and forehead, and as he worked I began to feel what he called the poisons, draining out of me. This made me sob and I cried for a long time.

"I had no idea!" I exclaimed in horror, as with his great paws he squeezed the area of my liver and then my spleen, and a drippy mass oozed out of me. A foul odor was rising up while a greenish black mess ran off. Quickly Bear submerged me in the pool again—briefly pushing my head under too. I bobbed around for a time and it was strange because though I could see the poisons pouring out of me, somehow this dark stuff didn't pollute the pool but was drawn off without changing the color of the water.

"**Poison comes from many lifetimes,**" Bear said. "**It is not you, not who you are. It is from many lifetimes. Things taken on, gone through, and carried in the body. No fault in any of this,**" he said, patting me. "**This is psychic material.**" He worked as he talked, preventing the gooey darkness rising out of my cell beds from lodging anywhere else in my body. He labored so hard, laying on so many packs and then quickly removing them that I began to weep again, but this time in gratitude. "**No time,**" he said, "**no time to comfort you.**" "I understand, Bear," I gasped between sobs, "and I'm so grateful."

Squeezing and massaging, he pulled layers of slime off me and as he worked, I silently cheered him on, willing as much of this horrid stuff as possible to leave. Finally he said, "**Don't be in such a hurry. Don't try to get rid of it all now. It would be more than you could 'bear,**" he said and grunted happily at his pun.

When he helped me out of the water, I folded my legs under me and sat at the edge of the pool. The sun felt good on my damp skin and I began to drift off, almost falling asleep. But I woke with a start when I heard Bear say, "**This is a period of accelerated change. Now it is time for work. This,**" he said, "**is the planetary shift you have heard about. It will affect everyone. Do your part,**" he said, giving me a look of intense seriousness. "**Come here every day, if possible. Here or to the Grandmothers,**" he added, "**three to one.**"

"Great change is coming. It will be felt by everyone."

Two days later I returned to the lower world, determined to again stick with that three-to-one formula. There was no question that I needed the healing of the compassionate animal spirits. I was already calmer and stronger since journeying to Bear and Wolf.

I entered the lower world the same way I always did and no sooner did I encounter Bear than he hoisted me onto his back, swung around on the path and began to run. He had said that this was a time of accelerated change and by his attitude I could see that this was so.

We followed a pathway that cut through a forest and before long it began to carry us uphill. Soon a pointed mountain rose before us that seemed to have sprung out of nowhere. It simply appeared, but undaunted by its steep slope, Bear plowed on while I hung on tight. After a while the atmosphere around us changed and instead of green trees and blue sky, now a grayish white light lay over everything. A wintry fog had dissolved the trees, hidden them from view, and now all I could see were indistinct shapes. My nostrils flared with the smell of cold and as I hunched over Bear, I heard the piercing whistle of the wind. Thunder rolled in the distance, and then swelled to a roar, as it rumbled nearer and nearer. At last a blast of wind was upon us, lifting the hair from my head and stinging my eyes, but I was able to bury myself in Bear's fur, so I was warm enough.

"**Storm Clouds,**" Bear growled, frowning, "**Storm clouds.**" "Oh," I gulped. We were in the midst of these clouds now, surrounded by them, and as the thunder roared and the earth beneath us shook, I clung tightly to Bear's back. "**Great change is coming,**" he said; "**this change will be felt by everyone.**" This, I realized was what he had alluded to the last time I saw him and as I held fast to his fur, the cells of my body began to tremble. Rocks that had stood beside our pathway now rolled, cracked open and dropped off the side of the mountain. A frightening dark shape, like some primeval bird flew over our heads. Yet all the while the earth shook and I shook with it, because I was on Bear's back, I knew I was safe. "**Destruction,**" he said at last, "**de-struction.**" "Oh," I murmured, "Is this is about taking apart the old?" "**Yes,**" he said.

Taking apart the old, I thought, and fear began to chew at the edges of my mind, but before I could give in to it, Bear said, "**You are here now to observe. That is all.**" He was reminding me that my job was to watch, to observe what was taking place and not be affected by the destruction occurring around me. Whatever was happening here was for now occurring only in this level of reality. I was to learn from it. Not react, but only watch.

I relaxed a little at this thought, but tensed up again when soot began to rain down on us. The air grew thick with it and when particles landed on my face and head, I cried, "What *is* this, Bear?" panic in my voice. "**Dirt,**" he pronounced, with disgust, "**dirt. It shows the condition of things.**" "The condition of things?" I asked, but all he would say was, "**This condition will clear.**" And then he patted me and said, "**Everything is taking place as it should.**"

I pondered his words. Something was changing, a big shift *was* occurring and this dirt was the fall out. Something big was about to take place on earth. This felt so serious, so frightening that my mouth got dry. "Bear," I finally asked, "what can I do to help as this change takes place? Please, Bear, how I can help?" **"Come here to the lower world,"** he said, **"and go to the Grandmothers."** He was repeating what he had already told me. To keep myself strong and steady, I must both learn and heal.

Gradually the ground stopped shaking, the dirt no longer fell on us and all was quiet again. When the birds began to sing, Bear stopped in the middle of the path and lifted his head to test the air. Then he breathed a quiet, rumbling sigh and slowly meandered down the mountain. He looked entirely relaxed now. No longer in a hurry, he actually seemed to be enjoying himself. He stopped to sniff at a flower; then rubbed his huge behind against a tree and again lumbered down the path. "Hummm," I mused as I watched him, "Obviously the lesson of this journey, whatever it was, is over." And then I wondered. "What did it all mean?"

Sitting astride Bear's wide body I let my dangling legs swing in rhythm with his stride. It was such a pleasure to rock along like this, especially after the race up the mountain and the panic of the ensuing storm. **"Slowly follow the path,"** he said as he glanced back at me, **"no hurry."** "Ahhh," I whispered. Bear was showing me how to slow down by letting me feel the rhythm of an unhurried pace.

He took his time coming down the mountain and I marveled at how relaxed he was. Then I marveled at how relaxed *I* was. It hardly seemed possible that just a few minutes ago we had been in the midst of destruction, turmoil and terror. I shook my head to clear my thoughts and wondered again what it all meant. I wasn't sure, but what I did know was there was a storm coming and when it came, I must not give in to fear. And, above all, I must *SLOW DOWN*.

Bear carried me to the edge of the forest where the river meets the trees and there he sat down so I could slide off his back. **"Go slow,"** he said and gently swatted me with a paw. "I will, Bear," I promised.

I was much stronger after these forays to the lower world; I was also newly inspired to share the Grandmothers' message with the world. My journeys with Bear had shown me that there was indeed a big change coming. The shift that so many had predicted would take place and the way I looked at it, the more people who knew about the Grandmothers' message and chose to work with them, the easier this change would be.

"Cover the world."

I faithfully tended to the Grandmothers' work and though spreading their message gave me great joy, periodically I became discouraged because not as many people as I had hoped would respond to the Grandmothers' message, had. Was their message only for a few? I wondered. Was it my fault that their work was not as well known as I would have liked it to be? Had I taken it as far as I could? And when I got really discouraged I would start to wonder if I should I keep going with this work and if so, why?

I wrestled with these questions many times and would periodically go through bouts of self-doubt concerning what seemed to be the slow spread of their message. A disappointment of some kind would often set me to questioning the relevance of what I was doing, making me ask if the Grandmothers' message was so important, why was it moving forward so slowly? This sort of questioning might go on for a while until eventually I'd say, "Oh, give it up, Sharon. You'll never figure any of this out." Then I'd think, "I love the work so I do the work," and like a cork, I'd pop out of the quagmire of doubt.

Around this time the issue came to the fore again but this time I didn't go to the Grandmothers to ask them about it. By now I'd been on the roller coaster of doubt so many times that I just decided to let it run it's course and keep working anyway.

Then one day while meditating, out of the blue my inner voice spoke to me, making the purpose of my journeys to the upper and lower worlds clear. Spreading the Grandmothers' message, it said, would keep me busy by giving me good work to do and helping my spirit evolve. This work would heighten my vibration and it would do this not just for me, but for everyone who chose to be on the ride with the Grandmothers. I hadn't officially asked a question, but the universe had answered the one festering below the surface of my mind. Clearly the worth of the Grandmothers' work was not to be measured in numbers, but in personal transformation.

After this communication, I went back to the Grandmothers to ask for more work. I wanted to be busy and I really liked the way 'heightening my vibration' sounded.

As I rose from my tree on my way to the upper world, I noticed this time I had white wings—lacy ones that appeared unusually graceful and wide. And as I lifted upward, I glanced back and saw that today I also had a new body, one I'd never seen before. I looked like a heron or a swan. As I sailed into their valley I also felt different, and when I stood before them, I noticed that I was perching on one leg.

I was fascinated by my metamorphosis but was determined not to let my unusual appearance distract me from the purpose of this visit. "Grandmothers," I said as I folded my wings, "I want work to keep me busy while my spirit evolves. I need a job. I've finished *"A Call to Power: the Grandmothers Speak"* and now I want to know if there's more I can do."

I bowed to them, bending forward like a ballerina, with one foot pointed while my wings spread over the ground. **"See how beautiful you are?"** they asked and began to lovingly stroke me. I stood quietly and let them do it because I knew they wanted to, but it was hard for me to stand still and simply receive. My mind kept going to embracing *them*, to giving to *them*. But whenever these thoughts arose, they whispered, **"No... receive,"** until I gradually relaxed enough to let their touch calm and ground me. And as I did, their love seeped into my feet and my wings too, all the way to down to my feathered fingertips.

I felt so relaxed, so naturally myself that I stretched; craned my neck, and my bird head began to rock back and forth. It was at that point that I began to sing. I hadn't decided to sing; suddenly I *was* singing. "I'm pulling the moon down into myself," I crooned, and no sooner were the words out of my mouth/beak than the silver light of the moon in the sky began to merge with the whiteness of my body. Amazed at what was happening, I lifted a foot to walk forward and as I did, my eyes fell on my bird toes. "Ah!" I exclaimed, overcome with enchantment.

I bent my leg further and watched as it came down in sections—knee, ankle, and heel. My wings were equally fascinating, and transfixed by the rhythm of the movements in my new body, I began to intone, "Maranatha, maranatha." I was calling Christ. "Christos," I uttered prayerfully, and startled by what I had just heard myself say, I said, "Wait a minute. What am I doing?" But no matter what I thought about it, I seemed to have no control over my voice, and again and again the word "Christos," rose up and out of me.

This went on for a minute or more until suddenly the sky filled with white birds. My eyes darted to the Grandmothers who nodded to reassure me and then watched the sky too. My cry of "Christos" had called them. Great white birds, very like myself, were winging in from every direction, the air growing thick with them. "It's like the Bosque del Apache when the snow geese are migrating," I said, "but these birds are coming to *my* cry!" And as I watched the sky, flocks of them began to land and spread over the ground.

"Christos?" I said to the Grandmothers, "why does this call bring them in?" Nodding like the wise teachers they are, they said, **"You are calling on the presence of the Christos, you are calling on the presence of the Christ consciousness."** Tilting their heads as they gave me a look of infinite patience, they said, **"You are calling on the human being to become God."** "Oh!" I squeaked, struck dumb by my temerity. "Where did I get this idea, Grandmothers?" I asked, "This never even occurred to me." But they smiled their secret smiles and didn't speak again.

I waited, but still they said nothing, so I tried again. "Grandmothers," I said, "this is terribly beautiful. The birds and all," I added, "but I don't know what any of it means. And Grandmothers," I said, recalling the purpose of this journey, "what I really want is for you to show me my work. This is why I came to you today." Smiling knowingly, they nodded to one another and said, **"This is your work."**

"What?" I asked, confused by their response, but although I stared at them with this question in my eyes, they said nothing. Finally, since they weren't being of any help, and not knowing what else to do, I began to walk toward the flocks resting on the ground. "There are so many of them and how lovely they are!" I said as I stepped among them. The birds watched me with interest and as I examined them closely I saw that their feathers were very like my own. "Grandmothers," I said, "what does this mean? Why are we so much alike?" Then, remembering to stick to the purpose of my journey, I went back to, "What is my work, Grandmothers? Show me my work."

Gradually the birds began to lift into the air. A flock of them arced to the right and as I watched them I realized that just before they lifted off I had moved my wings to the right. Now I gestured to the left and another flock lifted to the left. However I moved my wings, they moved. If I gestured left, they glided left. If I lifted my wings high, they lifted high. "I feel like an orchestra conductor," I said.

Suddenly and without warning, my wings rose too and lifted me off the ground. I glided forward effortlessly and as I did, the others followed me until we formed an enormous V in the sky. As we flew, I glanced over my shoulder and for as far as I could see, white wings were beating in concert. In a vast formation we circled over the land below and when at last we came in for a landing I felt my wings fan so wide it seemed they must cover the earth.

When I felt the ground underneath my feet I knew I had landed. Then I looked down and saw that my wings were still spread wide, noticed also that something was moving among my feathers. I bent my head to examine my wings and found babies nestling there! Little ones of every kind—newborn children, kittens, puppies, various small creatures were gathered together under my wings. As I peered at this strange sight I realized I had dreamed something like this the night before. And now here it was! My wings were spread so wide they were able to shelter hundreds of little ones. "Oh!" I exclaimed, "If all the birds here did this, everything on earth would be nurtured." And then it dawned on me. "Grandmothers," I asked, "Is this my work? Is this what you are showing me?"

Holding their sides, the Grandmothers doubled over as they gestured to one another. **"Did you think she'd ever get it?"** they asked. However, I was still too confused to join in with them. "Grandmothers," I sighed, " I'm tired of trying to make sense of all this; I still don't understand. All I can think of is, I'm supposed to lead a group and we are to do some kind of nurturing." They remained silent, but nodded their heads in understanding. Then they hunched their shoulders forward, fastened their eyes on me and waited expectantly.

Oh!" I whispered as understanding finally came, "It's in the spreading of the wings, isn't it?" I asked. "I must tell everyone about the power in these wings." **"Yes!"** they exclaimed, relieved that I had begun to understand what this lesson was about. **"Teach this to the women. They can become great birds and experience what it is to protect and shelter others. The subconscious mind has an innate understanding of symbols and, though it doesn't pay attention to words, it feels and knows the power of a wide wingspan. Understands that wings are for sheltering and nurturing,"** they said. Again they were illustrating the power of yin.

"First talk about the power of symbols," they said. **"Use the Pitcher and the Cup, the Net of Light, and our other teachings as examples. The great winged bird is yet another. This symbol will tap them into their power,"** they said, nodding wisely. **"It will free them from feeling alone by giving them an experience of their union and purpose with one another. In this way they will become instruments for mothering, nurturing and sheltering.**

"When they focus on their wings," the Grandmothers said, **"ask them to feel *our* light shining and filtering through them because our work is based on service, the power in these wings will serve the greater good. The wings are the vehicle for power and care-giving on earth."**

Then they showed me my human self, standing before the group of women in Laguna Beach, gesturing like a bird in flight. It was a ridiculous-looking posture, and when I glimpsed myself I looked beseechingly at the Grandmothers. "Don't make me do this," I said with my eyes. They pursed their lips, averted their glance and said, "**Let them try it and you try it with them. Yes, yes,**" they said, over my protestations, "**You must demonstrate it first to show them how. Many of these women have never sensed this power within themselves. Ask them to stand with their arms outstretched, and have them do this in silence. We will lead you.**"

"I'll play with it," I said, resigning myself to looking like a fool. "**Yes, play with it,**" they replied. "Hummm," I muttered, "Maybe if we all did this with our eyes closed it would cut down on our (my) self-consciousness." I was mulling this over when I heard the Grandmothers say, "**Cover the world.**" Quickly I glanced up, but their eyes were not on me, but on the horizon. They seemed to be watching something out there.

"This work we are doing with you is part of a movement, isn't it, Grandmothers?" I asked them, surprised by the idea, which had suddenly popped into my mind. "**Yes,**" they said, and then turned and pointed to a bird, sitting very still on a branch near us. I watched this bird for several moments and it didn't lift a feather until without warning, it flew away. Out of the corner of my eye I noticed smiles playing around the Grandmothers' mouths and when I turned to them, they broke into laughter. "A movement," I said to them, "Grandmothers, I get it. The bird moved. This *is* a movement, isn't it?" "**Yes,**" they said again, looking a bit smug. The Grandmothers love to play with words.

Now they pointed to a different scene. This time women were standing together underneath the trees in my back garden and as I looked, I saw a nimbus of light glowing inside and around each woman. The light grew so bright I could barely make out the figure it enclosed and I was staring with so much concentration that I'd stopped breathing. When I realized I was holding my breath, I purposefully exhaled then inhaled deeply and as I did, my back stretched wide while the reach of my arms became enormous. I glanced at the Grandmothers in surprise and they laughingly said, "**This work will stretch your idea of who you are, stretch you into greatness.**"

The drumbeat stopped then, and when its rhythm sped up again, signaling me to return to ordinary reality, it pounded a beat into my third eye. This rhythm reverberated throughout my body and concentric rings of light began to fan out from my forehead, giving me an odd sense of circling and expansion. And in this pleasant, but strange state,

I bowed to the Grandmothers and said goodbye for now. Eagle accompanied me, and when I glanced over to say goodbye it looked like he was smiling. "What?" I wondered, "Eagle doesn't smile," but as I landed in the topmost branches of my tree I caught a glimpse of myself and smiled too. I looked like a great white heron.

At the next Grandmothers meeting, I did exactly as they had directed—shared the potency of the symbol of the bird with spread wings. Then we stood outside and practiced it. First we closed our eyes and meditated on the way a great bird opens its wings, and then we opened our own arms/wings the same way. At first I felt self-conscious, standing in front of forty women like this and for a moment I nearly burst into nervous laughter. But I didn't, and neither did they.

The Grandmothers were right. There was power in this position, and when we stood with our upper arms stretched to the side, and bent our elbows so our hands pointed upward we felt the sense of command in this posture. It gave us a feeling of majesty and queenliness. This, I realized was the posture of the ancient goddess of Crete, the one with snakes wound around her arms. We felt the stance's power and, because we performed this exercise together, the experience was even more potent.

Afterwards, women reported what a sense of solidarity this exercise had given them—solidarity with one another and an "I will not be moved" feeling within themselves. Confidence too, enormous confidence. When you stood like this it was impossible to find fault with or think little of yourself. We recognized that we were taking yet another step into what the Grandmothers call Beauty/Power. Owning and honoring the presence of yin within ourselves.

CHAPTER 5

Taking On Power

"You must take power—now!"

Every time I went to the Grandmothers or to the helping animal spirits I was encouraged and sometimes even forced, to grow. Some of these experiences were gentle while others were fierce. They seemed to vary the menu just enough to keep me coming back for more. Too much drama at a time would have exhausted me while too much loving expansion might have bored me. Whatever they did served the purpose because I was always eager to learn more from them and never, *never* was I bored.

Bear often appeared in my dreams, now and then showing up several times in one night and, after one of those nights when he came more than once, I got out of bed the next morning determined to travel to him. I found him waiting at the other end of the tunnel with an intent expression on his face. "Bear," I said as soon as I saw him, "you've been coming in my dreams again. What is it you want?" He stood still for a moment, seeming to think over my question, then made a lunge for me, tossed me on his back and sped down the trail. When I felt his urgency, I wrapped my legs and arms around him, flattened myself against his fur and hung on. He scrambled down an embankment, dislodging rocks that came crashing into the water with us, but that didn't slow him at all. Undaunted, he plunged into the water and swam with the current, then bounded onto the other side and sped on.

We hadn't gone far when suddenly extreme peaks rose before us that reminded me of mountains I had once seen in Woolong Province in China. On a recent journey Bear and I had come upon a sharp mountain peak, but these were even more sere, with fewer trees. "Where are we?" I asked, but he ran on, his silence reminding me to stick to my original question. "Bear, why have you been coming in my dreams?" I asked and again he stayed mum while doggedly hauling us upward. The sense of urgency grew and grew until the hair on the back of my neck stood on end.

But nothing slowed Bear's pace. Now he clambered onto a high plateau and though I had many times stood on similar terrain in the American Southwest, I could tell the energy here was different. This was another place. "This is the steppes," I said, and wondered how I knew. "Asia—China, Mongolia, somewhere in the east," and as I surveyed the land spread before us, I saw what appeared to be banners in the distance. From where I stood, they looked like small sticks, poking up here and there on the plain. And when I shaded my eyes to see better, I saw that there were masses of people gathered around the banners.

"Bear, Why have you been coming in my dreams?" I asked again. In answer, he lifted his nose, sniffed the air intently, and growled, **"Evil is brewing."** This sobered me and I gasped as I took in a breath. "If this is what is happening, Bear," I said; "if evil *is* brewing here, show me what we can do. Tell me," I said, my voice catching. **"Evil is gathering there,"** he pointed to the banners. **"Watch!"** he said, and then, turning slightly to the right, gestured to the vast plain that stretched before us.

I glued my eyes to the multi-colored grasses swaying in the wind and watched. The swaying became more pronounced and then the grasses parted. "Horses," I whispered as herds of them poured onto the plain, running in our direction. Reds, blacks, tans, pintos, browns, and whites raced toward us. They whinnied and called to one another as they came on and the drumming of their hooves filled my ears. Onward they surged, throwing up a great dust cloud that hung in the air above them.

The horses advanced, racing along a diagonal, row after row galloping across the land. A group raced in from the left and was met by a cross current from the right. No sooner did one herd thunder toward us than another pounded forth. Wave after wave washed over the plain, overlapping as they came together. I watched the patterns they created as they ran, struck dumb by their majesty. Then my eyes fastened on a herd of white ones charging in our direction and suddenly I recalled the great medicine man Black Elk's vision and remembered the mythic significance of "horse."

"Horse is the symbol of power," I said, and turned to Bear and asked, "Why are horses appearing in this place?" Bear made a deep rumbling sound, thumped his chest and said, **"You must take power—now!"** He spoke with such ferocity that I jumped. **"Yes,"** he growled as I stared, my eyes wide, and nodding his head while his great body swayed from side to side he looked so serious that all the love I felt for him swelled inside my heart. Spreading his paws in a gesture of expansion, he said, **"You must step forward and be willing to hold more power."**

The intensity of his look told me this was something I must do. "Okay," I quickly replied, so quickly I surprised even myself, "I'm in." And with no further ado I took a little hop and swung a leg over one of the white horses near us. I couldn't believe I'd done it, but before I could reconsider, I grabbed his mane in one hand and jumped up onto his back. Now I was *standing*, and when another horse edged in, I placed a foot on his back too. So now with a foot on each mount, I began to ride. "This is crazy," I muttered, aghast at my daring. "How in the world am I doing this?" But my legs were rock solid beneath me, and each time the pair's hooves struck ground, power thundered into me.

"I'm a charioteer without a chariot," I said as I grasped their manes and galloped forward. The sun baked my back and as I felt its deep penetration I remembered a picture I'd once seen of the chariot of the sun. Then it came to me that the disc of the sun was forming the back of *this* chariot. "It's like the chariot in the Bhagavad-Gita, the one Lord Krishna drove onto the battlefield," I said. "Hum…a battlefield," I mused. Then my breath caught in my throat and I said, "what if *this* is a battlefield?" Chills climbed my spine and, with eyes wide, I turned my head and fastened my eyes on Bear. "Is it?" I asked him, "is *this* a battlefield? **"Yes,"** he said.

I leaped down from my mounts, ran to a stop before him and with all the force I could muster demanded, "Bear, *why* have you been coming in my dreams? Again he pointed to the plain, but this time I saw the hoards that had gathered there were now massed in one place, throwing up dust as they jockeyed with one another for position. Somehow I knew they were preparing for battle. **"Yes,"** said Bear, **"it is time to stand in the light,"** and facing me straight on, he locked his eyes on mine and roared, **"Stand in the light!"**

I was stunned speechless, and for a moment all I felt was the heat of the sun. Behind me burned the disc of the sun, what I had recognized as the back of the chariot. As I again felt its heat, I said, "The sun is the source; it is the light," and as I spoke, thousands of rays shot from its aura. At the same moment someone said, **"Array the forces of light."** I turned to Bear and asked, "What does this mean?" but no sooner were the words out of my mouth, than I understood. The people who are drawn to the Grandmothers' work *are* forces of light. Wherever they stand, wherever they go, they hold light steady.

Suddenly women who had practiced the Grandmothers' work for many years, appeared and as we stood together we formed a long line.

I watched as one at a time, each of us stepped forward and received a mantle. It was an armoring of sorts, and looked like a golden casement. As mine slipped over my head I noticed it had been designed to cover the core organs of my body, especially my heart. The mantle glimmered gold and was made of a flexible woven material that gave protection. Carefully it encased the heart but its aura also protected the head, arms, hands, and the rest of the body too, providing a light, yet complete, armoring.

Now the Grandmothers appeared and stood beside us. "**What you refer to as evil comes in many forms,**" they explained. "**When it appears, it doesn't reveal itself as a monster. It is seldom even recognized as evil. Evil is surreptitious and small, or at least initially appears small,**" they said, nodding sagely. "**It gnaws at you as doubt, as numbness or preoccupation with the unimportant details, dramas and traumas of life. *That* is evil,**" they said, "**because it leaches your energy. Whenever you lose sight of the One you create an opportunity for what you call evil to enter. This is why we are giving you this protective armor. This gold mesh armor of light will hold you upright and in alignment with the Divine.**"

"Ooohh," I exclaimed, "there is such *invincibility* in it." This was exactly the word to describe the safety I felt. "**Teach others how to watch the world from this place of power and protection,**" they said. "**When you are encased in the armor of light it will be easy to observe the creeping ways of evil and yet not be affected by it. You will notice how it distracts and draws you in, how it creates worry, fear, and busyness. You will able to watch as it tries to worm its way into your mind.**" "Yes, Grandmothers," I said. "Teach me."

"**You are needed to stand steady and uphold the light now,**" they said while Bear nodded in agreement. "**Avoid fearfulness, avoid gossip, and spending much time on petty matters. Do the work of your life,**" they gave me a level look; "**do what lies before you. And always stay within the casement of gold that we have given you today.**"

Now I became aware of the mantle that lay lightly on my body, conforming to the curves and shapes that are mine. "**The armor of light will feel good to those who wear it,**" they said; "**it follows the contours of the body.**" Then turning to one another, they laughed and I heard them say, "**We supply it; you apply it.**"

The Grandmothers cast loving looks at us, but after a minute or more they seemed to grow sober. "**The darkness on earth is increasing now. This is the storm.**" I remembered the furious clouds that had gathered over the mountain, the ones Bear and I had seen a few days earlier. "Do you mean the storm is upon us?" I asked, my voice high with fright. **"You have nothing to fear,"** they said and patted me with their wings. **"Stay in the light and do not be distracted by the storm. Let it blow and roar as it will, but you stay in the light!"** "Yes, Grandmothers," I said, but wondered if I would be able to do this. When push came to shove could I withstand the roar of that tempest?

Interrupting the doubts that had begun to wash over me, they said, **"Stop a moment and feel your body. Note the light surging inside you at this moment and feel the way it shimmers and vibrates. This light not only protects you,"** they said, **"although it certainly does that, it also serves as a beacon. And this aspect of the light is important.**

"When others see light, they resonate to it and begin to awaken to its presence within themselves. So whenever you clothe yourself in the armor of light you help yourself and you help many." Smiling, they gestured and said, **"You give people somewhere to turn.**

"You have been called," they said and looked hard at those of us who stood before them. **"Each of you has been called at this time to stand steady, to hold and be held by light.**

"It is also important to be aware of the tricks of the place of 'not light' to remember that these tricks are subtle and rarely obvious." They paused a moment to be sure I got the import of their words, and then looked into my eyes. **"Ask to be made aware of how evil approaches you. Ask to be shown how it tries to sneak up on** you." They watched me closely to see how I was reacting to this message. "Yes, Grandmothers," I said and then I closed my eyes and asked to be shown how evil approaches me. My stomach plummeted. As soon as I posed the question, fear engulfed me. I felt lost, alone in a world where no one understood me. The experience was so real, the feeling so strong that I got dizzy, even nauseated.

"This avenue of thought, the belief that you are alone in the world," they said, **"has many times sent you into despair. This is how what we call evil gets to you and feeds. It is important for you to know this,"** they added, **"so you can watch for it."** "Yes, Grandmothers," I said, so queasy that my voice was barely audible. **"This is *your* experience,"** they said, **"but each person who asks to be shown how evil approaches them will have a different experience. At the next meeting, tell everyone to be brave and ask themselves this question too. They will also get an answer so they too can be alert to how evil worms its way into them. This,"** they said, nodding knowingly, **"is the beginning of freedom."**

I was still shaking from my contact with evil, but focused with as much concentration as I could on what they were saying. **"When you ask the question, do not be distracted by the drama that evil creates but hold firm to the truth. This is simply the way evil enters your life."** And giving me a severe look, they added, **"This lesson is not for the faint hearted."** "Yes," I whispered. Indeed this lesson was not for the faint-hearted; I still felt queasy and light-headed. I sighed, took in a few breaths and asked, "Grandmothers, is there anything more you want me to know right now?" **"Know that we are with you,"** they said, and beamed at me with such love that my eyes welled with tears.

Too overcome to speak, I simply gazed at them and Bear and as my eyes rested on them, it came to me that whenever Bear comes into one of my dreams he is signaling. He may be calling me to the Grandmothers or to the compassionate animal spirits, but he is calling. "I need to remember that," I said. "Whenever He shows up, it's time to go and see them."

This lesson on the ways of evil and how to spot it was one of the most important teachings I received. And once I saw the route evil used to creep and crawl its way into my life I was on guard. Whenever that painful yet familiar feeling of being alone, of being an outsider in life, came up, I'd say, "Oh no you don't." Then I'd call on the Grandmothers, turn the sneaking thing over to them and proceed to move forward. This became easier and easier and though I still sometimes forgot, I learned that as soon as evil was unmasked, it lost its power and slunk away.

After this journey I became aware of a growing power inside me. This was something I hadn't known before—a feeling of steadiness, but more than just steadiness. Bear had told me I must be willing to take on more power because the task ahead demanded it. I had said yes to him, ridden the horses of power and after I did that I was no longer the same woman. Day and night a line from an old civil rights song ran in my mind. "We shall not be moved, we shall not be moved," I sang until the day I realized that for me the words were not, "We shall not be moved," but "I *cannot* be moved." There was a resolute quality inside me now that was fast becoming home base. Steady and grounded, I knew nothing could stop me from pursuing the work the Grandmothers were bringing forward. A sense of purpose had invaded every part of my life and now *I* was on a mission.

"You will introduce a balance of yin and yang to this place."

The presence of power and its accompanying steadiness became real and slowly and gradually seeped into every corner of my life. It wasn't a conscious thing. It just happened; like Topsy, it grew. And with this steadiness, of course came confidence. These were qualities I would need in spades as the Grandmothers pushed me to confront the more difficult areas of life. I had no idea how timely my last journey to Bear had been. He had taught me the importance of watching for fear and evil, watching carefully so I could be free from reacting to either of them.

All the time I was traveling to other dimensions of reality, holding meetings and writing *A Call to Power: the Grandmothers Speak,* I was also attempting to carry on a somewhat normal life: seeing clients, fixing dinner, entertaining friends, painting and working in the garden. I rarely talked with my family about what I was learning because the subject didn't interest them and there were only certain friends I could speak to about it. However, through daily osmosis, the Grandmothers' message seeped its way into my husband's and my life. Our children were out of the house by this time so the person most affected by the change the Grandmothers were working on me was Roger. Little by little he began to understand and appreciate the effect these wise beings were having on our lives. And rather than being threatened by my increased power and confidence, he liked it.

Throughout our marriage we had used our times away from work to travel to far off places, and before the Grandmothers arrived, I had looked forward to these adventures as much as Roger did. Because we enjoyed discovering the unexpected, we had a preference for exotic, out-of-the way destinations. But after I had spent time traveling to the worlds within non-ordinary reality, normal travel no longer held the same thrill it had. Roger, however, was still excited by foreign lands, so when it was time for a vacation, we went.

In January we would go to Angkor Watt in Cambodia and then on to Burma. This holiday had not been my idea, nor had I chosen these countries. Once again I was along for the ride. It was Roger who wanted to see Angkor Watt, 'one of the wonders of the world,' and since the political situation in Burma had shifted a bit, and the country wasn't too far from Cambodia, he wanted to explore it as well. The day before we were to leave it dawned on me that there might be more to this trip than the travel brochures promised; maybe there was something special to learn and/or do in these out-of-the-way places. So at the last moment, I went to the Grandmothers and asked.

With this question in mind, I landed in their valley and was surprised to see them standing with the holy man. The Grandmothers and the holy man didn't often appear together, but before I could greet them, they all walked forward and quickly surrounded me, coming in so close that the Grandmothers seemed to encapsulate me while the holy man rose to a point above my head where he created what looked like an umbrella of light. Though I was a bit nonplussed by this, I stuck to my question and said, "My dear teachers, we are leaving tomorrow for Cambodia and Burma and I want to know if I can be of service. I want to serve all the time," I added, "even on vacations." **"We know,"** the Grandmothers chuckled and stepped in closer, tightening their circle. Now I felt their protection as well as their love. I also liked the cozy, sheltering feel of that umbrella of light.

As they had done several times before, they walked me to the edge of a cliff and pointed into the distance, telling me to look. At first all I saw was an expanse of blue sky, but when I dropped my eyes I noticed the undulating canyons, mountains, and valleys that rolled in, one over another, all the way to the horizon. **"Many worlds,"** the holy man said as he pointed, **"and you go to a world tomorrow. We are sending you and Roger to another world."** I turned to him with a questioning look but he ignored me, so I looked to the Grandmothers. They, however, were also silent, regarding me with impassive looks until at last it came to me that this "vacation" was to be about the energies of masculine and feminine. I would be working with yin and yang. Was this right? I wondered. I looked up and the holy man nodded, yes.

"Sit and pray with Roger in these places," he said, **"and call on us."** And from this I understood that while on this trip, whenever I called on either the Grandmothers or the holy man, both would respond. This gave me a comforting feeling and I smiled my thanks to them. However, they didn't respond, but instead looked very serious.

"The energies of masculine and feminine in this part of the world have been out of balance for eons," the Grandmothers said and shook their heads. **"Woman has not been venerated as she should be."** This was clearly something that concerned them. **"Because you and your husband are in harmony with each other,"** they explained, **"you will introduce a balance of yin and yang to this place."** "Oh," I said, "it sounds like you are giving us an assignment." They nodded, smiled and, watching me expectantly, added, **"TARA will greet you."**

I took in a breath, "Tara!" I exclaimed. "Tara will greet me?" but they said nothing, just continued to smile and nod. Green Tara, black Tara, white Tara, I thought, the legendary goddess in all these forms. For years I had read and heard about her but didn't really understand who she was. I turned to the Grandmothers to ask about this goddess of the east, and I saw her. She was dancing in the space directly in front of them. Graceful in her movements, she had a softly rounded figure like that of an animated statue from the Kyber era. "She sits in Angkor Watt," I said with authority and as I spoke I was aware that once again I was 'knowing' something without understanding how I knew it. "**Emerging, emerging, TARA is emerging**," the Grandmothers replied.

"**Wherever you go, you will carry our message**," they said. They were changing the subject and as they looked away from the dancing goddess, she disappeared. "**Roger will flank and protect you as together you hold the work of the great yin**. "Roger will protect me?" I asked. "Why...why do I need protection?" but they remained mum. Finally they said, "**Yin and yang will once again sit in harmony in these places**," and they crossed their arms while they nodded their heads slowly up and down for emphasis. "**This is a sacred journey**," they said, and quickly added, "**Do not share all that we are telling you with him right now**." I saw the way they were looking at me and understood. If I were to speak about this now, it might feel like too much information. It might overwhelm him.

"**We will watch over you**," they said, smiling and nodding to reassure me. "**We are sending you on this mission in a similar way that we earlier sent you to France**. "Hummmm," I murmured, "I remember."

Less than two years after the Grandmothers entered my life my friend, Pat, and I took a pilgrimage through the mountains of central France in search of the Black Madonnas. Meinrad Craighead, the artist-teacher I had worked with in New Mexico introduced me to these pre-Christian Mother worship sites that are marked by medieval statues of the Madonna and Child and are usually, for some unknown reason, painted black. Pat and I were curious about the feminine principle of creation showing up in medieval Europe and wanted to explore the subject. I drew up a crude map, based on Meinrad's lecture notes, and we followed it, winding our way through cities, villages and hamlets in the mountains as we searched. We had only a few days, but because the country of France was once a center of Mother worship, we found a good number of them.

In the oldest part of Clermont-Ferrand, an industrial city in the mountains of central France, we came upon two potent Mother sites.

This was our first experience of their power and it was humbling as well as shocking to encounter the Mother in the midst of a rough, urban environment. But there She was. Medieval statues of the virgin and child marked both Clermont-Ferrand sites. One was situated in front of a well in the crypt of the old port church in the most ancient part of the city and the other sat in the cathedral, high on a hill where a statue of Vercingetorix, the Visigoth conqueror, also stands.

A cold April wind blew us in the door and we lit candles first at the port church and then in the Cathedral and sitting before the statue of the virgin and child, we called on the Grandmothers, the Virgin Mary, and the presence of the original Mother of this site, praying for the earth and asking all forms of the Mother to come forward at this time to save her children—to once again infuse this ancient spot with its intended power. Our prayers were answered and as waves rushed up and out of these vortices we sat there shaking. Now and then someone from the town would come in to pray for a few minutes, but we stayed on, sitting silently, so intent on our mission and absorbed in the waves of power rushing up from these sites, that when we finally left, our knees were weak.

We did the same thing everywhere we went, whether in the tiny hamlets of Orcival and Marsat, in the small city of Les Puys en Vallie, or high on the cliff at Rocamadour. And every time we called, the Mother responded. By now it was clear we had been drawn to these places to do a particular piece of work—to awaken the dormant power of yin that would now sleep no more. And everywhere we went, the Grandmothers led and protected us.

By the time we were once again on our way back to Paris, we had an understanding of what these sites of the Black Madonna were about. Because the elemental power of the Great Mother had been too much for the patriarchy of the Catholic church, the sites had been capped by placing a church, chapel, or cathedral on top of them. The power spots had been respected, but their purpose and potency had been masked. They belonged to the Mother and we had played a small part in restoring them to Her. We turned to Paris, wiser and full of awe for having been used in such a wonderful way, grateful to the Grandmothers who had opened the journey for us and led us all the way.

"**This journey to the East,**" the Grandmothers said, "**has a different purpose from the one you took to France. The purpose of this one is to balance the feminine and masculine principles of energy,**" they said, looking hard at me to be sure I understood. "**The energy** of yin is continuously infusing you now," they explained, "and that enlivened energy will greet the energy of yin still sleeping in Cambodia, Burma, Thailand and Japan. Everywhere you touch down the energy of yin will also touch down and as this happens, every place you visit will begin to awaken. Your husband's energy will stand guard as this work takes place," they explained and again I wondered about all this 'protecting' and 'standing guard.' "It is good to travel together in a sacred way," they said and as they spoke they seemed to study me. I was a bit overwhelmed, even dazzled by their explanation, and once again wondered what it all meant.

"They are looking forward to you coming," the Grandmothers abruptly stated, smiling and giving me a knowing look. "They?" I blinked, but they said nothing in reply, just continued to fix me with that penetrating look until I understood that "They" were the feminine goddesses and spirits of this region of the world. As soon as I realized this, I sensed the eager anticipation of these deities and was flooded with emotion. "Oh," I gulped, tears cracking my voice, "They have been ready to awaken for such a long time." The Grandmothers nodded in understanding and bathed me with loving smiles.

The holy man joined us now and together he the Grandmothers said, "When you pray in these places, speak of the harmonizing now taking place between the energies of yin and yang. Speak of the great need for harmony between men and women. Say this out loud," they chorused. "As a couple, you and your husband embody this harmony and will therefore carry it wherever you go. Ask Roger to pray with you at each place you visit and as you pray, call upon us and upon the Buddha. "I will, I will," I promised, understanding that the reason we must call upon him is because Lord Buddha is greatly revered in these lands. "Everywhere you go you will walk a sacred path. Be aware of this. This is a holy journey," they said, and they looked serious. "You have been called here—together."

I was stunned by the seeming import of what I had until now thought of as our vacation, but I bowed low and when I lifted my head and looked them in the eyes I felt my own dignity and power. The holy man and the Grandmothers were reflecting it back to me, asking me to own it, and I felt a sense of gravitas. "The Grandmothers will mantle you with light and power," the holy man said, "you have nothing to fear." "I have nothing to fear," I repeated and as I looked into his eyes, I knew it was true. He held me with his gaze, and the force of his message moved deep inside me until it made my arms and upper body tingle.

The Grandmothers spoke then. **"Write to everyone involved in spreading our message,"** they said, **"and tell them of the purpose of this journey. Ask them to hold you in the Net of Light as you travel."** "Yes, Grandmothers," I said. I would be grateful to have this support and share the journey.

Now the Grandmothers and the holy man pointed downward and as I followed their gesture, I saw our blue and green earth, orbiting in space. "Oh," I exclaimed, as they showed me the effect the awakening of yin in the Southeast Asian part of the world would have. The infusion of yin energy would create a cupped shape underneath the Middle East, buttressing it from one side. The work we would do on this trip would help hold this troubled part of the world too. Together with the Grandmothers, the holy man, and those who would work with us we would weave a basket of support underneath the Middle East. **"Yes,"** they said, **"this will provide a gentle corralling of the…warring energy there."** And when I quickly glanced up, they said, **" We will be with you."**

I was so thrilled by what they had shown me and aware of the import of this journey that my body began to shake, but at that moment the drumbeat stopped. This was my signal, and I turned to go, but as I began my return I noticed that somehow the Grandmothers and the holy man were still with me. Even as I dropped down through the levels of the upper world, I could still see them. "I get it," I whispered, "They are with me now and always will be." This thought brought me a comfort I would need in the weeks to come.

Throughout this trip I called on the Grandmothers and the holy man non-stop. The energy in and around Angkor Watt turned out to be surprisingly ominous; heaviness oppressed the land. Because I'd been focused on Angkor's physical beauty, its architectural significance and history, I hadn't thought of what the vibration of this locale might be like. But the temples, monuments, and countryside around this magnificent site have born witness to the most hideous tortures and sufferings invented by man, and I felt them. The sense of oppression was so strong that often I could barely get my breath. Wars, but especially the genocide of the Pol Pot regime in the 1970s, pressed down on the spirit of that beautiful land.

We visited the ruins around Angkor Watt, shrines sacred to both Hindus and Buddhists, and as we had been directed, prayed at most of them. One day, when Roger wasn't with me, I entered a temple alone with our guide. He spoke such poor English that I couldn't make out what he was saying, but he kept pointing to the walls of the temple, looking at me in a challenging way and laughing. I didn't recognize anything on the walls and didn't understand a thing he was saying, so I just smiled like the ignorant tourist I was and followed him inside.

The temple entrance was similar to others we'd seen, but after we passed through it, suddenly the hall turned into a tunnel. Quickly it became dark and stuffy, and as we made our way through tunnel after tunnel my scalp began to prickle. It was so close in there that it was difficult to take a full breath, and when I became aware of the presence of a spook-like energy I got truly frightened. Inwardly I screamed for the Grandmothers and the holy man and intensified my chanting of the Gayatri Mantra, the ancient prayer for protection and illumination. As soon as I called on them, the Grandmothers surrounded me, and the holy man covered me with that umbrella of light and in spite of the dark energy of the place I knew I was safe.

The guide kept watching to see how I was reacting to his 'tour,' but now that I knew he was playing a game with me, I wasn't about to let him know how affected I was. When I finally made out the word 'Yama' chiseled into the tunnel I began to understand. We were inside an ancient Kyber cremation ground, a site sacred to Lord Yama, the god of death.

When we finally emerged into the light of day, I could see how proud the guide was for having pulled such a good joke on the tourist lady while the tourist lady was just glad it was over. The energies of death and fear had hung in and around that temple, but the Grandmothers and the holy man had flanked, covered and protected me. I learned a lesson from that cheeky guide. From that day forward, whenever I enter a temple, church, museum, or any place where old energy might lurk, I call on the Grandmothers and the holy man. The stuck and darkened energy of these places creates a doorway for what they call "evil" to enter but I learned that with them surrounding me, that door never opens.

The feeling in Burma was very different from that of Cambodia— not as oppressive, but heavy in a different way. A totalitarian government controls the country and there is no freedom. Emptiness, hopelessness and fear are in the air, but at least Burma has not witnessed mass murder on the scale of Cambodia. And the people we encountered in both the cities and countryside were lovely and welcoming. Because they have been so isolated and cut off from the world by their military dictators, they are not bored with tourists, but were delighted to see our pink, western faces. I had never seen such innocence, such open people. Each time our car passed them, they smiled so completely, with their heart in their eyes that automatically I cried.

One day our Burmese guide took us on a walk through a jungle several hours from Yangon or Rangoon as it was earlier called. After we had gone far enough to be in the midst of the jungle he told us he had picked a 'safe' time for us to walk, because tigers prowl this jungle during 'unsafe' times. "Oh," I said, trying to act relaxed, while I called on the Grandmothers and the holy man.

Here on the banks of a river we came upon crude figures of Hindu gods and goddesses carved into the stones of the embankment. This work had obviously been done before Buddhism had become the predominant religion in Burma and since we met no one on our walk, we assumed that this spot wasn't much visited. There beside the river Vishnu and his consort, Lakshmi, had lain undisturbed for hundreds or perhaps a thousand years. We stood and prayed beside them, asking these aspects of Divinity to bless and harmonize the energies of yin and yang on earth.

The next day we boarded a steamship down the Irawady River, and later took a walk among the abandoned temples of Bagan. Then we returned to Mandalay and stopped by a monastery at the moment when a thousand Buddhist monks came pouring in for their one meal of the day. Our guide next took us to an impoverished nunnery where it appeared the gentle, smiling nuns never got enough to eat. That evening we watched a puppet show where the spirits of 'good' and 'evil' fought with each other. Everywhere we went, I walked with the Grandmothers and the holy man, praying for everyone we met and chanting the Gayatri mantra non-stop. This trip to Southeast Asia was no holiday, but rather a series of holy days and on the plane trip home, I realized I had never worked so hard on a 'vacation' in my life. Certainly, had it not been for the constant presence and protection of the Grandmothers and the holy man, and the fact that Roger was there beside me, I could not have done it.

CHAPTER 6

Hold a Sacred Space

"There is only one rock. There is only one God.
The same rock/God underlies everything."

Being on the ride with the Grandmothers was thrilling and fulfilling. That being said, there were times when it was almost more than I could handle. I never knew where or from whom my next lesson would surface, let alone what it would be. It might come from the Grandmothers, it might come from Bear, from another animal spirit, or from something I stumbled upon in 'ordinary' reality. Learning was everywhere, life was a minefield of surprises, and if one was thing certain it was that I was not in charge of any of it.

One day while going through a journal I'd kept a long time, I came upon a dream I'd had a few years earlier. In it I was traveling out of India by foot, carrying two stone tablets. I wasn't sure if I had discovered them or it they had been given to me, but they were precious and I had wrapped them in a gunnysack so I could carry them. They were spiritual teachings etched into stone, and *they were heavy!* I was lugging them up a hill when suddenly I arrived at the Indian frontier. In front of me rose a metal fence with barbed wire thickly spread across the top. I would have to climb it to get across the border. And as I eyed it, I knew there was no way I could get over the fence with this load.

In the dream I was aware I had to go on, so I was forced to make a difficult decision. I would have to leave the tablets behind. Beside the fence lay a pile of rubble—furniture, containers of various sorts, oddments that others had abandoned before they too crossed the border. With reverence I laid the gunnysack on top of the pile and, my heart heavy, I turned to go. But just before scaling the barbed wire, I turned and looked once more at the burden I had so treasured, and out of the corner of my eye I noticed something strange. There were symbols on the fabric of the gunnysack. Jumping down from the fence I had just climbed, I upended the sack and slipped its contents onto the ground to examine it. The writing on the tablets had somehow soaked into the fabric! Now the sack itself held the essence of these ancient teachings. I didn't need the stone tablets after all! The teachings were etched into the fabric. Stunned by this miracle, I picked up the empty sack, wrapped it around myself and climbed the fence.

This dream occurred more than a year before the Grandmothers entered my life and here I was, reading it for the first time. The hairs on my body stood at attention as I recognized what it was telling me. No longer did I need to carry the formal traditions and teachings of the past. I didn't need lessons etched in stone any more; their essence was enough. In the last fifteen years I had made seven trips to India. For over thirty years I had meditated regularly and studied most of the world's religions. The dream was telling me it was no longer necessary to carry the heavy burden of formal tradition. The Grandmothers' work was the gunnysack; practical and down-to-earth, it held the essence of all these teachings.

The dream confirmed what I had long suspected: that the Grandmothers' work is a distillation of the ancient spiritual truths of the world. These wise women have come to lay life's truths before us in the hope that this time we will listen and pay attention. Their message holds the essence of the Vedas, Sutras, and other sacred texts as well as the sacred beliefs of indigenous peoples. I had long wondered if this might be so, but as I read the dream, I knew it.

Shortly thereafter in another journal I found a different dream. This one was just as illuminating as the first. In it I stood high on a hill, looking down on islands in a bay. Some of the islands were tiny—barely rising above the water line, while others jutted far above sea level. The archipelago, speckled with hundreds of rock masses, stretched far into the distance.

Next I found myself swimming beneath the water, exploring the shores of the islands closest to me. The water was luminous, so clear I could see every fish, crack and crevice in the rocks. I dove deep and as I explored further I discovered that these so-called 'islands' weren't really islands at all. They weren't separate landmasses but were made of the same rock. Underneath the surface of the waves they were one unbroken mass of rock. It was only when I looked at them from above water that they appeared separate and distinct.

As I observed their underlying union, a voice spoke and said, **"There is only one rock. There is only one God. The same rock/God underlies everything."** "Yes," I agreed, "There is only one God. There is only one truth, but it shows itself in different ways at different times."

In the great sea of life, like the 'islands' I had seen, various religions rise up and show themselves from time to time, but it's important to remember that each one of them is part of the same underlying rock/God and each demonstrates only a piece of that rock.

These dreams were a gift, and I felt that by leading me to discover them the universe was saying "Yes!" Go forward with the Grandmothers' work." Their message is practical and universal, their lessons enhance day-to-day life, their Empowerment has a lasting effect, and their teachings are available to everyone. Not a religion, but a teaching of practical universality. "Yes!" I answered back to the universe.

"Hold a sacred space."

Shortly after making these discoveries, once again Bear began to show up as I slept. **"You stay away too long,"** he growled when at last I traveled to the lower world to find out why. **"Follow me,"** was the only thing he would say.

He turned and shuffled away and I followed close behind his dear, familiar figure. He was walking upright and as I trailed him, for some reason a horrifying story I'd seen in the newspaper popped into my mind—people in Siberia butchering tame bears. As I recalled it, I gasped and doubled over. Bear must have sensed something, because he stopped, gazed at me in compassion and then gestured for me to hurry. Quickly I snapped into the present and ran to catch up to him. "This is the first time I haven't ridden on Bear," I said to myself as I pounded down the trail behind him. When he dropped to all fours, I realized it was going to be difficult to catch up to him, and though I doubled my efforts, quickly I fell farther and farther behind his retreating figure. Finally he glanced over his shoulder and when he saw how hard I was struggling to keep up with him, he waited and took me on his back.

Now he *really* began to run. Forming a flash of fur in the forest, his strides extended so far that as he ran, he formed a straight line. I held tight to his back and hunkered over him like a jockey and as we flew along, we formed one body. When we finally emerged from the trees and the sunlight hit us again I heard myself say, "Bear, why did you call me? Why did you call?"

Before he could answer, suddenly it was dark. Bear hadn't varied his pace at all; we were still running, but now we raced under a starry sky. I was determined to not let this shift from light to night distract me and again I asked my question, but again he was silent. Finally he stopped so abruptly that I jolted from his back onto the ground.

"Come here," he said, and motioned me to follow. Then he turned, strode between two trees and disappeared into the forest. I squinted, peering around, but it was so dark I couldn't make out anything, so with a feeling of trepidation I stepped into the place where Bear had last stood. Complete blackness enveloped me, and with my hands flailing the air, warily I shuffled forward. At last I came to an opening with a faint bit of light where there appeared to be a clearing of sorts. There were no trees here, though hundreds of vague shapes lay on the ground, but I couldn't make out what they were. "Oh!" I cried as I bumped into one of them and fell down.

As I pitched forward my hand grasped something that felt like a human leg. I explored its contours and when I came to a foot, I gave a small squeak. I had stumbled over a body! I picked myself up, and now I stood in a weak, wintry light. Squinting and peering about, I was able to make out that all the shapes were bodies! Strange, distended and distorted forms lay everywhere—so many that I gasped in horror. Most were naked and though now and then one of them made a slight movement, the rest lay quite still. It was one of these I'd fallen over.

Suddenly Bear was back at my side. "Oh, Bear!" I shuddered and collapsed into him, whimpering as he hugged me to himself. At last I was able to speak. "Oh, Bear," I said, "What *is* this place? It hurts my heart. Please!" I cried, "I can't bear it," and no sooner were the words out of my mouth than I heard the double meaning of 'Bear.' Bear, the animal, and bear, to carry. "Bear does both of these," I whispered. "Bear *is* both of these," I marveled as I nuzzled my face into his fur.

He made soft rumbling noises in his throat and then pointed to the bodies lying around us. **"You must pass through this,"** he said, and gently massaged my back. Then he lumbered forward and this time I followed close behind, determined not to let him to get away from me. And with every step I took, I prayed for myself and for those pitiful beings lying all around us. Not once did I take my eyes off Bear's backside, but followed him closely, trusting that he knew where we were going until at last we made our way back in through the trees and once again passed into daylight.

"I don't understand what that was, Bear," I said as we stood together in the sun. The horror of the scene wouldn't leave my mind. I was about to ask why we had to walk though such a place but stopped myself when I remembered that I was not to lose sight of my original question, no matter what happened. "Okay, Bear," I said, and determinedly took in a breath and asked," Why did you call me?" Again he remained silent, but instead turned and strode forward and I followed.

Now we made our way into the midst of a crowd of people, but *these* were living, moving people. Some were talking with one another while others stood still and, shading their eyes against the sun, gazed upward. I tilted my head back too so I could see what they were looking at and saw that what they were staring at was a tall pole that rose far above our heads.

Bear and I stood among the crowd and watched as groups of dancers glided forward and began to weave in and out around the pole. "The pole?" I asked Bear, "What is it?" He looked at me with raised brows as if to say, "Well, what do you think it is?" until I said, "I get it! This is a Sundance!"

I watched intently as the dancers circling the pole pierced their skin and, hanging by rawhide strips, ran, leaped upward and seemed to fly through the air, so intent on what they were doing, so intensely *real* as they leapt and flew that my heart caught in my throat. From the expressions on their faces, I understood that this dance was an offering—being performed for the good of all. The dancers were dedicated, dancing like this to alleviate suffering.

The scene before us was riveting, and as I followed the dance I noticed that Bear and I were not the only ones watching. The suffering figures we had seen when traversing that dark place were also present. No longer lying on the ground, they stood watching with worshipful faces, their eyes locked on the dancers, and as I recognized the look of need in their eyes my heart stirred and I understood that an important reason for the Sundance is to assuage those who suffer.

"There would be no such dance if it were not for the suffering on earth," a voice said. "Yes," I replied, "Offering up the self for the good of all is a rare and beautiful thing. It lifts and transforms those who suffer at the same time that it lifts and transforms the dancers. Everyone is elevated by the purity of this sacrifice," I said. Once again truth was being voiced through me and though I didn't understand how it was happening, I was so happy to have something make sense that I didn't care. Now I understood that without suffering there could be neither great elevation, nor beauty. A sacred pattern was at work here, a plan, far beyond my understanding, and or a brief moment I glimpsed a bit of it.

Bear interrupted my musings when he turned to me and said, **"Prepare yourself."** His words jolted me back to the present. "Yes, Bear?" I said, wondering what he meant. "Please show me why you've called me." **"There is going to be a great deal of suffering,"** he said, and lowered his head to gaze directly into my eyes. **"Offer yourself as a light and stay within that light. Offer yourself as a pathway of** light," he said, **"as one of the Sundancers. Sing and dance in the light, bear your breast and offer yourself."** "What?" I said, shocked by his words; "What are you talking about?" He caught the look on my face, and chuckled as he shook his head. "Oh," I said, chastened, "When you say 'bear your breast' you're speaking figuratively. You don't mean I'm really supposed to stick something into my skin."

"You must pierce your breast—your heart," he explained, **"with truth. You must offer only truth."** "How shall I do this, Bear?" I asked, intent on what he was saying. **"You will be shown,"** he said, **"you are ready."** And then he laid his great paw on my third eye and gently pressed in.

All the while he talked, in fact, the entire time the Sundance was going on, the air was filled with a powerful singing. The atmosphere quavered as many voices rose and toned together. This singing seemed to charge the molecules in the air, change the vibration of the place and as the on-going sound rearranged matter, I felt a shift beginning in my body.

This was fascinating, and I wanted to experience more of it, but once again Bear pulled me back to the moment. **"Stand and love,"** he growled. **"Stand *in* love—no matter what,"** he stamped the ground for emphasis. **"Stand in love,"** he repeated, **"do not forget."** "I see how important this is to him," I muttered. "I *must* remember."

"Go forward with the Grandmothers' work," he said and as the crowd before us parted, behind those standing near us I saw the Grandmothers, sitting and drumming for the Sundancers. They were part of this rite of transformation; in fact, it was their presence that provided the framework, or foundation for the sacrifice.

Wrapping a paw around me, Bear pulled me close and we stood together, watching the dance, praying together and holding a sacred space. Suddenly I heard the words, *"HOLD A SACRED SPACE"* resounding from the rocks and the earth at our feet. **"Yes, yes,"** the Grandmothers said, smiling and nodding agreement; **"This is what each of you must do. Tell all who work with us to hold a sacred space, to claim and hold it."**

Just before they said, "Claim and hold it," I glimpsed the Net of Light sparkling in the background. It lay under the Sundance pole, under the dancers and drummers and when the Grandmothers said, **"This is what each of you must do,"** a downpour of colored ash poured onto the Net, changing its tint from blue to a deep pink. As I watched this transformation, billowy piles of ash continued to rain on the Net, weighting it so it dropped downward and fastened itself to the center of the earth. The Net of Light was now anchored to the earth's core! As I marveled at what I'd seen, I realized it had been the decision to hold a sacred space that had created this downpour in the first place. That had set the change in motion. I was so stunned by the enormity of what I was witnessing, I couldn't speak, but only stare at the Grandmothers.

They smiled at me, laughed with one another and then said, **"It doesn't really matter what activities you perform or what food you eat."** "What?" I said, shaking my head in disbelief, "are they talking about now?" I stood there a moment or two, waiting for them to explain themselves, thinking I must have misunderstood, but they ignored me. When they continued, they said, **"These things have some importance in life, but in the big picture, they are fairly inconsequential."** "Oh," I said, "they are telling me not to worry about being or not being a veg-etarian—things like that. Why?" I asked, "are they talking about this? What does this have to do with holding a sacred space?" **"It is the com-mitment to hold a sacred space that is everything,"** they said. **"This must be your intention.** "Okay, Grandmothers," I said, "okay. I get it. You mean *this* decision is primary. All others are secondary." **"Yes,"** they said.

"Step forward now," they said, **"and plant your feet on the ground."** I watched as they did this and noticed that as she came for-ward, each Grandmother stepped on her left foot first. **"The thought while stepping forward,"** they said, **"is to send energy downward to sink into the earth. Take only one step with each foot,"** they said, **"and as you do, think and say, 'Here I hold a sacred space.' You may also say, 'I hold a sacred space for the good of myself and all beings.**

"Don't forget to take this step," they said. **"In the times approach-ing, many will panic, but you need not. Simply choose to hold this space, and then do it. Hold,"** they said, fastening their eyes on mine, **"and tell others to do the same. Send out a request that those who feel moved to do so, commit to holding sacred space. Once you con-sciously make this commitment, no matter what occurs, no matter where you find yourself, you will not forget that you are holding this space."**

Bear listened as they spoke, nodding his head. I followed the Grand-mothers in this act, and as soon as I stepped down on my left foot I felt the rightness of it. I was rooted in the earth. Strength and resolution filled me and fear and hesitation left. "Yes," I whispered, "within a sacred space there is no room for fear. It feels like all of me is actually *becoming* sacred space," I exclaimed in wonder and Bear rumbled, **"Yes."**

"Great Bear! Great Bear!" I suddenly cried, my voice rising and falling in an incantation. I had never made sounds like these before and was shocked by my action. However, my voice continued. "Great Bear from the mountain," I chanted, "Great, Great Bear, I honor you." But the bear I was calling on now was not my 'Bear,' but a mythic one, a mammoth creature from another time. As I chanted on, calling this beast from the past, suddenly, towering above our heads, appeared BEAR, at least ten times larger than the one I was accustomed to. The colossus moved a left foot forward, and just as first the Grandmothers and then I had done, she too claimed sacred space. This was Ursa, the bear mother, and as I watched her take this step, automatically my body aligned with hers. The Grandmothers were aligning themselves too, all of us becoming one with the great bear mother and she with us. "What does this mean?" I whispered to the Grandmothers. "Can this really be happening?"

"**This is no time to doubt and equivocate,**" they said, pulling me up short, "**no time to second guess what you are being given. The time is Now!**" they said, their looks fierce. "**It is time to step forward and claim sacred space.**" "Yes, yes, Grandmothers," I said, "you're right. I claim it, I claim it."

"***This* is why I called you,**" Bear roared, raising the hair on my body and at last answering what I'd asked him over and over again, "***This* is why I came in your dreams.**" "Oh, Thank you, Bear," I said, almost weeping, "thank you for calling, thank you for not giving up on me." "**I will never give up,**" he rumbled and smacked me lightly with a paw. "**Come here again soon,**" he said and then growling happily to himself he lumbered away, sashayed up to the Grandmothers and began to step and bow with them.

For a while I watched Bear and the Grandmothers dance, so happy to see them with one another. They waltzed, circled and dipped with such joy and playfulness that I laughed with them and then sat down by myself and cried with happiness. Soon the Grandmothers walked up to me and said, "**Taking the step to hold a sacred space, and doing this in a public way, will strengthen your resolve. It will make you conscious of taking a stand,**" they said, "**of making a decision not to be caught in the ephemeral, willow-the-wisp activities of daily life, but to claim sacred space now and forevermore—for yourself and for all beings,**" they said, their voices full of feeling. "***This step,***" they pronounced, "**can only be taken in selfless love. *This*,**" they said, "**is what it means to become a Grandmother,**" and looking deep into my eyes, they added, "**this is what is needed now.**"

Tears cascaded down my cheeks as I listened. My heart was full to bursting and I wanted to tell them how very much I loved them, how much they meant to me, how wonderful they had made my life, but at that moment the drumbeat changed. They smiled then, letting me know they understood my feelings and that I didn't have to speak. Then they and Bear began to wave goodbye. I bowed to them and waved too and as I turned to go, Bear broke away from the dance, ran up to me and threw me onto his back. He would 'bear' me back. When we came to the familiar river we embraced. "I am so grateful to you, Bear," I said, and as we held each other it felt as if he was melting into me. "In a way he did," I later said to myself, "because I know I carry his strength inside me.

CHAPTER 7

Take a Stand

"Do not blow with the winds of change."

I was gaining so much, both from the Grandmothers and the compassionate animal spirits. Every time I visited non-ordinary reality, they showed me how to live truths I had previously only read or heard about. Then when I came back to ordinary reality and observed the world situation as it was, I noticed that besides teaching me life's great truths, these visits to the other realms were bringing a much-needed balance to my life.

The messages I received in non-ordinary reality gave me hope and purpose while the messages from the world at large sometimes made me feel defeated. Often I was so overwhelmed by negative news and lies that I began to wonder how I could possibly live the Grandmothers' message in 'this' world. "How," I asked myself, "Can I stay centered, and **"Love, no matter what?"** Finally I went to them to ask if there was anything I could do to be helpful, even during these times.

When I landed in their valley, my wings flexed and let me down gently and as I stepped into the center of their circle, I cried, "Grandmothers, help! "Is there *anything* we can do at this time—other than 'hold a sacred space that is?" I was so full of despair at that moment that I could barely get the words out of my mouth. **"Yes,"** they abruptly replied, and striding forward, they deeply marked my third eye.

"Take a stand," they said. "**Speak out, but voice your truth from a position of power.**" "Yes, Grandmothers," I said, "but how do I do that? How do I speak from a position of power?" **"Never speak in anger,"** they said and raised a finger in emphasis, **"but hold sacred space, stand proudly in it and *then* speak. If you cannot maintain your equilibrium and hold a sacred space, *do not talk*,"** they said, pursing their lips and shaking their heads. **"Do not contribute to the present agitation in the world. Instead, speak in wisdom, speak of peace and, most important, *be* peaceful."** They took in a breath, and as they eyed me, said, **"Until** you *are* peaceful, until you hold, live, and breathe a sacred space, do not speak." "Yes, Grandmothers," I murmured, nodding, my eyes big.

"Should you catch yourself going into anger or fear," they said, "stop whatever you are doing, retreat inside yourself and call on us. The times you are living in are a great test," they said, nodding solemnly. "Everywhere you look you see the energy of yang running amok." They spoke quickly now, gesturing freely. "Yang pulls and grabs at whatever stands in its path. It is greedy, always greedy for more. It would like to attach itself to you too, and whip you into a frenzy," they said, and now their speech carried such force that they looked almost menacing. "But being whipped into frenzy will simply feed the run away energy of yang," they said, shrugging their shoulders as their voices dropped.

"As the energy of yang gets more and more out of control, it becomes seductive and smart," they said, and now they wore cunning expressions as they pantomimed this. "It will attempt to hook you in a number of ways. So if you find yourself losing your peace, losing your sense of rootedness, and your stance of power, retreat!" They raised their hands high, palms outward. "Think of your original decision to claim a sacred space and then hold, hold, hold it.

"Call on us," they said, "always call on us. We will fill and anchor you until you become a colossus, a beacon of light that holds, holds, holds sacred space." I listened and watched, mesmerized by their performance. "Ommmm," they chanted. "Your commitment to holding sacred space is like the om. The stance you have taken will resound deep and wide," they spread their arms; "it will echo inside and outside your body. It will anchor the Net of Light," they pronounced, their heads rocking forward and backward, "and strengthen the Fabric of Being of this planet.

"What is happening in your world now will test you," they said, narrowing their eyes. "Everything you have previously been taught and experienced has come from a yang perspective and, because of your conditioning, at a time like this you want to *do* something. "We tell you," they nodded confidently, "don't worry about doing. Instead, *be* good. *Be* good. *Be yourself and live your life rooted in the Divine. Be this*," they smiled and covered me with their shawls. "The winds of change will try to knock you this way and that," they said, and lifting their heads, they seemed to be sniffing the wind. Then they said, "Yang energy is running crazed and inciting all to riot.

"Do not blow with the winds of change," they commanded, "but hold, hold, hold a sacred space and when you feel yourself steady, *then* speak. Say what is given to you at such a time. Give voice to the words that come. What you say at such a moment will be right. You needn't calculate it before hand," they added with a smile. "We will speak through you.

"At all times call on the Divine and pray for everyone. "'*Let everyone in all the worlds be happy,*'" they chanted. "Pray this over and over or say other prayers that you love. Recite the lines that bring you comfort. Such prayers hold power and do enormous good. Hold a sacred space and call on us," they said, again reminding me to always call on them. "We have told you before and we remind you now that often what in your world seems to be wrong bears within itself the seeds of right. Things are not as they seem.

"An immense shift is taking place now," they reminded me, "the shifting of yin and yang. And you are called to a great work," they nodded, their expressions thoughtful; "you are called to anchor the message we have brought. As you do this you will infuse your planet with the steadying energy of yin. And you will do this whenever you open to yin and hold a sacred space.

"This war that you are so upset about is not as important as the work you have been given," they said and I glanced at them in disbelief. "There have been thousands upon thousands of wars in the past," they explained, "and now war has come again." They were letting me know that the present act of war was not the worst horror mankind had ever committed; it was simply the latest. When they saw I understood what they were saying they lifted their heads and set their vision higher.

"We are with you," they said. "Do not forget the commitment of your heart to be at one with the Divine, your commitment to live in communion with the Divine, and hold steady. Then," they added, "should you feel drawn to take action, do it—as long as you can hold a sacred space. For instance, if you are with a group of people—pray. The good that goes out from prayers sent in the midst of a crowd is immeasurable. But if at any time you find yourself becoming angry or fearful and losing your center, then withdraw until once again you hold sacred space.

"Each time you choose to hold a sacred space your stance will get stronger and *You* will get stronger. At first you will catch yourself slipping in and out of sacred space—especially slipping out of it," they laughed. "Should that happen, return to your commitment to be at one with the Divine, no matter what. This is why you took the vow to hold a sacred space in the first place," they reminded me.

"We will help you develop your radar so it becomes easier for you to live in and hold sacred space and we will alert you whenever you are getting caught in the coils of yang energy. Whenever you become aware that you have lost your center, call on us and we will bring you home again. This *is* your home," they said, nodding and smiling. "You," they pointed, "are one with the Divine. "Holding this space feeds life; this is your work." Then they dusted their palms as if to broadcast, 'that's all there is to it.'

"Becoming a home place that others can resonate to will also help them. Whenever you make the decision to stand in sacred space, you create a center of calm in the world. When others see your example they more easily calm, center, and come home themselves. But without your contribution, without something steady to see and relate to, they are unable to remember who they are." I listened intently, so intently I forgot to breathe. My heart was singing as they spoke, but my mind was scrambling all over itself, trying to retain their lesson and at the same time, find the proper box to put it in. Every cell in my body was straining to receive what I was being given.

"Enter into any activity that calls to you," they continued. "We will support you in all that you do. This is our mission, and you have enlisted in it so of course we will support you. We love you deeply, and we will *always* help you." I saw the depth of love in their eyes as they spoke and I choked up. I was not accustomed to anyone looking at me with such naked feeling.

"Know that the pressure and pull of yang energy is very great now. For a long time the earth has known nothing but this pulling. All of you have been taught to live in a yang world. Be aware of that. But recently you have come to know the steadying power of yin too. Now it is time to live in *this* increasingly familiar place. You can rely on us," they reminded me, "and on the deep wellspring of yin within yourself." Then they wrapped me in their embrace and said, "We bless you. We bless you."

Again they pressed in on my third eye, their touch steadying and grounding me. "Thank you, oh thank you, Grandmothers," I cried and they laughed happily and hugged me to themselves. One called me 'little one,' as she smoothed my hair. "Our precious child," they said, "you are one of us."

I looked at them with a question in my eyes. They were calling me 'their precious child' and at the same time saying I was one of them. "How can both be true," I wondered. I stood there for a moment and then, like swooping birds, thoughts flew into my mind, and as they came, I spoke them aloud. "Here on earth at our very best we are precious children," I said. "We have a naiveté about life, although it's really only the limitations of a life lived on earth that create this naiveté. When at last we are able to expand beyond the illusion of our earthly lives, we are no longer naïve.

"It's all right to live on earth and be a precious child," I continued. And as I spoke, love for my naïve self welled up, making me realize how dear and tender this child-like part of myself was. Because at this moment I was able to see beyond the veil of earthly illusion, I was able to love, not condemn, the childlike one I am, the one who from time to time gets caught in the illusions of life on earth. "It's all part of the beautiful game of life," I said to myself, amazed that I was able to see it. "It's simply the way it is on earth."

The Grandmothers were teaching me to take a lighter hand with myself, and life; to observe more and evaluate less. Because what they taught always came as a surprise and went against much of what I had learned to believe while growing up, I was continuously jolted into letting go of old ideas and beliefs. I had once had some pretty strong opinions and ideas, but I couldn't take anything, certainly not myself, seriously any more. Nor was there anything I was actually sure I knew.

Thus, I was floating down a river in a boat with no oars and no ability to steer. I could wave to people as they passed by, and watch the strange things that popped up in the current around me—until the rivers' flow carried them and everything else away. Depending on the speed of the flow, sometimes my boat moved slower and sometimes faster, but however it bumped along, life was quite a ride, one over which I had no control. I figured the least I could do was enjoy it.

"Truth is in the greater vision"

My next visit to the Grandmothers was again focused on my reaction to the times I was living in. I came before them and said, "I am still anguished by the greed and dishonesty in my country, Grandmothers. I can't help it. How can I, how can all of us be of help in these painful times?" They turned to me and regarded me with such a serious look that I began to squirm but they didn't let up, just bored into me with their eyes until I realized they weren't judging or evaluating me, but were instead infusing me with their energy.

Finally they spoke. **"Focus on the real, not the unreal,"** they said; **"*the real is that which lasts. It is time to let go of your attachments and hold *only* to that which is real.*"** From the way they were looking at me I understood it was time to let go of how *I* had thought life should be. All my life I had worked for a fair and just world and stood up for those less fortunate than I. These were bedrock values—part of my identity, and now the Grandmothers were telling me to let go of them and broaden my vision. I had no idea what this would mean for me, but I trusted them enough to say, "Okay, Grandmothers. I'll try."

Now they brought forward "the Fabric of Being," the silky material that makes up the essence of life on earth. The Fabric of Being is the real 'stuff' that underlies what we take to be 'real' in our world. As the Grandmothers revealed it to me I saw that this beautiful pattern was spread everywhere and noticed movements taking place underneath it, what in *"A Call to Power: the Grandmothers Speak,"* the Grandmothers call **"pieces of gravel that get caught underneath the Fabric."**

As I stared in fascination at these small bumps I noticed how they rolled around underneath the fabric, bunched themselves together and then poked up in different places. I watched this play of movement and recalled the Grandmothers saying, **"Activities like these are what you mistake for reality,"** meaning we tend to focus not on the divine fabric that makes up our lives, but instead on the tiny movements underneath the fabric. We forget that we are one with God and instead place our identity in the temporary, saying, (and believing) "I am a secretary, I am too fat, I am an impatient person." Identifying with what the Grandmothers call "those little pieces of gravel," causes us endless pain and cuts us off from the truth of our being. We *are* the Fabric of Being.

The Grandmothers nodded in understanding and said, **"At the upcoming meeting we want you to speak about the *reality* of the Fabric of Being and the unreality of the movements under it."** I was to again share this lesson of the reality/unreality of life and as I talked about it, remember it myself.

"Do the Net of Light meditation first," they said, **"and explain exactly what it is. It is the Net after all that holds the world, and *will* hold the world throughout the changes that are coming. Remind them that they are part of the Net of Light and hold a lighted place on it. And from this place on the Net of Light they support the earth.**

"When you gather," they said, **"tell them to look around the room and remember that each of them is holding the Net of Light. There are many now who, having received our empowerment, consciously hold this Net, and thousands, no, millions more,"** they corrected themselves, **"who support the Net of Light. Each of you is part**

of something vast, something greater by far than your individual selves.

"This is the Net of Light that will hold the world," they repeated, "and steady the planet in the times that must come. The energies of yin and yang *will* shift," they said and held me with their eyes until they saw I understood them. These difficult times I had heard so much about were now upon us. Now there was no way I could deny it.

"Keep your vision grand. *Truth is in the greater vision*," they said, weighing each word. "Should you contract and collapse into your personal worries or the latest horrors of the world, you must catch yourself," they said, shaking their heads. I understood—this was exactly what I had done so many times, collapsed into what they were calling 'the latest horrors of the world.'

"When you have again regained your center," they said, giving me a reassuring smile, "step into your sacred space and hold the Net of Light. Unify with what is *real* and let the *real* support you," they said and resting their chins on folded hands, they gazed at me a long minute.

"We will surround each person who comes to this meeting and seal the space of this gathering. Each one of them will feel our presence and their alignment with us. This work is SELF-LESS," they said, fixing me with their eyes. "At this meeting, each of you will have the opportunity to breathe in selflessness and breath out selfishness," they said. "We will invite you to breathe in that which is greater, stronger and upright and breathe out whatever is wavering, small and needy. To breathe in what is expanded and grounded and breathe out all that is brittle, harsh and nervous. You will breathe in our loving embrace," they said, "as well as the power of silence—the *thunderous* power of silence.

We will help you hold the power of silence," they said, raising their eyes as if looking at something off in the distance, "for this is where we will fill you. You will be able to find us in the trackless, endless power of silence." I listened and quietly exhaled, feeling my body opening and relaxing as I did. Clearly my physical self understood what the 'thunderous power of silence' meant.

"Feel our touch upon you now." As they held me, their arms and wings folded around me. "You will experience this embrace whenever you turn to the presence within. Presence is held in silence." And as I listened, I began to 'see' the silence they were talking about. It was like the sky you glimpse through the leafless branches of a tree. The branches may be thick with twigs, but it is the sky (the silence), that frames them. I watched the silent sky as it held the pattern of tree and branch. It was background and foundation and though the sky didn't draw attention to itself, it held everything. And as I studied the sky, I felt that still place within myself growing larger and stronger.

"**In order to build a reservoir of power you must spend time in silence and there, in the stillness of your heart, turn toward the presence.**" Looking carefully at me to assess whether I was following, they said, "**Breathe in presence now. It is in your feet, in and on your skin. Presence is your own divine self. You can feel it in your hair and on your shoulders. It is everywhere. You hold presence and are held by it,**" they said, smiling at the look of discovery on my face. "**And as you focus on it, you will grow in power.**" Then they added, "**If we are to work through you, the presence within you *must* increase.**" "Yes, Grandmothers," I said, nodding and watching them.

"**As you sit within silence, become aware of your body,**" they said, and dutifully I turned my focus inward. I had become aware that whenever the Grandmothers plunged me to a new level of awareness, I noticed a steady humming or buzzing inside me. The hum was there again. They smiled and said, "**Think of opening further to presence,**" and the hum or buzz accelerated. When it grew stronger still I gasped at the force of it and the Grandmothers said, "**Now you are experiencing the power of union with the Divine. *Here* you can live**, they pronounced, smiling broadly. "**This is a natural place for you, and from here you can greet others.**"

I was so overcome by the sound and feeling in my body I didn't know what to say, and when they saw the state I was in they said, "**There is nothing you must say about any of this, nor is there anything you must *do*. We remind you to simply move into silence and live in presence. That is it,**" they said. "That's it," I repeated, "that's it." "**Each time you do this, you will become more aware of the depth and breadth of your being,**" they said, nodding wisely. "**You will become aware that you are one with the Fabric of Being. We have come to teach you this so you can assist in bringing yin and yang back into balance. The power of presence is one of the fundamental gifts of yin. It is now yours.**

"**Although the focus of our work is not on action, sometimes action will be called for. Neither is our work accomplished through words,**" they added, enjoying my look of puzzled concentration, "**although sometimes words must be spoken. Real work is done by *being*,**" they emphasized, "**not by doing. Instead of only talking and acting, move into the power of silence and once there, open to the** vibration of presence. **When you next meet, meditate on this. And, when the meditation is over and you again open your eyes, be aware that everyone who is sitting in the room with you is at one with the presence."** Smiling as they sweetly shook their heads, they said, **"Be at One."**

I wasn't sure I understood all they had said, but I knew what they were teaching me was right because something inside me answered 'yes' to it. I could feel truth in the cell beds of my body. At last I breathed out with a 'whoosh!' and smiled at the Grandmothers, and once again they pointed to the Fabric of Being. **"Whenever you meditate on the Fabric of Being, let your body soften and merge into it. The soft, flexible quality of the Fabric will teach you a great deal. The Fabric is able to expand, to contract, and do whatever is necessary to adapt to change."** I studied its deep blue color and observed its silky elasticity as it moved with one's movement and rested with quiet. And as I watched, I recognized that these were qualities I wanted for myself. "Yes," I said, "I will gladly meditate on the Fabric of Being, Grandmothers. Thank you. Thank you so much."

They smiled, nodded their approval, and then clasping hands with one another, they began to waltz. As they glided into the dance, a billow of blue stretched over their forms and, covered with this, they waltzed back and forth in front of me. I laughed when I realized they looked like Martha Graham dancers. **"See how the elasticity of the Fabric of Being lends itself to the dance?"** they said. "Yes, Grandmothers," I replied. **"Moving with the Fabric is an adventure!"** they laughed as they swooped and twirled.

I watched them at play, admiring their grace, and then they stopped directly in front of me and as they stood quietly, they seemed to be studying me. **"Your mind wants to control things because of *its* need,"** they said, **"but your spirit doesn't want to cling."** I cocked my head and squinted.

"*Your spirit knows its home,*" they said, nodding gently to reassure me, **"and its home is in expansion. The expansion of your heart will give you the greatest joy of your life. And the heart cannot be magnified,"** they said, **"in a static or controlled environment.**

"You are ready to let go of your attachments to the way you have always wanted things to be," they said, and as I listened I found myself hoping they were right. Hoping I was ready to let go of my old ways. I was tired of being controlling, tired of being afraid. I wanted more love in my life, more life in my life. I was still too attached to many, many things. I only hoped I could let go.

"**The mind fears expansion,**" they said, "**it wants to cling.**" They made rapid clutching gestures with their hands as they spoke this, demonstrating how my mind attempted to control my heart. "**Each time the mind clings to something it squeezes the heart and clamps it shut a little, so the flow of love and good feeling inside it lessens. The mind engenders fear,**" they explained, "**and now, as the times of accelerated change approach, it is fixating on fear. This is its nature,**" they said, shrugging and lifting their hands as if to say, 'well, what do you expect of a mind, anyway?' "**Its primary desire is to control.**

"**But your soul!**" they cried, and their voices rose in joy as they said this. "**It is your soul that speaks through your heart, and your soul is *happy* to move. Your soul is unafraid. It desires greatness, it seeks growth and openness,**" they said, pronouncing each word carefully. "**And whenever the heart and soul move into expansion, they flood you with love. *This* is the joy of life,**" the Grandmothers cried. "**You have *nothing* to fear.**" They shook their heads as they took my hands in theirs. "***You* are part of the Fabric of Being! *You* compose the Net of Light. Remember this and let the dramas of the world play themselves out while you love on.**" "Ah," I sighed, "while I love on."

"**We will cover you,**" they said, and as they folded that blue expanse over me I felt my heart lift high. Joy engulfed me and I broke into song. "**Breathe in,**" they said, "**and feel the expansion within the Fabric of Being. This is *your* expansion,**" they said. "**This is *your* essence!**" I must have looked shocked by the feelings flooding over me, because they suddenly began to laugh. This made me feel even more bewildered, and when they saw that I didn't understand their mirth they laughed even harder. Finally they began to shriek and hold their sides, doubling over in hilarity each time they returned to the stunned expression on my face.

"**You do not even have words for this,**" they panted at last when they were able to speak. "**When we say, 'of which you are a part,' even those words fall short of what we are trying to tell you. This *is* you!**" they laughed again, not able to contain their joy. "**The Fabric of Being *is* who you are. Your essence is joy! Ever increasing joy.**" "Oh," I said, my voice small. I was still bewildered, but I was beginning to grasp a little.

Sobering, they returned to teaching me again. "**Play your part in life,**" they said. "**Do what you are drawn to do. We know you want to play your part well; we know you want to be true to yourself, follow your inner promptings. This is the right thing to do, but just for now,**" they gave me a loving look, "**let your heart rest within the**

Fabric of Being. You need to rest a while so you can begin to feel at home here. You will grow into your spirit," they assured me. **"*This*,"** they said, pointing to the Fabric of Being, **"is what you are and have always been."**

When I returned from this journey, I climbed into bed, pulled the covers over my head and stayed there. This business of 'coming awake' was hard work. I wasn't accustomed to standing back and observing my mind. Standing back as the Grandmothers were advising me to do required a quality of detachment and objectivity I'd never had. Up until they came into my life, my mind had pretty much had free reign and had sent me chasing after ideas and judgments twenty-four hours a day.

The Grandmothers, however, had a different agenda. They consistently led me back to the position of the 'allower'—the observer and appreciator of life—all life. This position wasn't comfortable to someone accustomed to trying to control life—not that I'd ever been any good at it—and the tendency to control was still strong in me. I believe it was this inner battle—to control/to give up control—that was so exhausting. At any rate, after a journey like this one I ended up in bed.

CHAPTER 8

Dig In

*"Whenever you hold to the real, you strengthen
the Net of Light that holds the world."*

The Grandmothers were consistent. Never did they think small, nor would they tolerate it in me. They invariably called me to be all I could be, to expand as far as I was capable of stretching. And over and over again they told me, **"You are one with us."**

While I was adventuring with them I could feel this truth and even hold on to it a while, but once I returned to daily life, I quickly lost it. The Grandmothers were asking the same thing Jesus had asked of his followers two thousand years earlier: to be in the world, but not of it. Urging me/us to stop holding ourselves separate from the Divine while we lived our time here on earth. And although everything within me answered yes to this call and with all my heart I wanted nothing more than to live in this state of union, life kept distracting me. And each time it did, I lost my balance and forgot that I was one with them.

Long ago I had made up my mind not to be the kind of 'spiritual' person who lived with her head in the clouds. I had seen too many of these folks. They were usually lovely people, but they tended to float on the fringes of society, not functioning well in the 'real' world. Such a life did not appeal to me. I figured that each of us had come to earth for some reason. Being born on this planet couldn't be a mistake, so if I took my allotted time here and spent it in withdrawing from 'the world,' what good was that? Besides, I didn't have a monk's temperament. I wanted a life of practical spirituality—to "chop wood, carry water" *and* live in oneness with the Divine, to be in the world but not of it. That was what I wanted all right; I just didn't know how to live it.

Once upon a time I had taken pride in my ability to 'stay up' on the events in the world, to be active both politically and socially. Now, however, I found myself struggling with the avalanche of negativity that assailed me each time I opened a newspaper or turned on the television. I believed I should be aware of what was happening in the world but found that if I got too involved in 'the world,' I lost my hard-earned equanimity. Try as I might, I couldn't be philosophical about the daily horrors in the news and was sickened by the man-made catastrophes and cruelties I read about. "How?" I asked myself, "could I participate in this world and not be swallowed by the horror of the moment?" There it was again. How to be in the world and not of it?

I was embroiled in this struggle when I next returned to my wise teachers. "Grandmothers," I said, as I came before them, "please communicate with me in a way I can easily understand. We are living at a time of intense cruelty; cruelty to people, to animals, to everything—just everything. It's terrible, Grandmothers," I said, the tears running down my face. "You tell us to pray for everyone," I said, "and we do that, but Grandmothers," I asked, my exasperation showing, "does it really work? Grandmothers," I asked, "what good are these prayers of ours doing?"

Eyeing me with compassion they slowly stepped forward and wrapped me in their wings and as soon as they covered me, my breathing slowed and warmth returned to my chest. After a while, I opened my eyes and looked up at them, but all I could see was feathers; I was so enclosed in wings, I couldn't see their faces! When at last I wiggled myself free enough to get my head up, they smiled at me and said, **"Your faith must be strengthened."**

Immediately they began to work on my spine. Encouraging me to stand tall, they kneaded and stretched it until my spinal column pushed itself upward and sprouted out through the top of my head. At the same time, they lengthened it until it stretched past my tailbone, then continued down, right through the crust of the earth. Now my backbone formed an amazingly long line and strangely, this elongated connection felt somehow familiar. It came to me that once before the Grandmothers had stretched me like this; it was when they had first taught me about the Fabric of Being.

"Oh, Grandmothers!" I said in amazement, "I'm a column or maybe it's more that I'm aligned with a column (I couldn't tell which) that reaches into the sky and far out into space. I'm moving into different worlds," I said, full of wonder, "and at the same time I go down, down, down," I said, my voice growing quieter with each 'down.' All the way to the center of the earth," I marveled, "right to the magma layer." **"And farther,"** they smiled, shrugging, as if this happened every day.

Although I was astounded by what was taking place in my body, somehow I still held to my question, whispering under my breath,

"What good do these prayers do? What good?" I repeated to keep my focus on the purpose of my visit. I was chanting my question when, out of the corner of my eye, I noticed tendrils growing out of the column that was part of or fused with my spine! "What?" I exclaimed, shock in my voice, but as I watched, I cried, "Oh! I see. These tendrils stretch across time and space. They penetrate the past, the present and the future. They *link* them," I whispered.

As I scrutinized these spreading lines the Grandmothers said, "**It is the Net of Light that is real.**" "Oh!" I exclaimed, "Is this the Net of Light I'm seeing, Grandmothers? **"Yes,"** they replied, and when I looked again I noticed that wherever the tendrils crossed my spine, was a point of light. At last I said, "Grandmothers, it looks like I'm forming part of the Net of Light. My spine?" I asked them, "Is it connected to the Net of Light?" **"Yes,"** they said.

I turned to them expectantly, waiting for a more thorough explanation, but instead they said, **"Watch the dramas in the world from this place. The pillaging of the forests,"** they said, **"the wars, the greedy grabbing at everything."** I didn't see the connection between this, my spine, and the Net of Light, but they wouldn't look at me, so I couldn't ask more. "Okay, Grandmothers," I finally said, and turned my awareness to the dramas on earth.

As I observed the activities that invariably upset me, I became aware that I was linked with the Grandmothers and linked with all those who do their work. Together we formed and held the Net of Light, which, in spite of what they were calling "the dramas," still supported the earth.

I turned my attention to the vast Net and for a moment, I caught a flash of movement underneath it. There was a shift taking place. As I stared in fascination, I was able to see through the Net to flash floods, storms, fires, human grief, rages, killings, and traumas of every sort. The Net of Light lay above and below all these events and held each one. Trembling from the shock of what I'd seen, I turned back to the Grandmothers who calmly looked me over. **"Drama changes from age to age. It changes from year to year,"** they said as they held my eyes, **"but the pattern of life does not change. Nor does the warp and woof of light that holds life in place. What is needed on earth now,"** they stated and continued to keep their eyes on me, **"is the recognition of this warp and woof. *This is the pattern* that holds everything.**

"But the bad behaviors you are seeing now," they said, and I began to laugh uncontrollably. "Bad behaviors!" I cried, "Grandmothers, you're calling these things bad behaviors! The government lying to us—bad behaviors!" I was so astounded by the way they described such (to me) horrific behavior, that for a moment I lost what they were saying. "Grandmothers?" I finally said when I had calmed down again, and not missing a beat, they continued, **"...come from panic. Bad behavior always comes from fear,"** they explained. **"Those who are run by panic have lost their connection to the warp and woof of light,"** they said, their voices full of compassion. **"And in their lost state they grab at anything, hoping to hold onto something."**

They turned to face me then and said, **"As you stand in, are held by and hold to that which is real, you do many things. You demonstrate to others what it is to affirm life without grasping at it. That is a great thing,"** they said and nodded in affirmation. **"Whenever you hold to the real, you strengthen the Net of Light that holds the world."**

As soon as they said, "hold to the real," a humming sound started and grew to a singing inside me. And as I listened I became aware of the strong horizontal and vertical position I was in with my spine expanded far into the universe and down into the earth. "Oh!" I gasped. "I get it. Now I can see it and feel it. 'Strengthens the Net of Light' is not just a phrase. It's happening! I feel it!" There was such strong support at my back now it felt as if I had a steel cable inside me.

I also became aware of the horizontal cables I had seen a few minutes earlier, the ones that had started out as tendrils. As each minute had passed they had grown much bigger, more and more of them reaching out from this extended spine of mine. "Oh!" I exclaimed, "Now they're bisecting the vertical cable above my head and below my feet!" I was merging with the Net of Light. I could hardly believe it was happening, but it was. I had become a web-like creature, huge, and growing more enormous by the moment.

But the Grandmothers simply smiled and said, **"All the distress on earth is caused by fear and grasping, trying to control in some ridiculously small way that which can never be controlled."** They weren't going to be distracted from what they had come to teach. **"Wars are born in fear,"** they said, **"greed is born in fear."**

Then they turned to me and said, **"This work you are doing with us is deep and unseen."** "What?" I said. **"This work you are doing with us is, for the most part, unrecognized,"** they explained, adding **"and this is its greatest blessing."** "What, Grandmothers?" I said, shaking my head in disbelief. "This is its greatest blessing? It's a blessing that so few people know about you?" But before I could say another word, they spoke again.

"Others may not recognize what you are doing, but they feel it," they said. "They sense something affecting them, but aren't sure what it is, or where it's coming from. They just feel better," they said and smiled happily. "They feel grounded, they feel relieved, and something good awakens inside them. When this happens," the Grandmothers said, "they themselves become connected to the Net of Light. Just because you are there," they cocked their heads and smiled more.

"It is a great blessing that this work with us takes place surreptitiously. This way it doesn't feed your ego," they smiled as they watched for my reaction, "because no one notices you. And because no one notices you, people do not burden you by wanting to attach themselves to you. You can be about your Mother's/Father's, work with no time wasted. And while you're at it," they laughed, "you can move into deeper union with the Force of Life. With God."

They folded their arms across their chests then and said, "You ask us, 'what real good are we doing with these prayers?" Smiling knowingly they replied, "Pay attention to what comes to you. Much good comes to you every day and most of it you are unaware of!" they said with feeling. "Prayer always lifts your vibration, and whenever your vibration lifts, good is able to come to you."

Then they added, "Besides paying attention to all the blessings life brings, when difficulties come your way, pay attention to how you respond to *them*. Notice," they said, "how well you recover from the blows that life visits upon everyone. These storms move across all lives," they said, "but when they hit you, notice how *you* respond. This too will tell you what good you are doing," they said, and as they spoke their heads rocked up and down.

"Here is an example," they said. "When a blow from one of life's storms hits you and you recover more quickly than you have in the past, or don't react the way you have before, that particular storm dissipates a bit. It loses some of its force. Then," they added and smiled at the thought, "when this storm moves on, it will not be as devastating to the next one it visits.

"We suggest that another way you can measure your progress is by the way people respond to you. In short, people will feel good in your presence," and spotting the bemused look on my face, added, "Yes, it's as simple as that. Pay attention to how people respond to you, and if your ego tries to run away with this, saying, "Oh my, I *am* special! Look at me!" simply recognize that this is the sort of thing an ego does, and quickly affirm your union with us." Nodding and smiling confidently, they said, **"We will also help you detach from the grasp of the ego. First we will help you become aware of the progress you are making and then we will help you let go of your attachment to it."** "Okay, Grandmothers, okay," I said, "I think I'm following."

"You will get more enjoyment out of being at one with us than you ever got or will get from being romanced by the ego," they laughed and now I laughed with them. I *knew* this was true. **"We tell you that you are dear to us,"** they said, **"indeed you are special. No two flowers in a garden bloom in the same way,"** they said, looking me up and down, **"and it gives us joy to watch you bloom in beauty/ power. You bloom because you are at one with the Divine,"** they said and lifted their heads high, pleased with themselves and with me. **"You bloom because you are at one with us.**

"You are beautiful now and are becoming ever more beautiful," they said and though their words puzzled me, at some level I knew this was true. I was twelve years older now than I'd been the day they first appeared in my life. I was now approaching old age and had the wrinkles to prove it, and yet I *felt* more beautiful than I ever had.

They smiled in understanding and said, **"Enjoy your oneness with the Source, the source of your beauty/power. Then, when you see the world in upheaval—oh so many horrors, oh so much trauma,"** they pantomimed my reactions, **"and you begin to wonder what good you are doing, remember this oneness. We know you desire to help those who suffer and we commend that. You want to lift people. Your connection through the Net of Light impels you to want to do something.** "Yes, Grandmothers," I said, "I do have that urge."

"Feel us with you now," they said and held their palms up to stop my mind. **"We are present in the very fibers and nerve endings of your body. In one sense you are an electric field through which we move, give, and receive signals. We send love throughout this field, and we are giving you the power to love more. As long as you wish it, we will continue to magnify your capacity to love, to understand, to hold and nurture."** Tears poured down my cheeks as I listened and all I could do was stammer, "Yes, yes."

"We watch you as you move about your life," they said, and now they stood around me like hens intent on guarding their chick. **"We see that sometimes you forget your own greatness."** They waved away my protestations at the word and added, **"But we never forget. We see who you are. We are able to see you because you are at one with us. You are holding the world in light and you are at the same time held in light. You *are* the Net of Light. Remember this,"** they said, **"and now rest. Let us do all the work." And taking me in their arms/wings, they said, "**Today you have experienced a great expansion. You will grow into it, but for now, only rest.**" They smiled their most reassuring smiles and I took them at their word and rested. In fact, I fell asleep until the change in drumbeat woke me, signaling me to return to ordinary reality.

"Think of planting yourself firmly, your feet ground into the earth."

A few weeks later again I asked them to teach us a way to hold steady in this increasingly violent world. "I need shoring up," I said; "I think all of us need it. Grandmothers," I continued, "practically speaking, what would you have us do now?"

Not hesitating a moment, they looked me in the eye and said, "**Dig in.**" And then they began to scratch at the dirt like enormous eagle-chickens. Soil flew as they literally 'dug in,' and they looked so comical as they dug away that I started laughing, but stopped myself when I saw how serious they were. As they continued their strange dirt dance, I realized they wanted me to take them literally. "**Think of planting yourself firmly,**" they said, "**your feet ground into the earth. Let your bottom be anchored too,**" they said and shook and their tail feathers for emphasis.

"**We will send a rod of light through those of you who do this work that will travel through your central vertical axis and penetrate the earth. As you deepen your connection to your planet, you will be able to increasingly hold it in light while at the same time the earth will embrace and support you. No more skirting along on the surface of things,**" they laughed, "**but dug in and anchored, steady and still. "We shall not be moved,**" they sang, "**we shall not be moved from the light.**

"**You *are* a rod of light,**" they said and kept their eyes glued to me until I felt the force of their message. They were right. I was anchored deep, resounding with power. "Wow!" I whispered as the vibration inside made even my teeth ache. "What next, Grandmothers?" I asked, hoping whatever it was, I'd be able to handle it.

"**Feel the light,**" they said, "**flashing out your back, front and sides. It is shooting out the top of your head too and pouring out your feet. You are humming with light.**"

I was a tuning fork—almost rocking with the force that was surging through me. "**Your vibration will change whenever you focus like** this," they said. They had seen the stunned look on my face and spoke now to reassure me. **"Notice how energy vibrates in and around you. In the times to come, this vibration will become more familiar. It will begin to feel like home.**

"**Dig in,**" they repeated. **"Let what happens around you happen, and while it's taking place, recognize that** *you, yourself* **are unmoved. It's true,**" they laughed, tapping me lightly with their wings. **"You are anchored by light and you anchor light. Feel how the earth welcomes its connection to you—how it supports you. We can hear a collective sigh of relief going up,**" they laughed. **"***At last! At last she has come home.* **It's a wonderful partnership and familial feeling you have with the earth. This connection will feed you.**" "Wow, I whispered, shaking my head. Truth was evident in every word they spoke, but my mind was scrambling to make sense of it all, to somehow parse it up and *explain* it.

I was on the verge of asking them a question when they said, **"Recognize that the mind and all things mental have their place in the world. It is the nature of the mind to ask 'why?' The mental plane is a part of life on earth,**" they explained, **"but a mind not in balance with the heart and instincts will pull you out of connection with the Divine. "So,**" they pointed out, **"you needn't respond to every question your mind asks, to every road it tries to take you down.**

"**It's the nature of the mind to seek outside itself. Because a mind is in pursuit of sensation, it naturally looks outside itself for new material, whether physical or mental. If you allow your mind to control you,**" they said and puffed their feathers in outrage, **"it will focus all your energy on the outside world. And this constant looking outward will** *weaken* **your connection to the core of your being. It will also weaken your connection to the earth.**" "So the mind is not my friend, is that what you're telling me, Grandmothers?" They shook their heads, "no," and smiled grimly.

"**Now that you know this,**" they said, **"whenever you become aware of busyness, activity, buzzing, and rushing about, worrying or excessive planning—any of the things that remove you from the moment, remember the shaft of light that anchors you into earth.**" "Yes," I replied, " I will." And as I thought of being anchored to the earth I sighed with relief. "Ahhhh" we chorused together. "Yes," they said, "**Dig in. Maintaining your connection to the earth will keep you steady—no matter what goes on around you.**"

Then they shook their feathers, stretched their necks and tilted their heads so their beaks pointed upward. Strutting about, they said,

"Think of your connection to the earth as your hub, your home place. Always there for you. And should you travel from this home place into the world of mind and activity—as you will," they nodded steadily, "recognize you *can* come home at any moment. Home never leaves," they said, giving me a look of understanding. "It's always here."

"Always here," I said, "always here," and for some reason I thought again of the first part of the question I had come with today. "...is there anything we can do to help?" I turned to them with this thought in mind but they shrugged their shoulders and gestured as if to say, "Well...this is what you can do." "There is no more important work than this," they finally said and folded their arms/wings across their chests to let me know this was all they were going to say.

They stood quietly, regarding me from a distance, then opened their wings and covered me. "We bless you," they said. "Ahhhh," I sighed, as I eased into feathered softness. "Rest now. Rest with us."

I tried once more to ask about my feelings of being overwhelmed by the energy of the times I was living in, but all they would say was, "Dig in." And after that was silence until at last they uttered, "This is enough. This will do."

They strutted away then, leaving me to rest and soon they began to dance together, humming low in their throats as they stamped and stepped. When I heard them muttering under their breath, I realized they were speaking of the war in Iraq and Afganistan as "the rain cloud." "The rain cloud," they chanted over and over again and danced on. I watched them and it was clear that the rain cloud, whatever it was, had no power to stop their dancing. It was simply a dark cloud and as I looked on, drops began to fall, first softly and then sheeting over them.

They danced on, smiling, scratching at the earth and all the while humming low in their throats. Clearly enjoying themselves. "The rain cloud is a natural part of life," they said, and lowered their heads and hummed even louder. This was all they would say on the subject, and somehow it felt like enough. "Thank you, Grandmothers, thank you," I called and, as I turned to leave, one of them kissed the top of my head.

"By standing in your place of light, the entire template of life is lifted."

About a week later, while I was still thinking of their ability to dance on, no matter what the weather, an interesting thing happened. I was on my way to a spiritual bookstore where I volunteered each week. A lovely place with a prayer room where you can sit at any time of day and where the profits from sales are given to charity. On my way there, I decided to stop first at our neighborhood bookstore to see if they would be willing to sell the Grandmothers' book. I had thought this over and had decided that since I was a local author, perhaps they might even be willing to host a book-signing event.

About two weeks ago I had left a copy of *A Call to Power: the Grandmothers Speak* with the manager and told him I'd be back when he'd had a chance to look it over. I hadn't yet done anything to promote the Grandmothers' book—because I didn't know how, and because I had a dread of rejection—so as I approached the store, I was pretty nervous. I had put off returning to talk with the manager, and as I entered the store I gave myself a pep talk. "I am a local author and the Grandmothers actually appeared in Laguna Beach, so he should be happy to promote their book," I said to myself. "There is no reason he won't be happy to sell *A Call to Power: the Grandmothers Speak.*"

I couldn't have been more wrong. When I asked him how he felt about the book, he told me that not only was he unwilling to host a book signing, he didn't even want to carry the book in his store. *"A Call to Power,"* he said, was not the sort of work that interested him.

As I went out the door I tried to act like my heart wasn't breaking, but a blanket of rejection had dropped over me. The Grandmothers had assured me that *A Call to Power: the Grandmothers Speak* was a good book, one that would help many people so the reception I had just received was shocking. "What's wrong?" I asked myself. And then, "What am I supposed to learn from this rejection?" As I drove off, I poured my heart out to the Grandmothers—talked and talked, and after I'd gotten it all off my chest, I listened to them.

"We are not upset by this," they said, **"and neither should you be. Life is full of distractions. Keep your eye on the goal. The book is good,"** they assured me. **"Know this and hold to it,"** and this was all they would say. Afterwards, all I could remember of our conversation was **"keep your eye upon the goal."** That was reasonable council, but in this case what did they mean?

When I arrived at the spiritual book store, I parked my car, said hello to the other volunteers and got to work. I restocked the CD department and started cleaning up. There was a lot of trash to carry to the bin outside and as I walked back and forth I noticed a crow with grayed, beaten feathers crouching on the ground near the dumpster. She staggered in a strange way, weaving along the pavement, and after I watched for a while I decided she was sick—perhaps even dying. A flock had gathered in the trees nearby, cawed loudly to one another and now and then one of them sailed in and attempted to peck at the sick crow. I was furious that they would attack the helpless bird and dropped what I had been doing to station myself near the crow who was now moving very little. The others continued to call and scream to one another, but wouldn't come near her as long as I was on the scene.

Finally they flew away and when it was relatively quiet once more I resumed my work, left my charge and went back into the store. But I continued to check on her every few minutes to be sure she was not being harassed. This surveillance went on for over an hour and each time the flock returned, I took my place beside the now dying crow. Finally when she moved no more and had lain still for some time with glazed eyes open, the others left and all was quiet again.

I had been deeply touched by her struggle as she approached her death and felt somehow bonded with the bird. I left her there and went back to the prayer room where I gathered some flower petals and sacred ash, took them outside and covered her with them. I didn't move her body, because I had read you weren't supposed to do that soon after death. With a sweet sadness in my heart, I finished my tasks at the bookstore and before I left I asked the volunteer in charge if she would dispose of the bird's body before she went home. She said she would.

In the next few days I thought about the crow many times and when I went back the following week, the first thing I did was check to be sure that her body was no longer there. I thanked the head volunteer for disposing of it but she said she had forgotten all about it. "That's strange," I thought. "I wonder who took the body away?" I had to let the mystery go, however, and get back to work, but each time I took out a load of trash, I couldn't help glancing at the area where she had lain and wondering what hat had happened to her.

When it was time to leave, I walked out the front door and glanced one last time at the place where I had covered her with rose petals. There, where she had lain gleamed a black feather, silky and perfect. I stopped in my tracks, and with a feeling of reverence, picked it up and brought it home. Something had happened there, something magical.

My mind didn't understand it, but my heart did, and I felt the blessing of the crow.

When I got home I placed the feather on the altar in the garden where we hold the Grandmothers' Empowerment ceremonies. The spirit of Crow and Crow Mother, the feminine aspect of the Divine, revered by the Native Americans of the Southwest, would now be present at each of our empowerment ceremonies.

As I thought about what had transpired that day, my heart felt soft and full. The rejection by that bookstore manager now seemed far away. The dying crow had been a gift, jolting me back to what was real. With her, I had taken part in something true and this something had left me full of wonder.

Shortly after this, I journeyed to the Grandmothers and when I took my place in the circle with them, as I looked out at their beautiful faces, I noticed that our eyes were on the same level. I'd never seen the Grandmothers from quite this angle before, and as I sat there I realized they were showing me that we were equals. **"Share the story of the crow with those who come to the next meeting,"** they said, **"share what it meant to you. Talk about how important it is to keep your focus on the truth, to stay centered on moving forward, always moving forward. No matter what,"** they added, giving me a meaningful look. "Ah, I murmured, "This experience, first with rejection and then with the crow, was a test—an opportunity to keep my focus on the bigger picture. Thank you, Grandmothers. Thank you for this teaching."

"Let this lesson be the focus of your the next meeting," they said, **"so everyone can experience us guiding them. As each of you moves forward on your path you may become aware of the labyrinthine nature of life's distractions. But in spite of these,"** they said and held up a finger for emphasis, **"the guidance of the Divine will pull you onward, ever onward. As you voyage through life, be aware of the labyrinth,"** they said, **"it has an effect on your body. It is set up to confuse you. And it always comes to a dead end."** "Oh," I said, "You don't mean a labyrinth like the one at Chartres cathedral where you walk, pray and meditate. You can't mean that, because there you are using the labyrinthine pattern to help focus and turn within. You are talking about a maze like the one where the Minotaur of ancient Crete lurked, waiting to devour people." **"Yes,"** they said.

"The labyrinth of life is loaded with attractions and repulsions," they made a pushing and pulling movement with their hands to illustrate. **"Noises that offend you, annoyances of all kinds. Your reactions to beloved ones, your reactions to hated ones, your reactions**

to painful events in the past, to fears of the future—all of it. It all has an effect and it's all part of the labyrinth.

"In order to get a feel for this," they said, "become come aware of the longings that pull on you, along with all the distractions that lurk beneath the surface of your awareness. This will give you a feel for the labyrinth. These always seek to pull you away from the present moment," they chuckled ruefully; "they stand ready to frighten you, to urge you to do this or that. In short, within the labyrinth of life you will find everything to distract you from focusing on your union with the Divine.

"Layers of past and present relationships lurk within the labyrinth. Your dreams, ambitions, failures, excitements and hatreds," they added, "all of it is there. Each distraction a particular pathway in the labyrinth and each one leads to a dead end. A *dead* end.

"As you observe this, you will see your childhood, all the 'what might have beens' of your life as well as all the 'Why did this have to happen?' you will be able to view it all. But lying on top of the labyrinth," the Grandmothers said and gave me a secret smile, "is the pathway to God. This pathway," they nodded knowingly, "is present. It is calling to you.

"As you journey through life, we will be with you every step of the way, holding and guiding you. We are there at each moment and we stand ready to fill you with our presence. If you let us hold and embrace you, together we will easily move through the maze of pathways. It is a labyrinth," they said, "that is true. But you needn't walk it by yourself.

"The past is past—gone!" they cried and struck their palms together. "Do not waste energy looking backward at what is no more. We are here with you now and together we can easily go forward. You are growing more steady, and as you relax into our embrace, you will feel your psychic solidity. Yes," they said, "you are on the right path. And should you ever get lost and find yourself in one of the labyrinth's dead ends, simply call on us and we will restore you to the right way.

Taking my hands in theirs, the Grandmothers said, "As we walk together, notice how clearly defined and well-lit this path is. You are ascending, and because now you are far enough above what lies below, when you look down, it will be easy for you to see all the swarming activities and distractions within the labyrinth. That is what it's like in a labyrinth; it's a maze after all, and a maze is designed to confuse.

"**You see,**" they explained, "**When you are with us, you stand in another dimension. Here you can easily observe the labyrinth, walk, seemingly in the midst of it, and yet not be caught in its confusion.**"

I listened attentively and watched the labyrinth from this place. And as I watched, I observed that I was *actually in two places at the same time.* I was very much aware of the labyrinth, I was even inside it to some degree. I knew this because I was acutely aware of the distractions the Grandmothers had mentioned. With all the comings and goings in my mind, my brain was swarming with activity.

I also felt the presence of emotional triggers from my past. There was my father who had died when I was four. I had spent years and countless therapy sessions trying to make sense of my relationship with him. The quest for my father represented one of the dead-ends in the labyrinth.

I had also explored my ancestry, looking for something in my family line that would help me make sense of my life. One day I glimpsed of wave after wave of my ancestors, filing in one after another, the line they made reaching far into the past of central Europe. Coming up behind them was my mother in one of her uncontrolled rages and after her came an old boyfriend who had broken my heart when I was young woman. As I kept my eye on the labyrinth, these and many other scenes flicked into awareness. In the span of a minute or so I registered fear, regret, guilt, shame, longing, and a range of other unlovely emotions but the interesting thing was that I wasn't captured by them. It was again that sensation of being at the movies. I was present, but not attached to any of it. As I observed the labyrinth and viewed the familiar dead ends where in the past I'd gotten lost, I smiled. I wasn't caught this time.

The Grandmothers smiled too and said, "**You are doing fine. We are happy with your progress. We love you very much. Feel our love for you, feel it right down to the cell beds of your body.**" "Oh!" I exclaimed. Then I closed my eyes, turned my focus inward and felt how light my body was—and how much bigger than its usual self. The Grandmothers often caused this feeling of expansion to appear.

"**Let our love flow outward from you now. Let it flow to people who are trapped in the labyrinth of life. Let this love flow to everyone who is caught in a dead end somewhere. Don't try to rescue them.**" They held up a hand in caution. "**Each person has his or her own timing, her or his own path. You mustn't interfere with that. Just let our love and blessings flow through you to them. Let it flow,**" they repeated. "**This will make their way easier. It will 'unstick' them so-to-speak,**" they said, wincing at the thought.

I began to think of myself as a channel or a riverbed. The Grandmothers were the water while I was the place it flowed though. Quickly their love flooded my banks, swooshing, flushing and filling everything in its path.

"By standing in your place of light, feeling our love, then letting it flow, the entire template of life is lifted," they explained. **"It's that easy. We ask you to be a steady point of love on earth,"** they said, standing back and watching me. "Yes, Grandmothers, yes," I said. **"Let us hold you and, while we hold you, enjoy the love that is radiating from you to others.**

"We remind you to take time to enjoy this period of your life. Enjoy the book you have written. It's like an apple seed," they said. **"The book comes from beautiful fruit and will bear more beautiful fruit. This will then be multiplied many times over."** As they spoke, they lifted their hands in blessing, and when their hands rose upward, I saw the tree they were talking about. "Oh, Grandmothers!" I said. "It's the Tree of Life! And it *is* bearing wonderful fruit. The book is this sort of fruit," I said to myself and to them, and as I spoke, I heard truth in my voice. Then I said, "And because *A Call to Power: the Grandmothers Speak* is now finished, this truth is ready to be planted in many hearts."

CHAPTER 9

A Changed Woman

"You can be a woman of enormous power and wisdom."

After eight or nine years of Grandmothers' meetings, men suddenly started showing an interest in the Grandmothers' work. Now and then one of them would order a book or come to a meeting with his wife, mother or girlfriend. At first I wasn't sure what to do with them. Although I knew the Grandmothers' message was for everyone, I didn't know if men should participate in our meetings or just observe. I hadn't thought they would be interested in this work. In fact, when I was choosing the title for the book what I set up for the printer was *A Call to Power: the Grandmothers Speak to Women.* The Grandmothers changed my mind at the last minute and omitted "to Women" by reminding me that I was eliminating half the human population.

As I listened to the men who came to our meetings I began to understand just how hungry they also were for the loving energy of the Mother. That was when I asked the Grandmothers to give us something specifically for them. The Grandmothers had been clear that the Empowerment was only for women, but maybe there was something else for men. The Cloak of Comfort was the Grandmothers' answer, and when in a simple ceremony we covered men with it, many of them came to tears.

This proved to be a universal response, because after we held a Grandmothers' workshop in Lithuania one evening, a man who had been present that night called my publisher the next day to say he was so affected by receiving the Cloak of Comfort that he spent the whole night on the phone, passing the Empowerment and Cloak of Comfort to friends in Siberia and Moscow. When he shared this with us I didn't have the heart to tell him that only women were supposed to pass on the Grandmothers' Empowerment. He had been filled with love, had acted from his heart and I figured that had to be just fine with them.

At another Lithuanian meeting with a group of architects, builders, physicists and members of the military who wanted to know about the Grandmothers, we set up a ceremony under some nearby fir trees and passed the Empowerment and Cloak of Comfort on to them. The next day the phone rang again. This time it was a quantum physicist, a man made famous by his discoveries. He was quite emotional as he told us, "All my life I have lived only through my brain. I am famous for my mind," he said, "and so I came to think that my mind was all I was. And now since I met the Grandmothers for the first time my heart is open. I am so grateful that now I want to do something to help the Great Mother." As we listened, we looked at each other with tears in our eyes. The last I heard from him he was hard at work on a generator of some kind, seeking a way to amplify the energy of yin so that everyone could feel the presence of the Great Mother.

The Grandmothers' have come to shift the energies of yin and yang on our planet and these two instances in Lithuania were a good reminder to me of the pain men suffer from being cut off from the nurturing power of yin. They also reminded me of each person's deep down longing for the love of the Mother. And as I worked with the Grandmothers, I came to see that another valuable part of this energy shift has to do with rebalancing the relationships between as well as within individual females and males. This had been dramatically pointed out on Roger's and my trip to Burma and Angkor Watt.

Over time, the Grandmothers changed me in many ways. The remodeled version of my self turned out to be a calmer, kinder and more accepting person—one who cared more about everything and everyone, including herself. I liked her a lot better than my pre-Grandmother self. I also liked being her; the presence of yin in my life gave me a peace and contentment I had never before known. Now life felt like 'enough' to me. Instead of putting energy into chasing after the next goal, the next desire, the next thing, as I had so often done in the past, I found myself simply enjoying *this* moment. Gratitude became a frequent state and living became more a pleasure than an effort.

I was happy to let go of my personal baggage and become this new, improved self, but when I'd begun this journey I hadn't realized that as I changed, my relationship with my husband would also change. The first thing I noticed was, the power struggle that had dominated our marriage was dwindling until finally it nearly disappeared. Because of my work with the Grandmothers, I appreciated and almost understood my husband. I say 'almost' because I don't think I've ever totally understood anyone. People are too complex for that, but the sort of man Roger was now made sense to me.

What I hadn't anticipated, however, was his response to my appreciation of him. And his response exceeded all my expectations. As I stood back and accepted him as he was, *he* changed. Suddenly *he* understood *me*! At this point we had been married for forty years and here we were, closer than ever. There was more love, more fun and lots more understanding between us. What was taking place in my home astounded me and I gave full credit for it to the Grandmothers. But what especially thrilled me was the fact that my experience was not unusual. Others in the Grandmothers' group were telling me similar stories.

Carol had been married for over twenty years to someone I considered a very difficult man. I'd known her almost as long as they'd been married and had heard stories of his bullying, his tantrums and need to control. But in the last year she had several times indicated that "Richard" was softening. "You know," she said one day, "I think he's different now because I'm different. The Grandmothers," she insisted, "have made the difference."

This sounded a little too good to be true and I viewed her comments with a jaundiced eye. She insisted it was true, however, and said, "I don't argue with him any more, and now he doesn't get to me the way he used to." One day she reported, "Next week is our twenty-third anniversary and we had a good laugh today about what a miracle it is that we've stayed together all this time."

I listened to her reports, but because I had several times seen Richard at his worst, I didn't believe what she was saying. Was it truth or fantasy? I hung on to my dim view until the day she said, "I just can't get over it. Richard has turned out to be the easiest man to live with." No one, I thought, would say those words unless there had indeed been a change.

There were others who shared stories of softening, of healing and harmonizing in their relationships with the opposite sex. However, along with the good things I was experiencing personally and through the lives of the women in the Grandmothers' group, I was aware of plenty in the arena of female/male relationships that was not so good. I saw this each day, not only in the news, but in my therapy practice. And now that my own marriage was relatively harmonious, seeing and hearing about a lack of balance between the sexes *really* troubled me. It no longer seemed inevitable, (just the same old battle of the sexes), but unnecessary.

The next time I went to the Grandmothers, I approached them with this issue in mind. "Grandmothers," I said, as I stepped before them, "Please teach me what to say about the real power of woman. How do I present this so people get it and I get it too? I know every woman coming to the next meeting wants this." Then I paused and said, "I want it." As I searched for the words for my question, I became aware of how much I longed to understand the feminine principle. The subject of yin was still far beyond me. Now, as I spoke, I opened my hands as I stood before the Grandmothers and thought of laying the entire issue before them.

They smiled and pulled me to them, and as soon as they took hold of me, light began to flicker and sparkle in the air above us. Small globes bounced on my head and cascaded over me until I was completely covered in a shimmering glow and gazed out at them from within this fairy-like cocoon.

They studied me, chuckling and speaking quietly, and then said, **"Come with us,"** and took me by the hand. **"We are going to show you something,"** and giving me a tug, they hoisted me onto a flat bed train car where I sat down in the midst of them. I had traveled on a car like this once before, when I first came to the lower world. But because I was with the Grandmothers this time, I didn't feel the fear I'd felt then.

The train gave a chug and with a sharp jerk, we rolled forward. I peered at the landscape as we passed and noticed that, this time too the scenes were quickly changing. For a while, buffalo thundered beside us, running with the train, as if the Grandmothers and I were part of an old western movie. Herds of animals raced across the grasslands and as I watched them, I saw it wasn't only buffalo racing beside us, but other animals as well. Horses, elk, bulls, deer, and some I couldn't name.

The railroad tracks curved to the left as we began to follow a river valley and then they sloped downward. Far in the distance, through the trees, I glimpsed light striking water and as we drew nearer, I saw that it was a vast body of water. "Oh," I said, "It's the sea." When the train ground to a stop, the Grandmothers and I clambered down, walked a little way, and then stood at the edge of the water.

As we gazed outward, all we could see was the endless blue of sea and sky. I peered at the horizon and by squinting hard I was able to make out ships, ancient ships with full sails. We held hands and silently watched them grow fainter and fainter until at last they dipped over the horizon and were gone. All the while, the tide lapped at our feet, gently tugging at us, and I thought how lovely it was to stand quietly like this, sharing such a moment with the Grandmothers. And although I had no idea what any of it meant, it was beautiful, and for me that was enough.

I waded a little way into the sea and the water began to pull at my legs. As I felt its tug and listened to the plash, plashing of the tide, what came to me was the word 'sea.' Sea/see I said to myself. "Looking outward to sea," I murmured, "looking outward to see. Oh!" I said and started as I realized this was undoubtedly important, as the Grandmothers love to play with words. "That's it," I exclaimed. **"Yes,"** they said, regarding me fondly, **"But don't look outward to see,"** they corrected my interpretation, **"look *inward* to see."** "Look inward to see," I mused, and we sat down together on the sand. I closed my eyes and focused my awareness inside myself, willing myself to "see" as they had suggested.

The rhythm of the tide lulled me, and as I slowly relaxed, my senses came alive. Now I tasted salt on my lips, felt dampness lying on my hair and the wet sand underneath me. A breeze wafted in over the water, bringing a fresh, slightly acrid scent and the steady heat of the sun beat down on me. "Oh, how wonderful," I whispered, "to be here. Not looking for anything, not looking outward at all," I said. "Just being here." And at that moment all I felt was oneness with the sky, oneness with the earth, and the sea.

"Woman is the sea," they said, interrupting the silence. **"Woman is the earth,"** they added, and then, **"Woman is."** After that, all was quiet again and they turned, and looking into my eyes, said, **"Yin is."** They appeared unusually thoughtful and as I wondered about their seriousness they said, **"Be what you are,"** and then repeated, **"Be what you are."** "Yes, Grandmothers," I said and sat quietly, breathing evenly, listening to the lapping of the water. "It's all here," I said at last. "It's all here. Deep inside my body, deep inside my soul and mind—it's all here. I am complete," and taking in a full breath, added, "I am enough."

They stood up then and looked down at me. **"This is the gift of yin. *This* is what is real; *this* is what is lasting and eternal."** "Yes, Grandmothers," I nodded. "I understand." And I did.

"Women can access this state of consciousness and dwell here," they said, faces serious. **"This is a woman's nature. Once she stops being fooled by a world that tells her to seek outside herself, she can live in completion all the time."** They shook their heads, smiled patiently at me and said, **"Ask us to help you reach this place of completion within yourself. This is your birthright."** "Thank you, Grandmothers," I murmured, bowing low. "I accept. I accept my birthright."

"We are happy, they said as they gazed at me with love. And from their look I understood that whenever we let ourselves expand to receive what they have come to give, it makes them happy. They were happy because they felt my happiness. **"Whenever you call on us, we open the door for you,"** they said, and I smiled my gratitude. "Hold,

hold, hold," they said as they continued to look at me. "**Stay with us. Don't drift off, but hold this state of completion.**" They had caught me, I realized. I had been about to nod off. "Why?" I wondered, "Do I do that? Why do I often fall asleep in their presence?"

"**Take joy in finally being home,**" they said and shook their heads, letting me know they were not going to answer my question. "Yes, Grandmothers," I murmured, and then there was only silence, as I sat, absorbed in this gift of completion.

Finally they spoke again. "**Should your mind try to distract you and pull you away from this home place within yourself, call on us and we will embrace and hold you steady. Hold,**" they said again, "**hold,**" and as they pronounced the word, I felt a locking in take place inside. I had made a decision to occupy *this* reality, to hold *this* place of completion, and my body was letting me know that the shift had indeed taken place. "**Do this for yourself. Do it for the joy you were born for.**" "Yes, Grandmothers," I said again. I didn't want to waste time falling asleep and I didn't want to waste time wondering why I was falling asleep. Clearly it wasn't important—what was important was holding this state of completion.

They circled round me then and said, "*This* **is your place. Live in your place. It is the right one,**" they assured me. Nodding thoughtfully, they said, "**It is only the energy of yang that says you need something outside yourself, and** *that,*" they emphasized, "**is a great lie.**

"**Take whatever comes to you in life and enjoy as much of it as you can, and at the same time know there is nothing 'out there' for you to seek. Everything is already here,**" they said and gently massaged my back. "**You can live complete** *now.* **You can be a woman of enormous power and wisdom** *now.* **If you want this, we will give it to you.**" "Yes, Grandmothers," I said, my eyes growing bigger as I gazed at them. "This is what I want."

"**Notice how it feels to have access to the indwelling power/ beauty inside,**" they smiled knowingly. They were so happy, I couldn't help but smile back at them. "Grandmothers," I said, "I can feel this inside me and I'm so grateful to you." "**If you wish,**" they said and looked at me expectantly, "**We will give you even more.**" "Yes, yes," I quickly replied, "please give me as much as I can take." And no sooner were the words out of my mouth than I dropped into a deep sleep.

I woke when I heard them say, "**Some choose, to dissipate their life force by chasing after what the world tells them they must have.**" They shook their heads and I could almost hear them say, "what a pitiful waste." "**But chasing after the things of the world,**" they shook their heads even harder and wrinkled their noses, **"whether money, men, things, status or power—will only thin your energy. Fragment you, and make you brittle."**

As I listened I began to think of people I had known, (both women and men) who had spent their lives like this. Always in pursuit'—of something. I had seen what had happened to them and the Grandmothers were right. They had become brittle. I shook my head, thinking how sad this was and then a feeling of unease inched its way over me. Who was I kidding? These people weren't the only ones who had done this. The reason I understood what this was like was because I too had chased after the things of the world.

The Grandmothers must have read my mind, because they immediately said, **"Think of a time when you too were seeking outside yourself, a time when you were in pursuit."** They fixed their eyes on me as they spoke and though I waited for them to expand on this, when they remained silent, I realized they were expecting me to do it *now*.

Quickly I searched my mind for an instance when I had been in pursuit, when I'd been driven, a time when I'd been fully run by the energy of yang. I didn't have to look long. The stress I'd felt when building my psychotherapy practice immediately came to mind. The search for opportunities, the endless meetings and networking, the need to 'sell' myself—the anxiety that had weighed on me like an itchy blanket. "Ugh," I said as I shuddered, " I haven't felt this tense in a long time."

They smiled good-naturedly and said, **"As soon as you remembered that time, you registered its effect in your body. Your breathing changed and the tension inside you climbed. *This* is what seeking outside yourself does. This,"** they said, shaking their heads, **"is the great lie of the world. Seeking after something *out there* has never yet made one person happy."**

They took me by the hand and pulled me onto the sand with them. **"Feel the warm sun on you now and turn within to our presence inside,"** they said and gratefully I thought of them inside me, especially inside my heart and a comforting glow seeped through my body. **"We are with you and within you. We are the life force that vibrates inside you, the rhythm of life that circulates in the cell beds of your body/mind. Flow into harmony with us, flow into harmony with all that is. Expanding, expanding,"** they chanted as they rolled their hands in circles. **"Deepening into your essence."**

After a few minutes they announced, **"You are complete. At this moment and at every moment, no matter what the world tells you, you are complete."** "Ahhhhh…." I sighed and gratitude swelled inside me and I began to rock back and forth, back and forth. The Grand-mothers were right. I was complete.

"Ask us to teach you how to live this way," they said and held me with their eyes, **"to take you under our tutelage so this place of completion becomes home for you. We will do that,"** they promised, nodding their heads cheerfully. **"As you turn to this home place, you will become a blessing upon the earth."** "Oh, yes, Grandmothers, I want to live like this," I said and they opened their arms and scooped me in. And as they held me to themselves, blessings began to rain down on us.

I gazed at them, so full of love, so full of wonder, that I knew I was complete. And when the drumbeat signaled the time to return to ordinary reality, they came with me. When at last the drum stopped and I opened my eyes again, there they were, standing around me in my room. Catching the look of surprise on my face, they said, **"We will not leave you,"** and I felt so happy to have with me, to have them in my home, I thought I might burst. But they shook their heads lightly, as if this was the most common thing in the world and said, **"From now on, we will always be with you."**

After this session I was so filled with happiness that it took me hours to get back to 'normal.' I floated along and then began to think of the Grandmothers spending every moment with me—shopping with me, riding in the car, sitting in on my sessions with clients. "Life now," I told myself "is going to be even more an adventure."

It didn't take long, however, for my skeptical mind to kick in. A few days after this visit I caught myself wondering, "How can they be with me all the time? How can that be true? The Grandmothers, after all, are divine," I reasoned. "So how can they be a part of *my* every day life? They're divine. I'm ordinary. How does that work?" Old conditioning patterns of separation were rearing their heads and my mind was rev-ving into high gear.

Over and over again I struggled with this concept (was I sepa-rate from the Grandmothers or was I one with them), but whenever I brought it up, all they did was laugh. They understood how hard it is for a human being to get beyond conditioning but knew eventually I would shed these patterns. They would wait me out.

The wrestling match with my mind went on until at last I realized that whether or not I understood *how* they could always be with me, they *were* with me. I might worry about this forever, but the Grand-mothers were not going to go away. At last I was forced to accept that there were a great many things I would never understand and this was one of them. And as soon as my rational mind let go its death grip I started enjoying the adventure again.

"Your straight spine lets us know that you are ready to receive us."

The next time I went to them, I had moved far enough beyond this issue to get the focus off myself and ask something about the world in general. I wanted to know what we could do at this point in history, a time so beset by negativity that many were falling into despair. "Grandmothers," I asked, "what can we do to help ourselves and the earth move toward light and goodness, especially at this time? I need your guidance," I said, "and so does everyone else."

They nodded understanding and the first thing they said was, **"Feel your power."** Quietly they turned and pointed to a woman who was sitting behind us, sitting with her feet rooted on the earth and her hands firmly on her knees. I studied her for a moment and noticed how solid she looked. **"Yes,"** they said, **"sit like this at least once a day, with your back straight, your feet planted on the ground and your hands on your knees. *Then* call on us,"** they said with a knowing expression. **"Your straight spine will let us know you are ready to receive us.**

"When you take this position, you will *immediately* feel our power. *Your* power," they corrected themselves. **"And when you do this you will hold the power of oneness with the Divine. Call in the Divine and you will immediately feel your connection."** I did as they said, assumed the position and called on them. Then I closed my eyes and prepared to wait, but the response was so immediate, my eyes flew open.

"Waves of power will wash over you, pool around you and flow into the earth whenever you do this," they explained. Mutely I nodded assent. I had felt the power they were describing. **"You *are* feeling it,"** they said, reassuring me that I wasn't imagining anything. **"These waves will enter you from above, from below, from behind, and they will come in through the sides of your body. Whenever you take this position and call on us,"** they said, giving a firm nod, **"you make the choice to anchor great power."** "Yes, Grandmothers," I said, thinking, "this is an understatement if there ever was one."

"Each time you do this you become an outlet for others to plug into; you make the Source available to them." I must have looked frightened by this responsibility, because they quickly said, **"You don't**

need to worry about becoming depleted. **You will become a source of power. Power will flow through you to others, yet this won't drain you because *you* yourself are plugged into the Source. You won't be giving from your own supply,"** they explained, **"but from ours, and our supply is infinite. To think of yourself as an outlet for the Source is a good meditation for you at this time."** They gave a confident smile then and quietly watched me.

I thought about this—about being an outlet—not the source, but just the plug in the wall. I remembered the first time they had brought this up. It was in 1998 and I was standing in front of the Black Madonna in Chartres, France. I had gone down to the crypt of the old Romanesque church, beneath the cathedral and was staring in awe at the statue of the Mother when I noticed an electric outlet in the church wall. The outlet looked so out of context in that ancient place that I couldn't take my eyes off it. This was when the Grandmothers said that those of us who work with them are like this outlet. We provide access to the high current of the Divine, an outlet people can use to plug into.

I liked the idea of being an outlet. It let me off the hook. I, who had been so hyper-responsible, could at last let go. All I needed was to think of and call on the Grandmothers and then watch as *they* did all the work. And as I thought this over I again experienced the relief of being a receiver, not a 'giver.'

"When you put up your Christmas lights this year, remember this," they said and I glanced up in surprise. **"Notice how you hook one string of lights to another,"** they said. **"You can light a whole tree this way. As long as one strand is plugged in, the others will take power from that one. As long as you are attached to the Divine people will be able to access divine energy by being around you. There is nothing you need to 'do' for this to happen,"** they chuckled as they thought about my addiction to 'doing.' **"You simply go around lighting strands.**

"Each time you sit with your feet anchored, your back straight, and call on us, you will become especially aware of who you are. The people who come near you will feel good, and even those who aren't in physical proximity may become aware of a lift in their mood. And because you are united with the Divine," they explained, **"everywhere you look and everything you think of receives a blessing."**

"Wow!" I whispered as I recognized what they were describing. This was the posture of the statues of the Black Madonnas I had seen in France. Spine straight, feet firm on the earth and hands on knees. "This can't be an accident," I whispered to myself. "When we sit like this and then think of others, it allows these others to hook into the power of the Grandmothers. Not just me," I said, "but every person or situation I think of. This is the power of the Mother." I turned to them, my eyes big with wonder, but all they said was, **"Power naturally surges forth from anyone who is plugged into the Source."** They shrugged their shoulders as if this was something everyone knew and said, **"We encourage you to sit with a straight spine whenever you can, and especially when you cast the Net of Light.**

The Grandmothers were in teaching mode because they barely drew breath before going on. **"If at any time you find yourself distressed by what you see in the world around you, assume this grounded posture and go immediately into prayer. And we promise that as soon as you think of the Divine, we, or whatever form of divinity you love, will come in and link you with the Source. If a stressful situation comes up, chant the om and sit quietly. The humming vibration of the om will carry added power not only through you, but through the situation you are thinking of."** I nodded. This was starting to make sense. My vibratory rate would shift and the rate of anyone or anything connected to me would also shift. The sound of om would amplify the work. "What a difference this could make in the world," I said and began to imagine the possibilities. An elevated vibration, enough food for people, an end to violence, an end to cruelty, loving kindness....

Interrupting my reverie, the Grandmothers said, **"We are not saying it is *necessary* for you to sit in this grounded position in order to pray for and send blessings to others. Nor is it necessary to sound the om. However,"** they added, **"these two actions will enable your body to participate more fully in sacred events. And 'sounding' like this will amplify the work you do. You will feel more and more joy as you work in this way,"** they assured me, **"and whatever you experience at such a moment will go deep into your cell beds and memory banks.**

"Your body will enjoy this. Each time you do it, your body will receive healing. And at the same time you receive healing, you will also be sending it to others." Then they gave me a big grin and said, **"It will happen effortlessly.**

"This is simple, practical work," they said, **"that will help you and help everyone."** They smiled again and I could see how pleased they were with this teaching. "Thank you, Grandmothers for making it so clear," I said, and then I sat down and quietly began to om, giving myself over to an ever deepening state of communion. In a short time I became aware that I was becoming rock solid. This sensation grew and grew until I felt so grounded, so much a part of everything and everyone that I lost my sense of separate identity. And at that point I realized I couldn't move, not even lift a hand. As I sat there like a great monolith I finally said, "Of course I can't move. There's no longer any 'me' to do the moving."

As I ran all this through my mind, the Grandmothers sat quietly too, seeming to think things over. At last they spoke. **"The weighty problems and events in the world today are going to go on for a while. Do not give them over much attention,"** they shook their heads in dismissal. **"These events which seem so devastating mark the disintegration of old energy patterns and ways of life on earth. Instead of dwelling on these problems, become the divine outlet that you are. Full of power so all who come into your orbit can receive from the Source. Place yourself in union with us and as much as possible, stay there!"** they said, giving me a severe look. **"The horrors and depravities of this age that so distress you will pass. Hold to your union with us. We urge you to do this for your sake, and for the sake of everyone else as well."**

"Yes Grandmothers," I said and nodded, hoping as I said 'yes,' that I'd be able to do it. They narrowed their eyes then, and said, **"Whenever you unify with us, you will feel us lining up along your back."** And no sooner did they say this, than I felt it. A dozen Grandmothers stood behind me now, holding me so straight and steady that nothing could have knocked me over. This was the strength I would need to maintain my focus on the Divine—no matter what. I took in a deep breath, willed myself to drink in their power and noticed I was standing taller. "Thank you, Grandmothers," I said, "I *will* do this."

"Whenever you breathe with us, where you stand becomes holy ground."

On every visit, the Grandmothers deepened my understanding and my faith, but after this one there was a pronounced shift. I had always known their wisdom ran deep, but now I could feel the depth inside myself. I could hardly believe what I was becoming— this unshakable woman, one who was able to say, "yes" to life. This is when I made a decision. I wanted to live like this all the time—not just bounce in and out of union with them, touching in from time to time only to fall back into 'ordinary' life. I wanted to *live* it. A few days later I decided to return and ask for more.

As soon as I came into their presence, they took one look at me and said, **"We are with you. There is never a time that we are not."** "Oh!" I gasped. "They're addressing my question before I even formed it." **"It's your mind that denies you the experience of oneness with us. That busy, busy mind,"** they chuckled and looked fondly at me. "Wow!" I muttered, "They're doing it again—reading my mind."

"Recognize that at all times we cover you with our love. We are with you every moment. We are the very breath you breathe. The Divine breathes life into you *every moment of your life.*" I gave another little gasp because their words rang so true. **"Breathe with us now,"** they said, and I synchronized my breath with theirs. **"Allow us to breathe you. Fill your lungs with us and feel the joy and blessing this brings you. Every time you inhale, we will rush in and whenever you exhale, we draw you into ourselves."**

I turned my attention inward and noticed that I especially loved it when the Grandmothers drew me into themselves. Every time I exhaled, I felt a deepening union with them until at last I reached that place in consciousness I loved. There was the feeling of no barriers and as I felt this freedom, I wondered if this was what samhadi or liberation was like. I had read about samhadi and what I was experiencing now seemed to fit the description. "Humm," I mused, "I wonder if...." but before I could complete my sentence my thoughts trailed off into noth-ingness. Simply disappeared. And as that happened, I felt even freer, so uplifted in fact, that I didn't care what the state was called. I couldn't muster interest to pursue the question. Whatever it was, whatever peo-ple called it, I didn't care. I just wanted it to go on and on and on....

Gently the Grandmothers pulled me back to the present when I heard them say, **"We are within the very blood of your body."** "Oh," I said and started, "this is the Grandmothers I'm feeling. What I've been told is samhadi or whatever its name is, it's *them!*" **"Each cell in your body is vibrating with our presence,** they said, smiling at my reaction, **"and this is true at every moment of your life.**

"We will guide you, and we'll do it at the pace that's right for you. We will never overwhelm you," they shook their heads, **"but will always follow your lead, giving you as much connection with the Divine as you wish, as much as you are ready to receive."** Then they locked arms across their breasts and rocked back and forth on their heals—happy with their communication.

"Breathing with us provides food for your body, food for your mind and spirit. Whenever you breathe with us, where you stand becomes holy ground. At such a time the space you occupy is holy. And the only thing that prevents you from living in holiness every

moment of your life is not remembering to think of the Divine." Twelve Grandmothers cocked their heads, peered at me from the side and asked, **"Now isn't that simple?**

"If you think of us when you place your hand on a tree, that tree becomes sanctified. We are already present within the tree but recognizing the Divine is important." As I thought about this, I wondered. "Were they saying that the tree was sacred only *if* someone recognized it as such? I looked at them with that question in mind, but they laughed at me and shook their heads.

"If you don't have eyes, you can't see beauty; and if you don't recognize the divine presence in the world, you live your life blind. When you live your life blind, not only do you overlook the Divine, you lose the opportunity to amplify the presence of divinity for yourself and others. The goal of the Game of Life is to recognize divinity everywhere." And with secret smiles playing on their lips they said, **"We would like to see you become very good at this game."**

My head was reeling. "Think of us while you place your hand on a tree and that tree is sacred,... living your life blind,... the goal of the Game of Life...." What did it all mean? Overwhelmed, I stared at them uncomprehendingly, but they simply smiled, shook their heads and said, **"You must grow into your spirit.**

"Start by getting into the habit of calling on us all the time. Breathe with us, walk with us, and drive with us. Eat with us and sleep with us. We are the beloved," they said, smiling from their hearts. **"We are *your* beloved,"** they emphasized, **"and you are *ours*. There is no difference,"** they crooned as they took me in their arms.

"Be Lov-ed," they sang and then said, **"be loved. Let yourself be loved,"** they sang again as they swung back and forth to the rhythm of their song. I listened to them, hummed along until I gradually began to take in their peaceful state, and when at last I was able to let go my concern about understanding everything they said, my worry began to dissipate.

"Each time you allow yourself to feel our love, you will recognize that *everything* is beloved. Everything that lives has but one desire and that is to be loved. This is true for everyone and everything on earth. And...," they said, delighting in what they were about to tell me, **"There is nothing you have to do to make this happen.**

"You can't love by trying to love," they chuckled at the absurdity of the idea. **"In fact, loving in the way we are describing it will never happen by effort. You can't *be* good, nor can you *be* loving by try-ing,"** they laughed boisterously, **"but whenever you call on the Divine**

and then open to its presence, you *are* loving and you *are* good. You are all this and more. It happens automatically." Again they were reminding me of the power of 'effortless effort,' reminding me also to think of, and call on the Divine. "Why?" I wondered again, "is it so difficult to remember that?"

"The veil between you and the Divine is thinning," they said, continuing their explanation, "thinning more and more. And each time you breathe with us, for a moment the veil dissolves." Again I closed my eyes and as I felt the waves of breath rising and falling inside me, I became aware that this focused breath was carrying me ever closer to my beloved teachers. I shivered in excitement. "We are coming together with you now," they said, confirming my observation, "flowing into one. Just like Jello," they giggled and I giggled too. It did feel a bit like Jello—soft and connected in a floppy sort of way. "When you smile at a time like this," they said, "It is our smile. When you love someone, it is our love. We are one," they said and stepped back and quietly observed me.

"You never imagined your life could be this easy, did you?" they asked, tilting their heads and peering at me over the tips of their noses. "You thought you had to try—to *work hard* at life.

"Its not like that at all. Our work is easy. Long ago Jesus said, 'My yoke is easy. My burden is light.' *This* is what we are talking about. Once you make the decision to open to us, or to any form of the Divine, God will carry you every step of the way. We will do it all," they promised, looking into my eyes. "You can live in loving companionship with the Divine, and you can do it all the days of your life.

"When you come together because you desire a deeper connection with the Divine, and then turn within and experience the sweetness of our presence, you fill with and anchor the Divine on earth." They looked at me to see if I had anything to say to this but I didn't. The thought of anchoring the Divine on earth had stopped me in my tracks. I just watched the Grandmothers, waited, and breathed.

"We will touch your third eye now," they said, "to imprint this experience within you. That way it will always be with you. Notice what happens when we do this," and as soon as I felt their touch on my forehead, my mind stopped. No more mental scrambling, no more thoughts, only silence. Silence and a blanket of peace that lay over everything.

"Great love is flowing inside you now," they said as they observed me, "pouring outward from you and pouring outward from this group of which you are a part. Healing and blessing everything.

"Yes, Grandmothers," I replied, "yes," and thought of opening more to blessing and being blessed. There was a rolling fullness inside me that kept folding over itself, growing larger with every turn it made. And although I stayed in that place of rolling, swelling grace for what proved to be only a few minutes, it felt like days to me. Within this space was not only ever-increasing expansion, but also peace and a sense of completion.

"If you like, you can think of a place on earth you would like to receive the grace you are now experiencing. The blessing will go to everyone who needs it, but there may be specific spots on earth, particular groups of people or conditions that call to you. Experience how the wellspring of love and compassion from your union with us floods outward to them now." "Yes, Grandmothers, yes," I said, and I asked for this blessing to go especially to the continent of Africa.

"Many of you have specific work to do," they said, **"karmic connections, jobs you have taken on with particular areas, countries and beings. We have mentioned this before and we remind you now to honor these connections. These places may come to mind at this moment, and as they do you may realize you have known about them a long time. When a particular place or situation comes to you, ask us to send this blessing of union to it. We will,"** they said, and added, **"we are already doing it.**

"Together we make up one world," they said as they held a finger before my face. **"In actuality, together we form one body of love."** I looked and looked at them, shaking my head in wonder. "We are one body of love," I repeated. One. It sounded so right.

"Yes," they replied and nodded, **"Cast the Net of Light to all beings. Do this whenever you can. And when you have finished connecting with everyone through the Net of Light, take the time to feel how loved you are,"** they said, and I did. I felt this great tapestry of love of which I was a part—the Net of Light. **"At such a time,"** they said, giving me their sweetest smile, **"and having just performed such an action, you are undeniably one with the Divine."** Again I shook my head and as I gazed at them tears streamed down my cheeks.

By this time I had cast the Net of Light countless times—offering this connection wherever I saw the need. If I heard of a tragedy, I cast the Net of Light. When I heard people arguing, I cast the Net. When I came upon anyone in distress, I cast the Net. I'd done this so often and for so many years that by now I had a pretty good idea of the power and practicality of the Net of Light. It helped people; it eased situations. It worked! However, it often slipped my mind that the Net of Light was also holding *me.* So when the Grandmothers told me to **"feel how loved you are,"** after I had connected with the Net I got a lump in my throat. They were reminding me that the Net of Light was there for me too.

"It may be a relief to some to be reminded that they are not the ones doing the loving." "Un huh, Grandmothers," I said slowly, "I see why you're giving me that look." They were again reminding me that I was not the doer, or in this case, not the lover. The act of love was taking place through me, not by me. This was still a difficult concept for me to grasp. I had spent so much of my life striving to be good, trying to always do the right thing that it was hard to get myself out of the way. In fact I'd tried so hard to do the right thing that a friend had once referred to me as 'Sharon, the good,' and when she had said it, she hadn't mean it as a compliment. I remember how I'd felt when I heard it. It was like "Sharon, the goody-two shoes."

The Grandmothers shook their heads, chuckled and said, **"Whenever you desire a deepening connection to the Divine and then call on us, you will immediately experience the sweetness of our presence."** They were proceeding with their lesson and I needed to put my attention on them.

"This connection is holy communion. We commune with you as you commune with us." They watched me out of the corner of their eyes, waiting to be sure I understood. "Yes, Grandmothers," I quickly responded, I get it. "Communion," I said, "this is what communion is."

The Grandmothers dive to the core of a concept and make it simple. They were letting me know that there is no ceremony or paraphernalia needed to experience communion with them. All we need is to call on the Divine and then open to our connection. That's it. "The Grandmothers," I said to myself (probably for the thousandth time), "make God so *accessible.*"

"Whenever you gather together for the purpose of communing with the Divine," they said, **"the good that takes place from this shared purpose is magnified thousands of times over. One of you unified with us sets up a potent energy field,"** they said. **"Ten, twenty, or fifty of you unified with us multiplies power beyond imagining. When you gather like this, the energy field you form spreads over the world and does more good than you will ever know,"** they nodded. **"Deep love travels from your meeting place and flows outward—over the earth—flowing far into the universe.**

"What we are saying is real. *This* is real life," they said. **"It is not the busy, limited life of the mind, the busyness of so-called 'reality' that is real. *This* is real."** Then locking their eyes on mine, they said, **"Breathe with us and know the joy we feel. Enter more fully into communion and together we will commune with everyone and everything that lives.** *This* **is why you were born,"** they said, fixing me with a look of infinite tenderness, **"to live in love and** *be* **that love."**

Mutely I nodded 'yes,' and willed myself to harmonize with them, wanting so much to know the joy they knew. What they were telling me made the hairs on my body stand up. It was Power, it was Truth, and I wanted it. Inwardly I prayed, asking to know the joy of this communion and as I held to my prayer, I felt my hands growing larger and larger until they felt like mittens. Soon they expanded to a tremendous size and as I stared at them in amazement I realized I could no longer feel them or any other part of my body. I had no boundaries at all. They had dissolved and now I was limitless.

The Grandmothers shook their heads and smiled at the look of wonder on my face. Then they gently took me into their arms and as they rocked and sang to me, one of them whispered in my ear, **"Don't worry. You will grow into your spirit."**

I smiled at her, relieved to be reminded that *I* didn't have to do anything about this. Not even my personal growth was my responsibility. Growth would happen at it's own pace. All I needed was the willingness to go wherever the Grandmothers led, and that I had. I took a deep breath, rested for a few minutes and when the rhythm of the drum changed, I allowed myself to float back down to ordinary reality.

CHAPTER 10

Everything is Beloved

"Bloom as the Flower That You Are"

After many years of being the only one to hold Grandmothers' meetings and pass on their Empowerment, others began to step forward. There were women in Holland meeting regularly to study *A Call to Power: the Grandmothers Speak*. When I heard about them, I was impressed by their sincerity and diligence, but especially impressed because the books they were studying weren't even written in Dutch, but in English.

There was a Grandmothers' group in Florida and a woman from Santa Cruz, California had started one. Someone in Canada contacted me about beginning a group in her area and I had been asked to speak on the Grandmothers at a shamanism conference in northern California. The Grandmothers' website was up now and this allowed me to communicate with people around the world who wanted to know about the Grandmothers. In short, life was getting interesting.

One day I got an email from Lithuania. A woman asking permission to translate *A Call to Power: the Grandmothers Speak* into her language. She expected nothing for her work but said, "I ask to do this because your book will help my countrywomen." I was deeply touched by her request and immediately said yes. Someone wanted to know if she could translate the book into Portuguese so the people of Brazil could read it and another woman volunteered to do a Dutch translation.

All of these possibilities were exciting, and after keeping my nose to the grindstone for so many years it was fun to have something different to look forward to. But I reminded myself not to get carried away by the potential for the Grandmothers' work, not to lose focus of what was really important. Possibilities might come and go, but the Grandmothers had said that *living their message* was what counted, and that was what I wanted to do. Since we had a meeting coming up soon, I would ask them to teach us about living their message.

I made my way to them in my usual way, but this time I felt them before I saw them. When they greeted me, their colorful skirts and shawls spun around me until I felt as if I was in the center of a blooming flower. "Grandmothers," I said when at last they stopped whirling and stood still, "what would you have us do to move closer to God?"

I surprised myself when these words came out of my mouth but I realized that this after all was the point of "living" the Grandmothers' message. Smiling, they bowed in acknowledgement of my question, but didn't say a word. Finally, when I could stand the suspense no longer, I said, "Grandmothers, I don't know the answer to what I just asked, I'm just waiting on you." Patting me reassuringly, they smiled and said, **"We know, we know."**

After that the air around me quivered slightly, making everything look wavy and then a shimmering vibration sped up until at last I felt myself vibrating too. Quickly my posture became their posture and my gestures theirs. I was merging with the Grandmothers.

Smiling sweetly, they acknowledged our alignment and said, **"At this meeting, share the good things happening with our work. Share it all. New groups forming, the potential for the book to be published in other countries—all the good things,"** they said. **"People who come to these meetings want to deepen their connection with us, they want to move into oneness with that which you call God and they want to serve others. Take time to announce all the good news. This information will hearten them."** "Yes, Grandmothers," I nodded, understanding that whenever triumphs, difficulties and possibilities came up concerning the Grandmothers' work, they affected everyone and so they needed to be shared. These issues were no longer only my business as I had thought in the past, but everyone's.

"It's time to broaden your reach," they said, and I understood now they were speaking, not about me, but about the groups. The Grandmothers' groups had work to do. **"These groups must become touchstones and provide a matrix for others. It is good to take our message into the world, good to assist those who want to work with us. We will guide and bless everyone who does that."**

Cupping their chins in their hands, they nodded thoughtfully and said, **"Because our teachings are spreading, the work of these groups too must expand. Like a healthy plant, these groups must reach deeper and wider. As they grow in strength and depth, new tendrils will spring forth from them which will carry our message further and further afield."** I listened carefully and pictured the growing plants they were describing. How one person would tell another, how one group would provide a beginning place for another to spring from. The Grandmothers watched me as I worked this out in my mind and nodded each time I made a right connection.

"Once you have shared how our message is spreading, call on us and open to the joy of being part of such uplifting work. At this time of darkness, rigidity and despair, there is also this *joyous* bloom of love. And as you open to this joy, we will come into your hearts." They swished their skirts when they said this and once again colors flared around me.

I smiled at them, watching as they swung their skirts from side to side, admiring their grace and thinking how lovely they were. The colors and movements were mesmerizing. As they swayed and swung, they reminded me of flowers in a garden. All that swaying and…and…I started to feel a little strange—warm and almost light headed. The play of color from those swirling skirts was making me dizzy and now an uncomfortable fullness, an almost swollen feeling had grown inside my chest. I shook my head to clear it, took in a breath and sighed it out. Then in a very tiny voice I heard myself whisper, "Oh."

The Grandmothers had done exactly what they had said they would do. They had said, **"As you open to this joy, we will come into your hearts,"** and then quietly and with no fanfare at all, they had done it. *This* was what I was feeling in my chest. That full feeling, that warmth. Them.

I'd followed their words with rapt attention and when they had said the word 'joy,' I had automatically expanded into it. And no sooner did that happen, than my heart flew open. The force of that opening had taken my breath away, creating an abrupt feeling of release. This was accompanied by a sense of vulnerability that came on so quickly it was almost painful. I was mulling over how these involuntary actions and feelings had succeeded one another, trying to make sense of the sensations flooding my body, when I heard them say, **"And their hearts will open in full…bloom."**

"Whoa!" I gasped, as my already gaping heart flung itself wider yet. The suddenness of *this* unbarring stunned me into silence and all I could do was pant and blow as I struggled to take in air. I couldn't seem to fill my lungs with enough of the stuff. "Am I supposed to feel this way?" I asked, as this unlooked-for sensation continued, but they said nothing. Just stood quietly with placid looks on their faces while I continued to gasp. "Is this healthy?" I finally asked and then, "Maybe I'm having a heart attack."

The Grandmothers smiled benignly and watched me cope with

the waves of shifting energy, and then they began to breathe deeply and gestured for me to do the same. I continued to pant, struggling to control myself and they stood patiently by, waiting for me to regain my composure. At last when I was breathing normally again, they gathered round me, bent down and whispered in my ear, **"There will be an early spring this year."** I glanced up in surprise. "An early spring?" I asked. Again they smiled that benign smile. **"At this very moment love is blooming inside your heart."**

"Oh!" I exclaimed and exhaled in relief. Spring was coming awake inside me; this was what they meant. That was why I felt so strange. I was thawing out—awakening. It was a natural occurrence, "entirely natural," I said to myself. I wasn't having a heart attack after all. "It's all normal," I repeated to myself. And then I began to laugh—at myself and at my fears, and the Grandmothers joined me, happy to see I was beginning to understand.

They began to twirl around me then and after they had done this several times, they wrapped me in their shawls and drew me into a dance with them. Together we wove brilliant patterns of color as we dipped and glided round and round. At last they sighed happily and said, **"All is well,"** and gathered me into their embrace. I lay my head on their shoulders and gratefully rested a few minutes, enjoying the peace and good feeling flooding my body. "Wow, Grandmothers, " I sighed, "that was almost too much."

They rocked me back and forth and it felt so wonderful to rest in their arms that I wanted to stay there forever—to never move again. But all too soon they stepped away and said: **"Become aware of how your heart is expanding."** Sleepily I looked up at them and with some effort, I brought my attention back to my heart. "It's taking the form of a flower," they said, and as they spoke, they seemed to be peering inside me.

I followed their lead and focused inside myself too, and there, where my heart should have been, was what looked like a fully blown poppy or maybe it was a rose. **"The flower of your heart is expanding,"** they said and I caught my breath as I saw and felt it happening. There was a rosy/orangey blush inside my heart as this flower, behaving like a small sun, sent a glowing nimbus far beyond its petals.

"Experience its color," they said, as interested in what was happening to me as I was. **"The flower will appear in hues and tones that resonate with you."** "Oh," I said, "I'm seeing a pinkish/orange color." This was a combination I would never have thought of.

"Your heart!" they exclaimed, and the way they said it made me catch my breath. **"Feel its softness and living quality,"** they whispered, and as I listened and watched, my flower/heart began to undulate and swell with each beat, growing so gorgeous that I began to sob. **"How big it is!"** they exclaimed. **"How resonant, strong, and soft."** "Yes, yes" I said, "it is," and as I felt its strength, I was overcome with such gratitude to this organ that I had never paid the least attention that I sobbed even more. Crying and laughing at the same time, I alternately smiled at the Grandmothers and covered my face with my hands. But they stood by patiently and watched, and when at last I had cried myself out and was calm again, they spoke.

"The joy of this blooming flower is registering inside you. Your heart is beating and pulsing with joy. Can you feel it?" they asked, waiting for my response. But now *I* was silent. I had no words for the beauty swelling within me. My heart was full—beyond full—and because what I was sensing was so much more than I could express, I began to cry again. Over and over I silently repeated their question. "Can I feel it? Can I feel it?" answering, "I can't feel anything else. There *isn't* anything else."

The greatness of this heart of mine! I had no idea I possessed such an organ. Its purity and power was, was…. I was speechless. "How did this ever happen to me?" I asked. "All this beauty. Was my heart always like this? Was it like this all along and I never knew?"

"This room is full of love now," the Grandmothers said, ignoring my question and nudging me back to the present. "Yes, Grandmothers," I said, and as I took in a breath, I brought my awareness back to 'now.' And as soon as I did, I felt the love they were talking about. It was inside me, and it was all around. And as I glanced about, I saw flower petals everywhere. The scent of rose was in the air as velvety shades of corals and pinks fell all around me. Petals piled one on top of another until they covered the ground and formed a silky carpet of light.

"Place your hands over your heart to honor it. That Sweetness," they whispered, drawing out the word, **"and that depth,"** they shook their heads in wonder, **"may be a little painful for some hearts to hold at first."** "Yes, Grandmothers," I said, "I can testify to that." I was experiencing an enormous expansion as well as the greatest capacity for radiance I had yet known, my body quivering while my senses merged into the space around me. In a moment I was so full I could no longer speak.

One Grandmother lightly placed a hand on my shoulder and said, **"Sit quietly, sit with your own heart."** She closed her eyes after she said this and I followed her example. It felt good to go inward and be quiet, to be alone with my heart. I rested here and after a few moments

I heard her say, **"This is the core of your power/beauty, the core of your beauty/power. Beauty/power is one,"** she reminded me, **"and *you* are that."** As her words resounded in my mind, I inhaled deeply and sighed with satisfaction. "This is my core," I whispered.

I closed my eyes and rested in this place until my body finally stopped vibrating and when I began to feel somewhat 'normal' again I opened them to see the Grandmothers standing around, waiting and gazing at me with loving smiles. "Thank you, Grandmothers," I said and they nodded and smiled even more.

"The flower of your heart is perfect," they said. **"Take a moment and feel its gratitude for at last being recognized. Now that it has been seen, it can grow larger and even more beautiful. The petals of this flower within you will open wider and its colors will grow more vibrant. Each of you who does this work is unique in her beauty/power, in her power/beauty, each of you is a perfect expression of the Divine.**

"Each flower in a garden is unique, so as you go about your days, honor and revere the flowers in life's garden. And as you do this, notice how it is that *you* express the particular beauty that you are." Then they dipped their heads, made a quick little bow, and let me know that our time together was over.

At our next Grandmothers' meeting I shared all of this with the people who came and after we had passed on the Empowerment and Cloak of Comfort to newcomers, we meditated on the flower of the heart. Luckily I made a recording of this meditation because what became known as "The Blooming as the Flower That You Are" CD proved so useful that it went out to a great many people.

"The winds of change are upon you now"

The next time I went to the Grandmothers, before I had a chance to say anything, they looked at me and asked, **"Who do you think you are?"** That stopped me in my tracks. If a person had asked this, I would have thought they were criticizing, but the Grandmothers' look told me that wasn't their intention. "What?" I wondered, "do they mean?"

Since I didn't know what to do, I waited quietly for them to explain themselves and at last I was rewarded. **"Stand tall,"** they said, and motioned me to lift my head high. **"Sit tall; take your place with us."** "Oh," I whispered, "They want me to believe in myself." This was what "Who do you think you are?" meant. **"Yes,"** they nodded and said,

"You are one with us, and now we are going to sweep all extraneous things off you."

"Wow," I whispered, wondering what *this* meant, but before I could speculate, a strong wind whirled in, lifting dirt, paper and debris off the ground and in a second all of it was whisked away. I watched as the cloud of dust rose above me and instantly it was gone. "The winds of change are upon you now," the Grandmothers said, their faces grim. "Let them blow." I glanced at them in surprise but when I saw their sober looks, I too grew sober. "They will blow away the past; they will blow away the old and needless," and as they spoke, the wind lifted my hair and billowed my shirt.

"Now is the time to offer up the old versions of yourself. Those you have carried around with you," they said, and now I really looked surprised. "All that you have previously identified as 'you,'" they explained, "images of who you have thought you were." My mouth fell open. *This* was pretty extreme. They were asking me to let go of my identity, to let go of my *self*. As I realized what they meant, I felt a clutching sensation in my diaphragm and noticed that I had stopped breathing.

"Grandmothers," I squeaked, but they shook their heads and continued. "You have carried these images around a long time, images of who you think you are," they explained. "Carried them for so long now that *you* think they are real!" they laughed. "But they are not," they shook their heads and eyed me critically.

"Begin to release them now," they ordered me and gave a firm nod. They were serious. "First offer us all the versions of your hated self." "My hated self," I repeated and after a second, added, "oh. Her. The weakling, the one who's afraid all the time," I said. " I can do that. I don't like that part of me anyway. What do I have to lose?"

"Let all the things you have *not* loved about yourself—both in the past and in the present—come to mind," they said and stood so close, bending over as they seemed to examine me, that I got a good look at their serious expressions. "Take note of the attitudes and memories you have of yourself as angry, as needy, controlling, weak, overbearing, etc., etc.," they said, waving their hands in dismissal. "Let all the hated ideas about who you are or have been come up. You have identified with so many of these," they shook their heads in disbelief, "offer them up now." "Okay, Grandmothers, I agreed, my voice meek. I hadn't realized I'd carried so many ugly thoughts about myself. "I would love to get rid of them," I said, "but how?"

"Breathe in," they answered, "and as you do, recognize you are taking in air that has never before entered your body. New air. And when you exhale, you are letting go of stale air, letting go of old states of consciousness that have not until this moment been ready to leave. But they're ready now. At this moment you are renewing yourself with your breath. You are always doing this, but it is especially true now. At this moment you are *consciously* breathing in the new and *consciously* breathing out the old, hated images. And along with them, exhaling the patterns your mind developed in order to cling to them."

I listened and breathed, listened and breathed. I couldn't do more than that. Everything they said felt true, but they were moving so fast I found myself hustling to keep up with them. They truly were the teachers and I, the student.

The Grandmothers didn't take their eyes off me for a second and as they watched, they breathed rhythmically, all the while making rolling movements with their wrists and hands to encourage me to continue. After following them for a few minutes, I began to get light-headed, my eyes watering and my vision becoming blurry. I was also getting tired, but I wasn't about to give up.

"Breathe with us again," they said, "and this time as you exhale, allow the remnants of these old consciousness states to exit." "Okay, Grandmothers," I said, and as I mimicked them, my body began to relax. "When you breathe with us, you breathe in the power and peace of the Divine." They patted me gently. "Ah...." I sighed as their touch made my body relax even more.

"The winds of change move with your breath; they move on your breath." I wondered what this meant, but before I could ask, they said, "Invite the winds of change to blow through you now, to release the negative attitudes you've held about yourself. Attitudes like 'I'm not worthy," they explained. "I'm limited, there's something wrong with me," they chuckled, pantomiming my feelings of low self-esteem. "Not true at all," they laughed and shook their heads, "not true at all. You are so much more than *anything* you have ever thought about yourself." Then they brushed their hands together as if to say, "Well, that's done."

"Wow!" I muttered. I felt different—tired, but also lighter. It was a good feeling. "Thank you, Grandmothers," I said, but they smiled, wagged a finger at me and said, "You are not finished yet." "More?" I groaned as I looked at them in disbelief.

"Now allow the idealized images you have carried of yourself to rise. These too will poke their heads up," they laughed, brushing aside my fatigue. "These images may tell you, 'I'm a good person, I'm sensitive, I'm a practical person, I'm generous, I'm...whatever,'" they said, again making that dismissive motion. "**Invite these 'beloved' self images to show themselves and watch as they too come up. You may be tempted to cling to them,**" they warned. "**However, simply let them rise into your awareness and as they do, just as with the negative ones, offer them to us.**

"**Idealized images are sacred cows,**" they explained. "**You wonder, 'Do I have to let go of this one?' Although you may initially want to hang onto it, you are much greater than any of these remnants. Let them come up,**" they encouraged me, "**and offer them to us as well. And if, as you do this work more hated images also come to mind, offer them too.**

"**You can watch all this on the screen of your mind. None of it is real; none of it is you. And if you find that some images are difficult to release, ask us to help you let them go and we will. You see,**" they smiled broadly, "**there is much greater joy in store for you now—better feeling, greater truth than you have ever known, even in these cherished images.**"

Then they began to recite lines from one of my favorite poems, Theodore Roethke's "The Waking."

"**Clinging never keeps itself,**" they said.
"**What falls away is always and is near.**
I wake to sleep and take my waking slow.
I feel my fate is what I cannot fear.
I learn by going where I need to go."

"**You will learn by going; do not fear the process. Let us lead you, and as you relinquish both the so-called positive and negative attitudes about yourself, the winds of change will blow the old away. What can withstand the winds of change?**" they asked, gesturing with ease. "**There is a freshness in the air now—at this very moment you are becoming new. And as we continue our work, should you find more images lurking beneath the surface of your mind, ask us to take whatever is ready to go, and we will.**"

Then they wrapped their arms around each other and forming a tight circle, drew in close to me. "**As the winds of change blow the old away,**" they said, "**we look into your eyes. And as you look back at us, what is it you see?**" I looked and looked at them, studying their expressions and twelve serious faces stared back. "**What do you see?**" they asked again and then answered, "***What you see is your own self. You are divine.***" I smiled back at them then, murmuring to myself, "Oh well, it always comes down to this, doesn't it?" and they smiled too.

Dazzled by the power of their gaze, as I mindlessly stared at them, I heard them say, **"We will now wrap you in light."** They reached out for me and like a butterfly in a translucent cocoon, quickly I was swaddled in layers of light. Now I could move neither my arms nor legs, but my awareness was so sharp I could see and feel everything anyway. I was surprised that being encased like this didn't feel confining, but instead felt magical. **"What is it like for you to be enfolded like this?"** they asked, but when I couldn't find the words to express my feelings, they smiled knowingly. They had seen my joy.

I rested inside this cocoon, happy in a dazed sort of way, and in a few minutes they said, **"When you turn your awareness back to yourself, you may notice that you are much larger than you thought you were. Much greater,"** they said, nodding knowingly. **"In fact, you are lightening up and opening out so quickly that it may feel like you're about to lift off the ground."**

As if following their instructions, I began to expand. My chrysalis self tripled, then quadrupled and one after another, the layers of light that had encased me peeled off. Smiling, the Grandmothers observed it all, nodded their approval and said, **"From this place of true grandeur, with generous wings/arms you can embrace the world."** I saw what they meant. They had transformed me yet again. Changed and charged with beauty/power, now I was an enormous butterfly whose delicate wings tenderly batted at the world. And to be this beautiful creature gave me the most lovely and loving feeling.

"While you hold the world in love, we hold you. Embracing and being embraced," they said; **"the two actions one. Great love is flowing to you now, flowing through you, and out from you, and because you are at one with us, you are safe, secure and loved beyond measure."** Then they giggled and said, **"We tell you, your greatness is just beginning."** I listened and I shook my head in wonder—wonder at the Grandmothers and wonder at what they were leading me to.

They nodded an almost imperceptible 'yes' then and said, **"When you have absorbed enough of our teachings for today, and are ready to return to daily life, once again ask yourself, 'who am I? Who am I really?' The answer to this is obvious. Of the three you's"** they said, **"the one others think you are, the one you think you are, and one you truly are—right now you are present in the real one. And here you can live,"** they smiled brightly. **"We salute you."**

After I returned from this journey, I sat up slowly and stared out the window a long time. I felt like I was in a trance. I had returned from an alternate universe and here I was again in my own bedroom. "From the exalted, back to the ordinary," I said and sighed. By now I had made this transition many times, and usually I simply thanked the Grand-mothers or the animal spirits for what they had taught me, and after a minute or two, jumped up and went about the next thing in life. But now and then the adjustment from the inner world back to the outer was too disorienting to handle with ease. This was one of those times.

I needed something besides ordinary and non-ordinary reality. I didn't want to think about what they had just taught me and I didn't want to think about what to fix for dinner. I just wanted to float, to be that jello we had talked about. Although for several years I had lived with a foot in both worlds, at this moment I couldn't bring myself to hop from one back to the other. I remember saying, " Thank God there's no one in the house now but me because I couldn't talk if I had to." I couldn't think, let alone talk, and what's more, I didn't want to. My circuits were fried. So after staring out the window for a while I went into the back garden and pulled weeds for the rest of the afternoon. That brought me back to earth again, back to what passes for normal.

CHAPTER 11

The Winds of Change Are Upon You
"There is no more powerful work you can do;
this is the most important thing."

Women who had been coming to the Grandmothers' groups for a while decided to start meeting every two weeks to study *A Call to Power: the Grandmothers Speak.* As we studied the Grandmothers' teachings, we dove deep into ourselves and because we did this together, we magnified the learning for one another. Soon there was a Grandmothers' study circle in New England, one in the Pacific Northwest, and another in the Netherlands.

After our circle had been together several months it dawned on me that I had never come out and asked the Grandmothers what *they* wanted from this group. I had simply gone along, meeting-by-meeting, letting myself be guided by the challenges and impetus of the moment without consciously asking. Now I found myself wondering how *they* viewed this group of women.

I made my way to the upper world and barely got out the words, "Grandmothers, what do you want from this group?" before they replied, **"People who follow our teachings like this are the vanguard. They need to know this, and we do not say this to make them feel puffed up, but so they realize that what a group like this can offer is important. Not everyone gets the opportunity to work with us,"** they said and gave me a meaningful look; **"not everyone is called to spread our message. But *they* have been called. We want them to want what we have come to give,"** they said, **"to allow us to work with them and through them.**

"We call each person to our work and we will communicate directly with them. Although you can gather together to meditate, to pray and experience your sisterhood/brotherhood with one another—to recharge your batteries. Our work with each of you is individual. Whenever someone calls to us, we come. You don't need

an intermediary to work with us." As I listened, I felt my heart lift. Once again they were affirming that I was not responsible for making any of this happen.

Now they showed me women who had received their empowerment and gone on to start Grandmothers' groups and I recognized many, though not all of them. I remembered some from Slovenia, from Holland, Switzerland, England and Lithuania but there were others too who I had never met. The Grandmothers pointed to a map of the United States and showed me how it had become peppered with groups. I saw others in Canada, Australia, Germany and New Zealand. The Grandmothers' work had spread much farther than I had known. I shook my head as I marveled at what they had brought about and were continuing to bring and again I felt gratitude for being along on the ride.

Next I reflected on those who step forward to lead these groups. These women are linked by their desire to serve, their wish to share the Grandmothers' message of the return of the great yin. Many of them have never met anyone else doing this work and unless they communicate through the Grandmothers' newsletter, the website, or attend the annual Gathering of the Grandmothers, their only contact with fellow grandmothers takes place when they receive the empowerment. As I thought about this, I began to wonder if this was enough, or if, as a group, we should be doing things differently. **"This is enough,"** the Grandmothers answered before I could fully form the question. **"You are linked with one another through our love for you; linked through your love for the Divine and through your desire to work for the highest good. This is as it should be."** I heard the rightness and simplicity in their explanation and nodded in agreement.

"Whenever someone opens to us or to any form of the Divine, we will work *with* and *through* them. And *through* them we will reach others. It's very simple," they said. **"If you call on us, your life will become easier, and when we say *us*,"** they explained, **"we mean *any* form of the Divine. All forms of divinity work together, so if you call, we come. It is that simple. It will save you so much energy, error and time if you stop first and call on us. Call us in the morning when you awaken. Start your day with God,"** they smiled, **"and then throughout the day, think of us or any form of the Divine you love and we will be with you. We are always there, so call us. There is nowhere you can go,"** they said and smiled from their hearts, **"that we will not be. But you need to think of us.**

"The world will ensnare, distract and pull you away from your

own deep down nature which is to be at one with God," they explained and I listened intently, willing myself to drink in every word. **"Don't let yourselves be distracted like this,"** they shook their heads. **"Don't waste your life."** "No, Grandmothers," I said. "Don't let me do that."

"We have come at this time," they announced, drawing themselves to their full height, **"and there is great purpose in our work. You are needed,"** they said and locked eyes with me, **"so do not disappoint yourself. We will love you no matter what you do, but you will be disappointed in yourself if you forget who you are, if you forget that you are one with God."**

I listened, my eyes wide and hung on their words, my head nodding up and down all the while. They knew me so well—knew how dedicated I was to following the path to God. Once again I was on the verge of tears.

"Feel us now," they commanded and extended their wings til the tips touched me. **"Sit or stand up straight and *feel* us,"** they said. **"Whenever you straighten your spine,"** they reminded me, **"you invite us to come in, to hold and uphold you.**

"Think of the straight spine as your alignment with the Divine, and when you have pulled yourself tall and are aware of this alignment, let your mind dwell on those you love—your family, friends and neighbors. Whenever you think of those you love, you connect with them through your heart," they explained. **"And then we, who are at one with you, can also connect with them. We bless all these people you love, you can be sure of that. Whenever you call on us, every thought you send out and every word you speak carries our love.**

"The difference between this way of operating and what your mind usually does (worry and blame)," they laughed, **"is simple. When you think of and call on us first, *whatever* you think about— our love goes to that.**

This is a form of prayer but you don't have to 'work' to make anything happen. It's simple. Call on us and once you have, our love will flow to every person you see, to every thought that comes to your mind. We will saturate you with love. This is what we mean," they said, **"when we speak about the effortlessness of this work."**

The only effort involved in any of this is to remember to think of the Divine. It's deceptively simple, this method. It's also the antidote to the unbalanced state we live in. Those who have chosen to work with the Grandmothers are fortunate because we can call on them and immediately rectify imbalance, not only within ourselves, but also around us. And the more we do this, the more the healing energy of yin infuses the earth, blessing everything. **"There is no more powerful work you can do,"** they said; **"*this* is the most important thing. You are making the energy of yin available to all."**

I reflected on the issue of calling on the Grandmothers—how it seems so simple, but isn't really. Why, I wondered, is it so difficult to remember to call on the Divine? Is it an effort, as the Grandmothers say, simply because we seem to have trouble remembering? "But why?" I asked myself, "Is it difficult for *me* to remember to do this? I'm communicating with them all the time and still I often don't realize when I need to call on them. "Grandmothers," I said, "why is this so hard for *me*? I want to know."

"We will show you," they said and then there was a whirring sensation and for a moment things seemed to fly by me. Quickly the Grandmothers transported me back to the little house in Indiana where I had grown up in what would today be called a dysfunctional family. By the time I had started school I had learned that when the world proved confusing and frightening to the child I was, there was no one to call on. This was a frightening way to grow up, but it taught me to be self-reliant. I *had* to take care of myself if I was going to survive, and early on I learned how to do that.

As the years went by I grew accustomed to leaning on myself, accustomed to having no one to turn to. Now I rejoiced that the Divine had at last become clearly and fully present for me, but I still hadn't developed the habit of turning to God first. Somewhere inside me lay the old belief that I was alone, that I was the one responsible for everything. "How," I wondered, "Can I get past this?"

The Grandmothers smiled lovingly and said, **"Sometimes you forget we are here. It's an old habit with you."** And when they saw the look of distress on my face, they added, **"But don't worry. In our presence old habits fade away. Each time you remember to call on us, you form a new habit. We will help,"** they promised, grinning to reassure me. **"By the way, this problem is not yours alone. There are very few today who truly trust in the Divine. This,"** they said, **"is why we have come.**

"Whenever you become distracted, forget about your connection with us and get caught in fear or negative thinking of some sort, as soon as you notice what has happened, think of us and we will surround you. We will fill you with our presence," they said. "Thank you, Grandmothers," I sighed in relief, "thank you."

"Should you make a mistake and catch yourself holding critical thoughts about yourself or someone else," they said, **"as soon as you**

call on us, we will come in and mitigate the situation. We will pour our love to every person, thing and condition with which you are connected," they said and I sighed again, tears starting in my eyes.

"Let your thoughts return to us as faithfully as birds coming home to roost," they said as they gazed at me with love. "Return to the nurturing embrace of the Mother that we, the Grand Mothers give, and nest in this endless love. This is your home," they said. "A nest is a good analogy for our love because a nest surrounds you on all sides while at the same time it cushions and shelters you.

"As you feel the peace of this nest, the safety and nurturance of being held in love," they said, "gradually you will learn to trust that it is always there for you." They paused a moment, then said, "As you sit in this place of love, think again of those *you* love, whether they are in physical bodies or no longer in physical bodies. Think of the ones you love and, as soon as you think of them, we will hold them too. You see," they said, beaming with happiness, "*within the play of love there is no separation*; there is no time and space. There is only instant union. And because you are held in union with us," they said, "whenever you think of those you love, you bring them into union too. They also become our own," they said, gazing fondly at me. "We care for them just as we care for you." "Oh, Grandmothers!" I cried, and overwhelmed by the generosity of their love, broke down sobbing.

"Thoughts that go out from you are not material," they explained; "thoughts don't require a set amount of space, or a specific roadway. They simply go where they go. Whenever you think of a place where any living thing is suffering and then think of us, our love instantly goes to that place. Whenever you think of the fighting in the Middle East, in Africa or anywhere," they said, "and then think of us, love flies to that place. This is a form of prayer," they explained; "this is what we mean when we speak about the effortlessness of this work." I listened and slowly shook my head. The economy and depth of their explanation had stunned me into silence.

They began to laugh. "*Now* we have something for you," they said, giving me a sly smile. "Think of those you do *not* love," they said, arching their brows, "the difficult ones," they nodded wisely. "These are your greatest teachers, the ones whose lessons you haven't yet figured out. Think of them," they continued, "and as soon as you do, ask us to love them—even though you may not be able to. As soon as you invite us in, we will embrace *them*."

They stood back, seeming to size me up and said, "Try it, and notice how it feels—that is if you can bring yourself to turn them over to us.

Whenever you turn these 'difficult ones' over," they explained, **"you free yourself."**

I saw the way they were looking at me, almost daring me to try this. I didn't want to think about "these difficult ones" (I *really* didn't), but I couldn't escape their penetrating gaze. Finally I relented. "Okay, okay, Grandmothers," I said, "I'll do it." And as soon as I spoke, my mind flew to where I didn't want it to go—to my friend, Elaine. She and I had been close for many years when suddenly and for no reason I knew of, she began to treat me not as a friend but as an acquaintance. This had been like a knife in my heart and I had tried several times to talk with her, asking what had gone wrong. But although she was invariably polite and treated me with superficial friendliness, she wouldn't open up. I had no idea what had happened to cause her to shut me out; I missed her friendship, and felt the smart of her rejection. Her initial pulling away had taken place eight or nine years earlier and to this day we remained acquaintances.

As the memory of this wound came back, my energy dropped and sadness enveloped me. I looked up from my misery and saw the Grandmothers waiting to see what I would do. Finally I took in a breath and said, "Okay, Grandmothers, you take her. I can't do anything about this. I've tried and tried and it's out of my control." They smiled their sweetest smiles then and reached their arms out, first to me and then to Elaine, letting me know that as of now, this problem belonged to them. As I watched them work, I took in another breath, and when I exhaled I was surprised to notice that I felt lighter.

"You will need to do this over and over again. The mind doesn't easily relinquish something it has grasped for a long time. It will try to dredge up this drama again and again," they said, wrinkling their noses in distaste, **"so you must be resolute in renouncing ownership of it. Whenever she comes to mind,"** they said, **"call on us. We will come immediately. We will love her as we love you and will heal and bless you both,"** they said and folded their hands to let me know this was all there was to it. The 'problem' now belonged to them. "Thank you, Grandmothers," I said, relief in my voice. I could hardly believe I would no longer be carrying this weight around.

They beamed at me. **"Feel yourself contained within the nest of love now,"** they said, **"surrounded and enfolded in it. Relax into it,"** they said and as I did, I became aware of their overweening love. My body softened and so did the defended walls around my heart. **"The people with whom you have difficulty need our love too,"** they reminded me, **"and whenever you allow us to take over and love them as well as you, you free yourself from negative attachments to** these 'difficult ones.' Our love will heal you," they said, "and in time our love will heal them too. It is your connection to us that makes all this possible," they explained as they gently patted me. "Just as our love changes you, it will also change others.

"This is what we want from you," they said as they held my eyes with theirs, "to let us work through you, so you become our vessel. Fully our vessel." What they wanted for me I also wanted for myself— to be their vessel, their instrument. I was awed by their explanation, awed also by the practical power of love. I wanted nothing more than to live my life in that and knew whenever my small self got in the way, I couldn't do it. "Lead on, Grandmothers," I said with feeling, "lead on."

"We have more to teach you. Notice that as soon as you let go of whatever you have been holding onto, no matter what it is, love and beauty come in and fill you. This is the way it works," they said. "Feel it now," they said. "*Joy!*" they exclaimed, "The joy you were born for. Whenever you make the decision to be at one with the Divine," they said, speaking in a confidential tone, "your life will fill with joy." As I listened to them, I felt it, felt the joy they were talking about. Happiness, lightness, a sense of freedom.

"This is something few understand, but from the moment of letting go, your smallest activities and even your worst times will be upheld by joy. Joy will underlie every thing you do," they emphasized, "and you will walk in love, in beauty and power. *This* is what we want for you," they said, "to be who you are—nothing less.

"All you need to live this way is to call on us. Throughout the day, throughout the night, call us. If you awaken in the night, call us. If you are overburdened during the day, call us. When you are lonely, call us. When you're lost, call us. When you're full of happiness, call us. Whenever you do this," they said, "we will magnify the love and goodness lying within you, just waiting to awaken."

Taking my hands in theirs, they looked into my eyes and said, "We are not separate from you." They shook their heads and smiled. "It is only old ideas and thoughts that make you believe we are separate. For thousands of years you have been conditioned to believe this fiction," they said. "It is not true," they stated.

"The good news is, that *each time* you call on us, those old conditioning barriers melt a bit. The false separation between the Divine and your own divine self dissolves. *Each time*," they said, smiling broadly. "So whenever you remember to call on us, be glad!" they cried. "Be glad you remembered. At that moment, more conditioning is being dissolved.

"Isn't this what you want?" they asked, "to be free to be your divine self?" and I nodded mutely. "This, after all, is why we have come. Remember," they said and held a finger to their lips, "It is not by doing that you become one with us. No!" they declared. "Doing will not give you joy and oneness with God. Action is part of the energy of yang, and yang energy has its place in the world," they said, "but *doing* will not bring you into union with God."

"Being will," they said. By *being* who you are; by being at one with divinity, you will save yourself. This is also how you will save your planet," they said. "We remind you that you have been called to us, and this is no accident, nor is it an accident to have received our empowerment."

They stood quietly with their eyes on me, watching to be sure I was with them. "I'm okay, Grandmothers," I said, "I think I understand." "Good!" they exclaimed. Then they said, "Take a moment to focus on your union with us. Let yourself again feel what it's like to be held in this nest of love." Dutifully I closed my eyes and thought of open- ing to the nest they were describing and immediately I was ensconced in coziness. Warm and safe, comfortable and comforted. As I nestled in, my mind calmed, my body hummed, and my heart began to sing. "Thank you, Grandmothers, thank you, Grandmothers" I sang over and over again. This would be my new mantra. "Thank you, thank you, thank you."

"The joy you are feeling," they said, "is more than you can con- tain. You are living in a sea of energy," they said, nodding, "and right now that sea is full of joy. Let it flow.

"Watch as joy pours from your heart, flooding throughout this city, throughout all of Southern California. It is washing over the entire earth now and then over the universe, filling everything. Holding all forms of life in love," they said. "Oh, Grandmothers," I whispered, my voice barely audible, "I don't know how to describe it. I feel like I've been amplified many times over, or maybe it's more that I've been dissolved. I don't know which, but whatever it is, there's no 'me' here any more." And as I stood before them with my mouth hang- ing open, I *was* the cosmos. The joy they had evoked was now both far away and near, and all of it at the same moment. I was the light waves I saw bouncing through the air and I was the one who stood back and watched them bounce. "I wonder where I am," I said, but I felt so happy I didn't care.

They gathered around me then and said, "Feel your body. Note the expansion within you and keep your focus there. From this experience of union, will come great good." I had read of people having this experience—yogis and such—but now I was living it. Waves of energy were rising and falling inside me, coming on so fast they made it impossible to talk.

"What you are feeling marks a change in your vibration," they said, speaking softly to reassure me and help me ground myself. "You will get used to it," they said. "Notice that the wave of loving energy that you sent out into the universe when you opened to joy is cresting now and rolling back. It is ready to rush into your body," they said, "so open up and receive it."

I glanced at them in disbelief. *"More?"* A few of them held my hands while others patted my back. "Each time you open like this, they said, "the reservoir of beauty/power within you will grow." They looked on with love, continued their gentle pats and said, "Sit quietly now and recognize your true identity."

Wave after wave of love, wave after wave of awareness washed over me as I sat on the ground. I was flushed and filled, flushed and filled until every cell in my body vibrated. I couldn't talk, I could barely think, but somewhere I recognized I didn't need to. "Just receive," I told myself, parroting the Grandmothers, "just receive."

I stayed in that position until all my parts calmed and flowed into harmony with one another and I felt okay—almost normal in fact. But there was something about me that was different. If I were a singer I would have said that I had just added another octave to my range.

Give thanks," the Grandmothers said when I shakily rose to my feet. But before I could express my gratitude for this amazing experience, the drumbeat changed, letting me know it was time to return to 'real' life. As I gazed at them I tried to convey my gratitude through my eyes and once more they said, "We bless you." Then tears scalded my cheeks as I recalled it was always they who did the giving.

When I returned from this journey I went to bed. I was full to bursting with wonder and happiness, and I felt blessed beyond imagining, but I was so tired I could hardly hold my head up. Some visits to the Grandmothers were monumental in intensity and this was one. When I finally played back the recording, I understood why I had been so exhausted when I returned. I had traveled to the farthest points in the universe. Gone there and come back. But more stupendous than this had been my experience of the power of love. Small wonder that I had needed to rest.

"Sometimes you forget who you are, but we are here to remind you."

The next time I went to them, I wanted to know about the potential of the monthly Grandmothers' meetings. Their message was spreading faster. Women and a few men too were now gathering each month in different parts of the world to study *A Call to Power: the Grandmothers Speak* and help one another learn to live the Grandmothers' message. Because so many groups were forming in so many corners of the world, I knew the work had to be important, but I wanted to know the real purpose of these meetings.

When I came before them, before I could get the question out of my mouth, they said, **"Know the greatness of your beauty and power."** Then they bored into me with their eyes and said, **"Do not underestimate yourselves, but remember the core of your being. Your core is beauty, power, truth and goodness,"** they said as they held me with a fierce look.

As they continued to stare at me, I became aware that there were others with me. I was one of a large group of women and as the Grandmothers walked toward us, we drew ourselves up very tall. They stopped directly in front of us and dropped a transparent covering over each woman, a covering that enabled the beauty, power, truth and goodness within her to shine forth. Although I couldn't see the covering, I could feel it and as I looked at the women with me I saw that whatever the Grandmothers placed over us made the special qualities of each woman more evident. Some radiated kindness, and others good humor. It was fascinating to see each woman's gifts exposed.

"Own your own gifts," the Grandmothers said. **"Sometimes you forget who you are, but we are here to remind you. And each time you gather in a group like this you will be reminded of who you are. Only truth is spoken at these meetings,"** they said, **"only truth is experienced. There is no place for falseness of any sort at these gatherings.**

"Whenever you come together, we encourage you to freely express your beauty, power, goodness and truth. There need never be pretense, performance or holding back," they said. **"The meetings are an opportunity to learn to receive, and whenever you are fully yourself, you can do that. You can receive what we have come to give. Take this opportunity.**

"We embrace and cover you with this transparent covering," they said, **"transparent in that others cannot see it. It will protect you as you**

move about the world and will at the same time magnify your beauty/power/truth and goodness. And each time you meet," they said, "our gifts to you will go deeper and become more fully manifest.

"This is why we come to you—to continuously strengthen your beauty/power/goodness/truth." Then they smiled at one another and said, "As you sit wrapped in this covering, ask us to show you the way you were before we gave it to you." I looked up in surprise but when I saw the expectant looks on their faces, I said, "Okay, Grandmothers. Please show me." "Notice the change in the beauty/power of your presence in the 'before' and in the 'after,'" they said. "There is a measurable difference in the amount of power/beauty within you now." I watched as they showed me my 'before' and then my 'after' self and I immediately saw the difference. I also felt it. The 'before' version of myself looked and felt smaller and weaker than the 'after.' She was also a bit disjointed—not all her parts were as harmoniously connected as they were after I received the covering.

"If you like, you can ask us how much have we increased your beauty/power in just these few seconds," they said with a glimmer in their eye. "Ask, and then observe as a percentage or a graph comes to you." "Okay, Grandmothers," I said again, really interested. "After you receive it, ask your mind to file this information," they said. "The mind is good at recording. And as you continue to assimilate this experience you may see your percentage climb."

"Okay, Grandmothers," I said, "I'm ready," and immediately 25% flashed on the screen of my mind. "Twenty-five percent!" I cried, "That's a lot." They shrugged, demonstrating that to them this was no big deal. But I was amazed. "Imagine," I said to myself, "I now have one quarter more beauty/power in me than I had before. They accomplished this within the blink of an eye. Grandmothers," I whispered, "*This* is really effortless effort."

They smiled indulgently and said; "Our work with you is cumulative, so your capacity to receive what we have come to give you will be continuously increasing. This is only natural," they explained. "If this is what you want," they added, "we will be happy to give it to you." "Yes, Grandmothers," I said. "This *is* what I want."

"All right then," they said. "As we increase the love, beauty, power, truth and goodness within you, these qualities will show up in your presence. The center of love lives in your heart," they explained, "and from this center love pumps throughout your body until every part of you is bathed in it. It floods your mind too, your thoughts as well as the storehouses of information within your brain. At this moment

your memory banks are filled with love. Your entire emotional system is filled. They stood back and looked me over. **"You are so much greater now than you were a few minutes ago,"** they said, **"and you will continue to grow in your ability to effortlessly receive and give.**

"You are an organism of love—that's why you feel oneness with us. All barriers eventually dissolve in love," they explained, **"because love expands throughout everything, flowing like water."** They playfully nudged one another then and said, **"Bathed in love like this, you are both the bath and the bather."** "Yes, Grandmothers," I replied, but suddenly I was so tired I could hardly keep my eyes open. I struggled to shake off the fatigue that was enveloping me, but soon my head dropped forward and I fell into a sound sleep. And although I only slept a minute or two, I knew I had, because when I played back the tape, I heard myself snoring. The Grandmothers frequently had this effect on me. When their lessons went especially deep, my circuits overloaded and I dropped into sleep.

I started awake when I heard them say **"You are fast becoming your true nature—awakening to what you've always been."** I blinked, determined not to miss another word. **"Everything you do and say, everywhere you go, and every thought that comes to you now, comes from love,"** they said. **"The more you think of us,"** they gestured broadly, **"the more your particular manifestation of love will impact life. As your vibration rises,"** they explained, **"you will lift everything around you.**

"Remember your percentage," they said; **"and how much more you are now than you were ten minutes ago. This lesson carries a blessing with it. You have received an enormous gift."**

"Tell the women they are needed."

The next time I went to them I didn't have a specific question, but what I most wanted was a deeper understanding of their message. I wanted to really get it, to anchor this truth in the cell beds of my body. This was what was on my mind as I stepped before a dozen very tall, very imposing Grandmother eagles.

"Say this," they said. **"Tell the women they are needed,"** their great raptor heads rocked up and down. **"They are important; sometimes they forget this."** As soon as they spoke, a great presence descended from above my head, moved through my body and anchored me into the ground. It was shaped like an inverted triangle, with the downward point imbedding itself in the earth.

As I watched this take place, the Grandmother eagles spoke again.

"If ever you doubt the efficacy of our words," they said, "or the rightness and timeliness of our message, turn away from the outer world to the center of your being. Focus in the middle of your chest," they said, tapping their breastbones, "and go quiet. As you do this," they breathed in and slightly lifted their wings, "presence will grow. It will deepen and penetrate the cell beds of your body, fill your consciousness and awaken all the lifetimes that you have lived. At that moment everything within you will awaken.

"Whenever you open like this," they said, "your karma will be burned." I gasped. "Yes," they affirmed, "your karma will be burned. This is because both the past and the present are drawn together and merge in presence."

Then they began to strut about, thinking on their feet. "As you open like this, you will stop leading a fragmented life," they said; "you'll no longer be drawn away from the now moment, no longer fixate on the future or chase after your latest desire or worry," they explained, pacing as they talked. "Nor will you be drawn backwards to gaze in fascination at your past and wallow in regret. No more of that," they said, shaking their heads in dismissal. "When you move into *presence*," they said, smiling at their own cleverness, "you fully occupy the present.

"We have spoken before of 'presence,'" they said, "and we introduce it again because you have more to learn. The presence we speak of is so deep," they explained, "so full, that it goes beyond what you think of as goodness. At each moment of life you are given the choice to expand into it. This," they said, nodding emphatically, "is why we have come. The purpose of our mission is to turn you away from the toys of this world, toward that which is real. The fleeting fascinations of the moment will never satisfy you," the great eagle mothers wagged their beaks. "They never have. And they never will.

"We are with you, within every breath you take. We surround you in our love. We are truly, as you say, 'here for you; we flank, guard and hold you in our embrace. Whenever you call on us, we will create a protected space for you," they nodded. "We will always do that. This protected space will make turning within yourself easy.

"Turn within now and open to the core of your being," they said and I breathed deeply and dropped into my center place. "Each time you do this," they said, "you will feel the Divine's love for you and sense how you are held, always held. And because we are here now, holding you and everyone on earth," they explained, "it will become easier and easier to feel and know your oneness with us and with others.

"Whenever you open like this you awaken to love. Love, after all, is what you are," they said. "Love is your true identity. Although many are asleep to this fact, love is flowing through the veins of every person on this planet," they said. "In the eternal, unchanging space within, you can sit quietly and let love flow. You are part of that flow," they said. "You are blessed. Your life is a blessing. This is the truth.

"Once this center place becomes home for you, the work you do will be easier. All the problems that need solving will be solved," they said, lifting their wings as if to say, "Well, isn't that obvious?" "Once you take up residence in your home place, everything benefits. In time you'll come to know this," they said, nodding to reassure me, "and you will occupy this centered place all the time.

As they tilted their bobbing heads they looked like they were concentrating on something important. "And whenever you feel the pull of worry, regret, or frustration, instead of collapsing into the drama of the moment, call on us and turn toward your home place. As soon as you call on us, we will instantly mend, heal and dissipate any states of worry and fear within you." They looked me in the eyes and said, "Because you are a deathless, changeless being you can live within the flow of presence all the time."

I was fascinated, listening with my mouth hanging open, but at the same time I was aware that my 'rational' self was beginning to nag. "Yes, but," it said, and then, "this sounds impossible! How will I ever get anything done if I spend all my time sitting in *presence*?" I knew the Grandmothers would tell me to, "Turn within," if I asked about this, and I was tired of hearing the same resound. "What about action?" I thought, "What am I supposed to *do*?" But before I could speak, twelve Grandmother eagles responded. "Everything that needs to get done will get done. When you turn within," they gave me a slightly disapproving look, "and open to your core, you will find *nothing* missing in your life. Things will happen the way they have always happened," they said, "but you will live in an exalted state. "An exalted state?" I asked and then in a different tone repeated, "an exalted state." I loved the sound of that.

"You are not the little personality you think you are— full of needs and quirks," they laughed, indulging me. "You aren't a compilation of events and genetic material from the past," they shook their heads and laughed even harder. "Those are only connections you made once upon a time," they explained. "As you awaken to the greatness of your being and move into oneness with the presence that you truly are, you will quickly move through all that." I was trying to take in what they were saying. If I wasn't my past, if I wasn't my inherited traits, and the particular attributes and deficiencies of my personality, then what was I? *Who* was I?

"**Tune in to the core of your body,**" the Grandmothers said. "**Whenever you occupy your center, everyone and everything connected to you lifts,**" they explained. "**Every form of life is part of the same seamless whole,**" they said, "**so when you accept the fact that you are an exalted being and allow yourself to lift up, everything lifts. Whenever you take this centered place and feel it, you salute the truth of life and the truth of life salutes you back.**" As they spoke they puffed out their chests and drew themselves to their full height.

Twelve majestic raptors stared down their beaks at me and said, "**No matter how cut off from this state of being a person may seem to you, no matter how contorted their personality, how sick, crazy, or even evil they may appear,** *presence* **lies at their core. So instead of spending your life worrying about the layers of conditioning and karma you carry around with you, (and everyone else carries around too), open instead to the center of your being. Come home,**" they said, slowing nodding up and down, "**come to center.**" "Yes, Grandmothers," I whispered, my hand over my mouth as I nodded.

"**As soon as you tap into presence, pure energy will cascade outward from you. This outward flow produces a domino effect,**" they said. "**The process may sound simple,**" they said, "**but it is not. The truth is this—your vibration can lift everyone on earth.**" I started and looked up in surprise. Patting me with their wings, they patiently explained, "**Basically, you are an electrical or energy body, so whenever the vibration within you moves to a higher frequency, the energy** that **surges outward from you affects everyone. Everything benefits.**

"**Call on us,**" the Grandmother eagles said. "**Let us surround and hold you as you turn to the Divine within. Your energy will automatically rise upward when you do this.**" Then they cocked their heads, gave me a beady-eyed stare and said, "**Haven't you had enough of living in the basement of life?**" I almost choked at their language, but smiling their raptor smiles they said, "**Rise up now and be happy.**

"**There is so much beauty/power present in you, so much is surging outward from this presence we speak of. We are sharing this information with you,**" they said, "**so you can know how energy works, so you understand why we have come. And we are sharing this so you can know who you are.**" "Yes, Grandmothers," I said. "I am very grateful."

I meant that. I was grateful for their explanation of how energy works, the idea that each life is part of a seamless whole, and their statement about how moving into presence burns karma. All of it fascinated me. But I also knew this lesson would take me a while to absorb. There was much to study here. Finally I looked up at them and they tilted their great heads and said, **"If you want to learn more about this, let us know."**

When I came back from this journey my mind kept jumping from one thing the Grandmothers had said to another. When at last I sat down at the computer to transcribe my visit I realized this one wasn't *a* lesson, but a *series of lessons*. The depth and complexity of what they had shared was not something I could quickly assimilate. I also felt a sense of urgency about getting this message out to others. It was at this point I realized I was actually working on a second book of their teachings.

"This is a time of awakening and expansion. Go big."

I had assumed that because it was so packed with information, I would spend a great deal of time pouring over this last lesson. I intended to do that, but life intervened. All of a sudden I began to receive emails predicting upcoming catastrophes on earth. Not just a few of them, but a lot. I knew announcements like these were well meant, but unfortunately they broadcasted fear. I wondered what I could do in response to the avalanche I was receiving. What was the best way to deal with stuff like this? After I thought about it for a day or two, I went back to the Grandmothers to ask them.

As soon as I landed in their valley the first thing I noticed was this time they were in human form. A group of lovely older women standing together and waiting for me. "Grandmothers," I said as I joined their circle, "There are a lot of bad things happening on earth now and people are sending me predictions of more to come. Please, how do we deal with fearful predictions like these? How can we be helpful?" They nodded thoughtfully and from the looks on their faces I could see that they liked this question.

Immediately they pointed to wings that expanded far into the distance, spreading over the horizon, and I watched in fascination as these great wings folded over everything in sight. **"Expand,"** they said, **"feel your oneness with us and with one another. Focus on your union with the Grandmothers' groups all over the world. You are expanding,"** they said and rocked back and forth with the power of their words. **"This work is also expanding.**

"**Fear is small**," they said, narrowing their eyes. "**It is fear's nature to contract into a ball of tightness. Expansion, however,**" they explained, "**has no room for fear. You are expanding,**" they stated, regarding me with matter-of-fact expressions. "**Feel your oneness with the winds. Feel your oneness with all the places on earth: the seas, the mountains, deserts, valleys, farmlands, cities, and rivers. You can easily do this,**" they explained, chuckling under their breath, "**because your wings (those were *YOUR* wings you saw earlier, by the way,)**" they laughed, "**are that broad. Your wings now cover the earth. They protect and shelter everything.**"

My jaw dropped when I heard, "Those were your wings, by the way." I was so amazed that I didn't know what to say. But before I could venture anything, they ordered me to "**Stick your chest *out*, and expand your wings,**" a knowing expression on their faces.

"Oh!" I exclaimed, as I attempted it and in a minute, I heard the surprise in my voice as I whispered, "I can feel my wings. They are actually physical." "**Feel this sensation in your body,**" the Grandmothers said. "**Where is fear now? Don't give fear anywhere to live,**" they said, shaking their heads. "**This is a time of awakening and expansion. Go big,**" they challenged me. "**Don't go small; go big!**

"**Wherever you go, this expansion will be with you,**" they said. "**The consciousness of connection, of oneness, of all inclusion is something you carry,**" they said. "**Feel it. This…is…who…you…are.**

"**We are calling you to greatness,**" they said, and shouted, "**NOW!**" I jumped, startled by their abrupt delivery and truth to tell, I was also startled by my size. I had become huge, expanded beyond anything I had previously known. "**As your chest expanded, your wings unfolded and many of the little contractions you had carried with you cracked and dropped off,**" they explained. "**Shedding,**" they shrugged as if this sort of thing happened every day, "**you are shedding the old. That explains your change in size,**" they said and gently patted me on the back.

"**We are moving forward,**" they said and no sooner did they say this than they began to rush past me. As they flew past I was carried along in their wake and together we raced forward, a great wind at our backs. "**Our work is expanding and moving forward,**" they said. "**Isn't this where you want to be?**" By now I was flying so fast I didn't have the presence of mind to reply. All I could do was mutely nod 'yes.'

"**Pay no attention,**" they said, making a gesture of dismissal, "**to those who are caught in fear. Love them, but place your attention on expanding, not contracting,**" they said. "**Include those who are caught in fear in the touch of connection, but remember that your** work is in expansion. We have called you to this," they said, giving me a meaningful look, "and we are moving forward. Move with us.

"Notice how your body feels now." Ever practical, even in the midst a rush like this the Grandmothers were reminding me to stay grounded. "It may feel different after this experience; recognize this and honor your body. The body is a great helper, a good teacher, and you may sense a new feeling within yours now, a change in color or vibration," they suggested. "Greatness," they said, nodding firmly; "what you are noticing is the feeling of greatness. For a while now we have told you that we are calling you to greatness and we always speak the truth," they said. "This is what you're feeling now. Come forward with us."

They gestured off to the side and when I turned to look to where they were pointing I saw all the women involved in spreading the Grandmothers' message. Together we began to move forward en mass until at last we come to a stop underneath the over-reaching wings of the Grandmothers. Feathers were everywhere, feathers from our wings and theirs. So many feathers that my eyes were drawn to the layers upon layers of them as they interlaced with one another. It was the Grandmothers who had first formed this mantle and covered us with it, and now, together with them, we were creating a mantle that enfolded the entire earth.

"The Grandmothers are right!" I said as I marveled at our out-stretched wings, "we are great." "This is where we are going," the Grandmothers said, gesturing to the mantle that now blanketed the earth. "Experience what it's like to be surrounded and covered by us, and notice how your wings blend in with ours. Let all old bits of consciousness slough off you now," they said. "They will fall away. The movement is forward—forward into greatness," they swept their arms wide. "Come with us!"

Suddenly I became aware of eagle consciousness; inside me was the presence of the Other, "the great speckled bird" of the old mountain song. And now the spirits of the native peoples who inhabited the continent of America long ago also made themselves known. "Honor them," the Grandmothers said, "and honor one another. Honor the commitment you share to expanding into truth, to opening and opening still further. Forward," they said, "forward, and dance! Dance this freedom, dance this greatness," they cried, "dance! There is great momentum now. Together we are rolling forward into greatness." Then they tilted their heads, smiled their raptor smiles and said, "Enjoy the ride."

CHAPTER 12

Moy, Man and Boy

*"The basic difference between
a man and a moy is selfishness."*

Men—the number one subject on women's minds as well as their number one problem. In my years as a marriage and family therapist I had seen a number of variations on the female/male conundrum but over and over again one consistently came up. Women reported feeling let down by the men in their lives. These men either wouldn't commit to a serious relationship, or they 'committed' and then in some way betrayed their wives or girlfriends. To quote my female clients, "they don't act like men. They're little boys." When a number of these cases showed up at the same time, I began to wonder if there was a message for me. Then the Grandmothers began to pester me. Popping into my mind, nagging at my consciousness—they wouldn't leave me alone.

I was busy with various projects, so I put them off, but they were so insistent that eventually I could no longer ignore them and ended up going to them before I had formulated my question. I made my way to the upper world the way I always did, and when I arrived in the Grandmothers' valley, I noticed that the holy man was there too.

He stood beside them and as soon as he caught my eye, he began to nod his head up and down. He was quite emphatic about it; **"Yes, yes,"** he stated. I looked at him questioningly but now he shook his head, letting me know he wasn't going to talk. Something was in the offing, but I wasn't going to find it out from him. I'd have to get it from the Grandmothers. So I turned to them, waited to catch their eye, and when I could no longer stand the suspense, said, "Okay, okay, Grandmothers, what do you want to teach me?"

Turning to me, they spoke as one person. **"Speak!"** they said and stood with their hands on their hips. "What?" I replied, dumbfounded. "What do you want me to say?" **"Moy,"** they answered and repeated, **"moy."** "Moy?" I asked, contorting my face, "moy? What is moy, Grandmothers?" "**Moy**," they said and took in a breath as if they were preparing to lecture. "**A combination of man and boy—but mostly boy**," they said. Now I was stupefied. "What in the world are they talking about?" I muttered.

"**This is what many men are**," they said, and as they spoke, they nodded in concert with the holy man. "**They are large**," they explained, "**all of them are powerful to some degree or another**," they added. "**Large in body, also in strength, and they have big voices. They are able to do hard jobs, but most of their energy is not man energy**." And shaking their heads with glum expressions on their faces, they said, "**It is boy energy, and we specifically include a 'y' in the word moy because there is a lot of "my" in moy**." I turned my head and looked and looked at them, my eyes growing big as they pantomimed, "*My* **truck,** *my* **house,** *my* **child,** *my* **money—***mine.* **This is young energy**," they explained, "**the energy of a child in the size of an adult**."

"Oh!" I exclaimed, a glimmer of understanding coming. "Oh, my gosh, Grandmothers, I think I get it. This makes sense." I had experienced what they were calling the 'moy' many times, but had never put it together the way they were now. Their description had drawn a clear picture. "Hummm…" I murmured as I thought it over. "Grandmothers," I asked, "why didn't I see this? It seems so obvious now that you have laid it out. Why didn't I put this together myself?" I thought more and then said, "Why don't *women* see this, Grandmothers? I know I'm not the only one who hasn't put this together. Why don't we see this 'childish' behavior and call it for what it is?"

"**Women have some confusion about their** *own* **essence**," they replied, "**and this confusion prevents them from seeing themselves clearly, let alone seeing men clearly. Women are even confused by the construction of the word 'wo man**,'" they said. "**You especially find this sort of confusion in languages like English where the term for the female contains the term for the male**," they explained. "Humph," I grunted and then said, "I'm thinking, Grandmothers, I'm thinking." And I was. Laboring to make sense of what they'd told me.

Finally I said, "Not all languages are like this, Grandmothers, where the feminine word contains the masculine." "**That's right**," they replied, "**and there is more confusion within language groups where the feminine form of the word does contain the masculine form. This sort of word construction adds another dimension to the issue of female/male differences and to the female/male balance of power.**

I tilted my head, straining to understand. "**Language has been** *manipulated,*" they said, cutting to the chase. "Hummph…" I grunted again. "It is interesting," they continued, returning to lecture mode, "that within the English language you are given an opportunity to tie into the truth of the Great Mother, the truth that She contains both the primal aspects of masculine and feminine. You find words like wo man and god dess in English," they explained, looking me over and smiling wisely, "where the feminine form contains the masculine. In these words," they said, "language imitates an elemental truth.

"Such words can put you at an advantage when you consider them," they said, "because they illustrate the feminine principle as the container. Simple words like these can increase your understanding of your place in the universe," they added, nodding and smiling. "Use your language as a tool to remind yourself of the truth."

I cocked my head to the side and studied them. "Grandmothers," I said, "I'm wondering about something. Does what you're teaching me about the feminine being the container and all have anything to do with what you mentioned first today? About moys, I mean," I explained. "I don't see the connection, but I know you never do anything arbitrarily. So does this subject of moys have something to do with the power of women, the real power of woman?" I corrected myself.

"Yes," they said, pleased that I was looking for how these subjects fit together. "Woman has not owned her power. For too long women have listened to moys instead of to themselves and then been disappointed when these boy/men don't treat them with respect, don't act like what women think of as men. It is time," the Grandmothers said as they drew themselves to their full height, "for women to *expect* men to behave like men. It is time," they said, "for women to *require* men to behave like men.

"Women need to stop rewarding moyish behavior," they said, brows furrowed as they shook their heads. "A moy is a case of arrested development," they explained, "a child in the body of a man. "For example," they said, "Why in the world, do you elect what are basically teenage moys to public office?" My jaw dropped as I looked up at them. "And you do it not just occasionally," they said, "but over and over again. Why," they asked, looking genuinely bewildered, "do women look to moys to lead them?" In response, I could only stare. I didn't know the answers to these questions and the way the Grandmothers were phrasing them was making me uncomfortable. They were hitting the nail on the head and it made me cringe. "Why, I asked myself, "do women *do* that?"

"Love them," the Grandmothers said and I blinked. They laughed at my response and said, "You can appreciate a moy's playfulness and

energy, but don't be fooled by him." They took my hand in theirs, and sitting down beside me, said, "**Women must learn to recognize a moy when they see one. You need to be able to tell the difference between a moy and a man. We are asking you to develop discrimination. This is something every woman can learn,**" they assured me. Then, in a conspiratorial manner they whispered, "*The basic difference between a man and a moy is selfishness.* **A moy does everything for his own benefit, to puff his ego, to make** *himself* **feel secure, for his...**" they rolled their wrists, making small, birdlike motions as if to say 'and so on and so on.'

"**Most politicians today are not men but moys, and this is true all over the world. They are selfish, they pander to special interests, and they always quest after money and popularity. Greedy and needy,**" they said, their expressions screwed tight in disgust. "**Your cultural icons—the sports and entertainment stars that people idolize are pretty much the same, and they consistently disappoint you too. It is rare to find a true man in these professions. And moys who get themselves elevated to positions of power will always do damage. They can't help it,**" they added; "**after all, they are only moys. They aren't men. What do you expect?**" they asked, and shrugged their shoulders.

"**A man stands for greater things than does a moy,**" they said. "**He looks beyond himself; he even looks beyond his own generation. In a man,**" they said, "**there is a quality of generativity, an understanding that life goes on long after he is gone. A man seeks to create good for those who will follow in his footsteps.**

"**Moys,**" the Grandmothers said, "**are** *only* **interested in what suits them for the moment. Children do not have the long view,**" they explained, giving me a patient look, "**so it is to be expected that moys will not have the long view. Their decision-making is based solely on** *their* **need of the moment. 'I want this NOW! I want it for** *me*,**" they said, stamping their feet and pulling a face. "**This makes** *me* **feel good,**" they thumped their chests. "*I* **want it now!**" they demanded. Then they shrugged their shoulders, slowly shook their heads and said, "**There is great immaturity in the moy.**

"**Women do not understand this about the man/boy and it causes you great pain. You expect something different from him, but after all, he is just a moy and this is all a moy can do. A man,**" they said, "**can do great things, but a moy can do only selfish, childish things. The problem is,**" they said as they studied me through narrowed eyes, "**When you are fooled by a moy's appearance—his looks, size and deep voice,**" they explained, "**you take him for a man.**

"As a woman your essence is beyond selfishness. Woman is made to be the container of life—physically you are formed that way," they explained. "Woman is open both emotionally and spiritually," they added: "open to holding, loving and embracing diverse ideas, people and groups. Your essence naturally expands.

"Women must follow their essence, listen to the truth within themselves and encourage one another to do the same. A woman who lives from the core of her power will encourage men to follow their essence too, to listen to the truth within themselves. And she will respect men who do this," they said, nodding wisely.

"We ask you to own your own power, to live from the center of your being and encourage the men and the moys in your life to do the same. Encourage each one to live from the core of their being and walk their own truth. However," they said, "do not expect moys to do this right away. And most of all," they added, measuring each word carefully, "*do not wait for them to lead you.* Never expect a moy to guide you," the Grandmothers said, "because he cannot. He has not yet developed beyond a primitive self-focus, so he is unable to see other people's needs. How could someone like this possibly guide another?"

They stopped speaking then and sat quietly, and as I watched them, I heard myself moan, "Oh my God." How many times had I been fooled by a moy? How many times had I not seen what he was? Mistaken him for a man? My father had been one of these and he had died young—before he'd had the chance to even try to become a man. Both of my stepfathers had also been classic moys, needing so much attention from my mother that they had been jealous of my brother and me—her actual children. My husband's stepfather had been the same way. I was seeing a pattern now and as I recognized it, I saw that my life had been riddled with the presence of what the Grandmothers were calling "the moy."

The Grandmothers interrupted my reverie and again changed the subject. This was something they did whenever I got bogged down by feelings from the past. "There are women who have also become attached to selfish behavior," they said, "women who, seeing the power and sway of the moys of the world, try to emulate them. For many thousands of years the world has rewarded the one who grabs and takes, serving only himself," they explained, "and we are sorry to say that women have also learned to grab and take. They have learned to think only of themselves too, telling themselves, 'This is the way of the world.'"

They shook their heads, their faces sad as they thought of how women had fallen into emulating moys. "**Do not be fooled by the world,**" the Grandmothers said. "**What you call 'the way of the world' does not lead to happiness.** *Especially* **for a woman. This is true because it is not a woman's nature to be selfish. This is not what women are made for. Look at your body, look at your biology. You are the bearer of life,**" they said, raising their heads and looking directly at me. "**Deep within you lies the tendency to care for others, to be interested in them, to love and reach out to them. It is encoded in your DNA. Look at that,**" they said, gazing into my eyes; "**it is the truth of who you are.**

"**There is a quality of ripened maturity in a woman who lives according to her nature, and a woman who chooses to live counter to her nature will be miserable. Just like the moy, she too will never be able to grasp and grab at enough to fill the emptiness inside her.**" They shook their heads and fell silent and I sighed a big sigh as I watched them; aware of the pain they were feeling. "Thank you, Grandmothers," I said, "thank you for explaining this. I want to learn whatever you have to teach me." And then I took in a breath, folded my hands in my lap and waited for them to continue.

"**A moy breeds destruction,**" they said, extending the subject; "**he brings it on himself and brings it on those in his path.**" "Yes, Grandmothers," I nodded, "I know. This is what has recently happened to our country. I've seen it. Actually," I said as I thought about it, "everyone has seen it."

"**You can love a moy, but always know that this is what he is. And….**" they said, faint smiles playing around their lips, "**when you cease to reward moyish behavior, you will find that many times he will grow up. Whenever you withhold approval and attention for his less-than-good behavior, you give him an opportunity to morph into a man.**" "Oh!" I said, relieved that the situation wasn't entirely hopeless.

"**Moys have been in charge of the world for a long time,**" they explained, "**pouring their energy into amassing piles of money, kingdoms of influence, and hording all the trucks into their corner of the sandbox,**" they said. "**Whenever power and success are equated with 'having more,' moys win because 'having more' is what they care about.**

"**Look at where this moyish way of life has taken the world. Look at the accumulated tragedies and the silly waste of life that follow in the wake of a moy,**" they said. "**Think about what today's robber barons have done to the world economy,**" they said, "**and what the** moguls of the sports' industry have done to the world of sport, not to mention what the politicians have done. "A moy's insatiable quest for 'more' destroys everything in its path. You must stop rewarding this behavior," the Grandmothers said, looking at me sternly. "And most important of all, you must stop expecting moys to lead you." Then shaking their heads back and forth in bewilderment, they giggled, and burst into laughter at the absurdity of the idea.

"Within yourself you know the truth," they said. "You know good when you see and feel it; you know the right way. It is woman's nature to know that. You are the creators, the reservoirs, as well as often the preservers of life," they added. "A *woman*, by the breadth and depth of what she is, does that. Trust your inner knowing; let it guide you. And as you do that, you will become a light to those around you.

"A man also preserves life," they said; "a man upholds and preserves life, right down through the generations. But a moy does not," they said, their tone final. They threw their heads back then and lifted their eyes heavenward. They would say no more.

"Thank you, Grandmothers," I said, and in reverence for them and their wealth of wisdom, I bowed and turned to make my way back to ordinary reality. "Discrimination," I said to myself. "We need more discrimination."

"Because you do not anchor your own power, you look for someone else to anchor you."

What the Grandmothers had told me about women, about moys and men kept going round in my brain. It felt true and yet I had no idea how to communicate it to others. I would have to speak delicately on the subject because I didn't want to encourage male bashing. *And* what the Grandmothers had said made sense. I just didn't know what to do with it. Finally I decided that just for now I would let it go, put it out of my mind and give it time to settle in by throwing myself into a painting I had begun.

I worked in the studio for several days, sandwiching painting between clients and household tasks. And when at last my need to understand the 'moy' eased up, I decided to go back to the Grandmothers to find out more. But when I closed my eyes to focus on the Grandmothers, all I could see was that painting. Now I was no longer obsessed with understanding the 'moys.' I was obsessed with the painting!

"**The mind is like that,**" the Grandmothers explained as they appeared. "**It tries to hold on to one thing or another. But we like to see you happy,**" they interjected, "**so paint when you want to paint, and come to us when you are ready to learn more.**" "Thank you Grandmothers," I said. They always made me feel better about myself, better about everything.

I closed my eyes again, and there was that painting. Laughing good-naturedly, the Grandmothers said, "**Don't worry about needing to see us. It's not important. We're here, whether you see us or not.**" This made me laugh too and as I relaxed, I was able to let go of trying to do this the 'right' way, and let the Grandmothers lead.

"Okay, Grandmothers," I said, "Here, then is my question for today. Why are so many men moys instead of men?" This time when I looked up I saw them observing me impassively. With deadpan looks, they remained silent, so after a moment I said, "Well Grandmothers, maybe my question is wrong."

I tried again. "There are so many men who are moys, not men," I said, wondering if I had it right this time. "Can anything be done about this?" and though they didn't speak, inwardly I heard them say, "**It has to run its course.**" What? I wondered, does this mean?

I was getting frustrated, but I wasn't about to give up. Finally I said, "Women (me included, Grandmothers), have a hard time accepting moy's behavior. We think there's something wrong with it." I looked at them and still they remained silent. Now I was beginning to wonder if there was something wrong with my premise. I had assumed there was something wrong with these boy/men. Maybe it was something else.

"**Because you do not anchor your own power,**" the Grandmothers said, breaking their silence, "**you look for someone else to anchor you. Because you do not think you are** *enough,* **you look to someone else to be more than you. Foolish,**" they said, shaking their heads, "**foolish. It doesn't work that way.**

"**You haven't wanted to accept your own power,**" they said. "**You haven't wanted to accept reality, and by not accepting reality,** *you* **have behaved in childish ways.**" I gulped as they spoke, my head nodding up and down, up and down. I didn't like what I was hearing, but by my body's response I knew it was the truth. "**Thinking the world should be different than it is, that the males in your life should be different from the way they are is foolishness. They are....**" the Grandmothers paused and looked around, "**as they were made to be. At this point in evolution only some of them are mature. Most males have not truly been men in many thousands of years. This moy** behavior is not new," they said. "Moys have been running the world for many centuries.

"You must wake up. You *must* wake up. You must look at life the way it *is* and claim your power. Much depends on you. Much depends on women. You, Sharon," they said, "can talk about this. We heard your unspoken question about how you could help women awaken," they said as they looked into my eyes. "Be yourself, and through your example many will take heart.

"You are married," they said; "you are *happily* married. You have accepted your husband as he is. You enjoy him as he is but you do not expect him to lead you on the inner journey. You aren't looking to him to be your moral compass, for you are your own moral compass, you are your own centering pole. After many ups and downs and much learning, you finally survey the world from where you stand," they said. "You look through your own eyes and no others. This is what all must do.

"For the most part, men do not know the things women know. They lag behind insofar as the deep questions of life are concerned. They know a great deal about particular things. They are good at amassing knowledge and figuring out specifics. Let them do those things," they said, "and enjoy and support them in their pursuits. Your support is helpful to them.

"It is a great secret," they laughed, "but by *not* trying to change men, you help them change. Accepting men the way they are helps them change because when you accept them, they don't have to put up a fight against you. Then they don't put energy into battling or undermining you. We are encouraging you to accept men and men's behavior. Men behave differently than you would, but a man is not selfish as is a moy, he is just a man—different from you." Then they repeated, "Accepted, accepted, the power of being accepted," and I sighed deeply as I took in what they were saying. They were right. I knew it because I had consciously accepted my husband, my son, and the other men in my life.

"As for the moys," the Grandmothers said, "let them be moys for as long as they need to. Let them be as they are, but do not reward their behavior. Love them from a distance and lead your own life." "Grandmothers," I asked, "why is it so hard for women to lead our own lives?" Immediately they replied, "You have been taught to distrust yourself. For thousands of years you have been forced to follow men, to look to them and give your power over to them. You know the history of all this," they said, shaking their heads and fixing me with a serious look, "**But don't do that any more**," they said. "**That time is over now. Men do not know what is best for you. We have already explained why this is true.**

"**We have come to help you take your power back, to bring your power home where it belongs. We have come to teach you how to stand and live in power.**" Again I breathed a great sigh. "What an enormous shift standing in our own power would create," I said. "**We will walk beside you as you do this work,**" they said "**and the situation is much simpler that you have thought. There is nothing wrong with men, only that you must not look to them, but to yourselves. Look within. Let us guide and teach you about your power. Every man in your life will appreciate this, by the way,**" they said and chuckled. "**Unless there is something terribly wrong with him, he will be happy to see you standing in your power.**"

"Thank you, Grandmothers, thank you," I said and as I bowed before them it came to me that some women might use this explanation of the 'moy' to go into opposition to men. The Grandmothers laughed then and said, "**Should this happen, should what is going through your mind take place, this kind of thing can be addressed through your background as a therapist.**" "Oh," I gulped and nodded. Then I laughed again at my mind's tendency to fixate on worry. "Thank you, Grandmothers," I said again, and I meant it from the bottom of my heart.

This message pin-pointed for me the most basic problem between men and women and explained why women are so often bewildered by the behavior of the opposite sex. Somehow I felt lighter after this session, freer. The Grandmothers were asking women to love men and moys, but not be guided by them. To trust ourselves and be guided by our own radar. "We need to develop more discrimination," I said to myself and reflected on what the Grandmothers had said to me early on. "**Women must lead,**" they had said. "**It can be no other way.**"

CHAPTER 13

It is Time

"This is the Kali Yuga, the Age of Destruction"

Once again I had become disturbed by the news of the world, haunted this time by an article on the suffering of children in Chechnya. The horrors I read about were so overwhelming, I couldn't get the images out of my mind. Because I knew that there are others like me, deeply affected by the cruel events so common in our world today, I decided to journey to the Grandmothers and lay this issue before them.

"Dear Grandmothers," I said, "the tragedies taking place on earth are almost too much to bear. I long for peace and so do most people," and as I said this, to my surprise I began to sob. "We long for love," I gasped when I had regained some control, "and it's so hard, Grandmothers, because there are such awful things happening that sometimes it shakes me to the core. You know all this," I added, "so I won't explain more, but please, do you have a message that will help us hold on to the Divine at this difficult time? It feels like our world is being over-taken by horror."

They smoothed my hair back and said, **"We know, we know."** Then they gathered around and, stroking my arms while they rubbed my back, reminded me that I was one with them. As they encircled me, I looked outward and saw that the earth was shaking. I glanced back at them, my eyes big, but they nodded calmly and continued rubbing my back. The earth was being shaken just the way the agitation cycle in a washing machine shakes up clothes to loosen the dirt in them. **"This shaking loosens the old, reified constructs on your planet,"** the Grandmothers said, **"cracks them open,"** and as I listened, I recalled a picture a Dutch woman had sent me. After receiving the Grandmothers' Empowerment she had painted a tree with a heart at its center; the heart so huge, it was forcing the tree open, and in the process, cracking dead wood off. She had done this painting, to show how the Grandmothers' Empowerment had opened her up.

"Breathe," the Grandmothers said, recalling me to the present. "Yes," I nodded and purposefully inhaled. **"Whenever you are assailed by the traumas of the world and become frightened, know it is not you, yourself, who is upset,"** they said as they looked into my eyes. **"Your Self cannot be upset,"** they said as they held my gaze.

"Your Self is steady and eternal. You have simply," they said as they paused, shrugged their shoulders and smiled, **"picked up the shaking of the world you are living in. It is not your shaking,"** they explained, **"but the world's."** My mouth gaped. "Do you mean that when I get upset by the latest horrors in the world, it's not really me who is upset?" I asked. "I'm just picking up the agitation in the world?" They nodded, **"Yes. Come to us at such times and we will enclose you in love.**

"You can be 'in the world and not of it' as Jesus said, if you make it a habit to call on us, or any form of the Divine," they said. **"Your consciousness will then begin to live in the Divine and when you live in a place of high frequency energy, although the world may pound on your door, threaten you, and even shock your personality, it will have little effect on you. After a period of time,"** they said, smiling confidently, **"it will have no effect at all.**

"As we told you earlier, it's a question of paving the road to God; a question of keeping your focus on what is real. And when we say, 'real,'" they explained, **"We mean that which is eternal and unchanging. Your connection to us never changes,"** they said, shaking their heads. **"There may be war in the Middle East, there may be famine in Africa. Such things will happen at this time of shifting energy,"** they looked sad, but resolute, **"but no matter what happens in the world, you can still be with us.**

"Living in touch with the Divine does not mean retreating from the world. You can go about your life—you can work, be with your family and contribute to the human community. You can do all the things you have always done," they said, **"but in addition, you will automatically bring our presence to every place you occupy, to every person you encounter. This is not a small thing,"** they said and searched my face to be sure I understood. Then they nodded and said, **"feel our embrace, as again we surround you. We are always surrounding you, but we say 'again' to remind you to think of this again.**

"Yes," they said, **"this is a time of destruction—destruction of evil, destruction of cruel and limiting ways of living. These old patterns are being destroyed and will be destroyed. This is the Kali**

Yuga, the age of destruction," they said, heads nodding. "**You are living in this age, and destruction is occurring.**" They gazed at me, waiting for my mind to catch up to them and then, cocking their heads,
said, "**Isn't this destruction a good thing?**" I goggled. A Good thing?
I didn't know what to say.

"**If the old ways were to continue,**" they said, "**if the limiting
and destructive ways of life were to continue, they would kill off
everything on earth. Bit by bit these ruinous patterns would snuff
out the life on earth. They are doing that now. The trees, the animals, and the waters would die and the very air would thicken. This
has already begun to occur and, should it continue, eventually you
would all die.**

"**These old ways must crack off,**" they said, "**and yes, you will feel
it. Life on earth will move through these changes, and on the physical
plane there will be earthquakes, floods, fires, tornadoes, storms and
other manifestations of the energy shift. You will also feel these shifts
emotionally and you will be aware of them mentally.**

"**The foundational concepts upon which much of your culture is
built are crumbling and cracking off. Many 'sacred cows' you have
long held dear and believed real, are now dying. They never were
real!**" they exclaimed, swiping the air to dismiss the lie; "**the false is
being destroyed. It is time,**" they said and folded their arms across their
chests. "**If these changes do not take place, all life will eventually die
out and this cannot be allowed to happen. The destruction of the limitations you have lived under, the destruction of the dead-end ideas
you have believed in—all this must take place. It can be no other way.
But you have a choice,**" they said. "**You can fear this process and contract into that fear or you can rejoice that the old is going.**"

As they said this, a song from the *Wizard of Oz* played in my mind.
"Ding dong the witch is dead. The wicked witch is dead." I giggled
when I recognized it and when I looked up at the Grandmothers, they
were laughing too.

"**We are not asking you to do this work by yourself,**" they said,
shaking their heads to reassure me. "**That is why *we* have come. You
need not go through this experience alone, nor is it necessary for
you to be inordinately brave. Simply be mindful of your connection
with us and call on that connection. Your contact with the Divine
will make you brave, brave in an effortless way,**" they added with
broad smiles. "**You won't have to ramp up your courage to face these
times; we will do it for you. Just call us,**" they said. "**We will carry
you, hold and enfold you throughout all of it.**

"**Think of what we gave to you a long time ago,**" they said and instantly the Pitcher and Cup meditation from *A Call to Power: the Grandmothers Speak* came to mind. "**Before you is a scene of plenty and beauty,**" they said and as I remembered the meditation, I saw a sunny room with a table set before a window. The room was flooded with light and seemed to glow. Sunlight poured over everything and in the middle of the table sat a large pitcher with curved sides, graceful and over-sized, the color of cream. And next to the pitcher sat a cup. "**When you look inside the pitcher you will see that not only is the pitcher the color of cream, it is filled with cream.**

"**We will pour from the pitcher into the cup until the cup too is full. Now look into the pitcher again. Yes, it is still filled to the top. This pitcher cannot be emptied. No matter how many times we pour from it, it will stay full.** *You* **are this pitcher,**" they declared, "**and we will not let you empty, but will keep you ever full. And from this place of fullness,**" they explained, "**you can give to others. You will fill them....effortlessly, and you will never suffer depletion.**"

Again they grew serious. "**The world must go through this shift now; these changes are mandated. This is divine will at work,**" they spoke quietly, nodding as they rocked back and forth on their heels. "**We ask you to stay connected to us while it takes place. Why not? You needn't suffer during this time of earth change. You can actually enjoy yourself. After all, you are a vessel of light and love,**" they laughed; "**that is who you are. Be that! We will fill you full....always. Let us.**"

"Mother is Awakening"

The Grandmothers' work was really spreading. There were several groups meeting regularly in California, a few on the east coast and a few in the Pacific Northwest. I was continuing the monthly meetings in Laguna Beach.

Shortly after the Grandmothers' book, *A Call to Power: the Grandmothers Speak* came out I received a letter from a woman in Lithuania. A friend had sent her the book and now she was asking permission to translate it into her native language. She said she wanted nothing for her work, but was offering to do the translation because the Grandmothers had spoken to her heart and she felt their message would help her countrywomen. I was deeply touched by her offer and gratefully accepted.

Not only did Antanina translate *A Call to Power,* she found a publisher with a small company in Vilnius, the capital city. One day, Vilma, the publisher wrote me, "…at my publishing company we are dedicated to bringing the new thought to Lithuania. I would like to publish the Grandmothers' book." Again I gratefully said yes and the Lithuanian version of *A Call to Power: the Grandmothers Speak* hit the bookstores before Christmas.

As this drama played out, I sat back and wondered what the Grandmothers were doing. No publisher in the United States had wanted my book. I wrote, designed, and put it out myself, but now it was selling in Lithuania of all places. And the publisher said it was selling very well! I had to pull out our old atlas to see where Lithuania was. A small former Soviet block nation, it sat on the Baltic Sea. Poland, where my ancestors had come from, was next-door.

Next came an invitation to fly there to promote the book. I envisioned myself sitting in bookstores, signing books (that's what I assumed I was supposed to do) until the Grandmothers began to nudge me to pass their empowerment on to the women of that country. We would hold empowerment ceremonies in the cities there. Vilma agreed and asked if I would do a workshop too. People wanted to learn to journey to the Grandmothers. Would I teach them how?

Here is where the fun began. I didn't want to teach journeying. Shamanic methods were potent and could be dangerous to those not stable enough to handle them. I had seen this happen when I took training eight years earlier. A woman in my intermediate class fell apart and had to leave in the middle of a session while I watched a man go through what looked like a psychotic break. When I saw what happened to these people I promised myself I would never put anyone in jeopardy like that. I didn't want to be responsible for bringing this sort of danger to another human being. I would persevere and learn this stuff in order to do the work, but I would not teach it.

Until the spirits of the land of Lithuania began to call me I stalled and avoided Vilma's request to teach journeying, attempting to placate her with other suggestions. I'd never experienced anything like it before, but these spirits were insistent. They talked to me during the day; they came to me at night. **"You must teach them,"** they said. **"The people of Lithuania must reconnect with the spirits of their land. There has been so much wounding in this country,"** they said. **"This work will bring about a healing."** After repeated visits to the Grandmothers and to Bear, whereby they each showed me how important it was to teach this method to the people of Lithuania, I gave in and scheduled the journeying workshop. I made the commitment out of faith in the Grandmothers and the helping spirits. Because I didn't speak the language and would have to work through an interpreter, there was no way I could screen participants to determine who was or was not mentally strong enough for this work. I would have to leave it in the hands of the Grandmothers.

I invited Jane, a Grandmothers' group leader in Rhode Island to come with me. I also talked to a Native American friend from California who generously taught Jane and me how to create a sacred space to work in as we moved from town to town, sharing the Grandmothers' message and passing on their empowerment. She also encouraged me to follow the Grandmothers' guidance and teach journeying to these women and men. "It will do only good," she said, and her words heartened me. Later on, when we were in the midst of a ceremony in one of the cities in Lithuania, we would often feel the comforting presence of Native American ancestors with us, cheering us on. Although I have no Native American blood running in my physical veins I have a great affinity for their culture and their presence made me feel at home.

About a week before we left the USA to fly to Vilnius, I journeyed to the Grandmothers and the spirits of Lithuania to ask about the real purpose of this trip. By now it was obvious that this trip was not just about selling books. What follows is the response I received.

As I rose into the upper world I was quickly taken to a place I'd never seen before. Before me spread a great meadow where all the beings—people, animals and nations of the world had come together. They were gathered at one end of the field with some sitting up on a dais; this was the Great Council for planet earth. I had never imagined that anything like this existed, let alone that I would see it; and as I stood before the Council, I shook with excitement and fear. The Grandmothers were beside me and my other teachers were there too—and many more.

I took in a breath and willed myself to calm down and focus. I didn't know why I had been brought to this place or what I was to do, but although this was not something I had engineered, it was happening, so I had better get a grip on myself. "My dear ones," I finally stammered, overcome with reverence as I stood amongst them, "I want to ask something," I said. "I am about to leave to take the Grandmothers' message and teach shamanic journeying in Lithuania. Please bless, guide and protect Jane and me at every moment." When I looked up and saw them nodding their heads, I added, "I also want to be able to talk about this trip with people in the Grandmothers' groups so anyone willing to work with the Net of Light to support us on this venture, can." They nodded "Yes," to this too and later, when Jane and I were preparing for an empowerment ceremony in the cities in Lithuania, we would feel the group members from America standing with us, holding sacred space.

I took in another breath and asked, "Please tell me, what is the *real* purpose of this trip to Lithuania?" Again heads nodded in understanding, and then the council motioned to the Grandmothers who turned to me and drew me off to the side. We walked a little way together and then they said, **"Come with us and we will show you."**

They took my hands in theirs and together with Eagle we sailed up into the night sky. Clouds swept past us and we lifted above them, so high that I could see the curvature of the earth below. In this way we crossed over the North Pole and then dipped closer to the earth. Now I could see mountains, ocean and waterways, woodlands, as well as voluminous clouds, and gradually everything took on an ominous cast. The clouds around us thickened, and thunder rolled in the distance. **"The Northlands,"** the Grandmothers said, and repeated, **"the Northlands, the Northlands."** They were showing me the area of the Baltic Sea, near St. Petersburg, Russia, the Scandinavian countries and the Baltic republics of Latvia, Estonia and Lithuania. "The Northlands," I repeated as I watched fog envelop gray water, rivers and forestland. **"Boglands in the past,"** the Grandmothers said, **"much is buried here."**

"Boglands," I said and remembered a story I had read in the paper about the boglands. Archeologists had discovered the remains of a young girl who they assumed had been sacrificed in some rite in the boglands of northern Europe. I shuddered as this came to mind and tried to dismiss it, but Eagle stepped in front of me and fixed me with a glare. **"This is real,"** he said, **"all manner of things have happened here."** "All right," I said, "teach me," and I repeated my question. "Teach me the purpose of this trip to Lithuania," I said. **"Much is buried here,"** the Grandmothers replied.

I looked down and noticed a soft golden color glowing in the earth below. Light was coming up from inside the ground. "Hum," I said. "There's a glowing there. Something down there is shining. I don't know what it is, but I suppose it might be amber." I was straining to make sense of what I was seeing, trying to use my mind to figure out the cause of this radiance. I knew that amber was found in this area of the world but I had never seen the stone glow. "I don't know what it is," I finally said, "I give up." After this, there was a moment of silence, and then I heard myself state with conviction, "There is light here within the earth," and no sooner were the words out of my mouth than chills covered my body.

"What you are seeing," the Grandmothers said, **"is correct,"** and when I looked again I noticed that the light was actually coming from and was at the same time, imbedded in the land. Patterns, beautiful light patterns were part of the earth here. "Art," I said. "This is art—prehistoric art. Pre-human art!" I exclaimed, "made of light."

"It's growing," I gasped, as I watched the light expand. Forming what looked like spotlights, it now flashed from different places on the earth and flooded set areas. Suddenly I burst out laughing. It was now bright enough to see figures moving about as up out of the earth stepped animals—bears, cats, wolves, rabbits and others. Some of them stood on four legs, and some stood on two. They stretched and yawned as they climbed out of the earth and tumbled about in play. Animals and other beings were awakening and rising up out of the ground. As I watched I saw a few human figures too. "Coming awake," they said, "coming awake, we are coming awake now."

"They are greeting the day," I said to myself, noticing how happy they were to be awakening and stepping into the light of day. As they came forward I saw that they were also bringing the light from the earth with them. "The doors of the earth have been left open," I reported, "so the light from deep within is pouring upward and outward, illuminating everything." I could hardly believe my eyes, but now the animals had begun to dance with one another, roll on the ground together and play. "There is such happiness in this scene," I said, my voice quavering. "I can feel it in the center of my body." Thrilled and warmed by happiness, I observed their joy.

"We have been sleeping," the animals said as they rubbed their eyes and yawned anew. Then they pointed to a pall of darkness that had lain on top of the land. "That!" they said, "has been here a long time," and when I heard this, I understood that this pall had lain on this part of the world for more than a thousand years. Like a dark blanket, it had covered the ground; but now it was beginning to lift. This covering had been so heavy it had been difficult for the animal spirits to breath. They had been smothered and drugged by its weight and had fallen asleep. Repeated yang excesses had produced this thick, multi-layered pall and the gray weight of it had built up over thousands of years, each layer blanketing the one beneath it.

Next the animals showed me waves of armies that had swept in over the land. One dominated until a new one came in from another direction. Wave followed wave, and as I watched, I saw hordes of horsemen riding in from the east, tribes sweeping in from the northwest, the southeast and from all directions. Waves of domination swept over the land; and on and on it went. "Grab and grab," I said. "Rape and pillage, pillage and rape—down through the ages all the way to the Nazi and the Russian occupation." "But not now," the animals replied.

The beings now rising from the lighted earth had waited a long time for this moment. "These are the spirits of the earth," I heard myself say, "that embody the life force of the planet here—beneficent, blessing spirits. They are spirits of joy and fun," I whispered, as I watched them roll and frolic, and with every moment that passed they appeared to become larger and happier. They brought good and goodness with them as they stepped onto the earth. "Joyous," I said, "they are joyous and they're dancing, dancing, dancing." Each time one of them encountered another one they laughed uproariously and I laughed with them. "Laughing, singing, dancing," I said.

"Thank you for coming," they said to me. "Oh," I choked, "Thank you for calling me." I shook my head to blink back my tears and said, "This is my joy." "And ours," they corrected me.

At that moment I became aware of Native American spirits with us. They too were happy—so pleased to see the spirits of life coming back to the land of Old Europe, and when I saw the joy on their faces I broke down sobbing. The spirits continued to greet one another and as I watched, I recognized that spirits from all the lands on earth were present at this awakening; they were talking, listening and sharing with one another. But it was the spirits of the Native Americans and of the ancient land of Lithuania that were embracing one another and I was so moved by this sight I could not talk.

"Awake," they said again and again, "we are coming awake" and I began to giggle as I watched the Grandmothers interacting with them. "The Grandmothers are like queens here," I said, "they are so loved." **"This is because we embody Her,"** they said to me. **"The Great Mother, the Great Mother,"** they joyfully repeated. **"Her body is here,"** and when I heard this I began to cry in earnest. **"She *is* this land,"** they stated.

Then I saw her. "She is so beautiful," I murmured, stunned by the sight before me. "And Oh! She is rising up!" I exclaimed, and as I watched, a primal figure, clothed in white sat up. She was huge, a monolithic form. Graceful in her movements, She had an almost featureless face and her neck and head formed one enormous oval. **"She sits here,"** the Grandmothers said with reverence, **"Ancient Mother."**

"She is h-u-u-u-g-e," I gasped as the Mother came to her feet. She towered over me, towered over the Grandmothers. **"She is the elemental power of life on earth,"** the Grandmothers replied and as I gazed at her I felt awe and a feeling of utter helplessness. I was little more than a speck before her. She was so enormous, so potent and majestic, that in spite of my best efforts to remain calm I felt an inkling of fear. And for a moment I understood why mankind had turned away from the Great Mother. She had been too much for them.

"God bless you, daughter," She said, speaking in a deep, comforting voice; **"do not fear me."** "Oh Mother," I sighed, my fear evaporating with Her gentle words. "Oh, how we need You," I said, and shook my head in wonder. "Oh, how we love You," I said and realized as I spoke, that these are the words the Grandmothers sing to welcome people to their work. **"I will send my blessing back with you,"** the Mother said. **"My presence will go with you."**

I watched then as the Grandmothers assembled in front of the Great Mother. They looked so small compared to Her, but they were communicating as dear friends. "The Grandmothers came to Lithuania to awaken the Mother," I heard myself say and then started laughing at how far beyond my wildest imaginings this work had taken me. Naively I had thought I was going to this country to promote my book. "It's already happening," I said, "they are awakening Her now. What is taking place now is beyond time, my travel to Lithuania is just an earthly confirmation of something that is already taking place." As I spoke my mind was scrambling all over itself, trying to make sense of it all.

"This is similar to when the eagle landed in my garden," I said. "His presence there confirmed for me that the Grandmothers truly had appeared two days earlier. When he showed up and Roger and my client saw him too, I knew it wasn't just my imagination, but that the eagle was anchoring in normal, every-day reality what the Grandmother had brought from non-ordinary reality.

"And now the spirits of *this* land have begun to awaken," I said, again hoping that by talking this out, my mind could get a grasp on it. "The Great Mother has already begun to rise up, so when Jane and I come to Lithuania," I said, "we will simply be anchoring in ordinary reality what has already begun to take place in the unlimited realms."

Suddenly I felt immense fatigue. Yawning and stretching, I could hardly stay on my feet, and all I wanted was to lie down. "I've got to rest," I said, "but the Mother is so huge, I can't really lie down on Her lap. If I lie down, I will touch only a small part of Her. Just like when I lie on the earth, I only touch a part of it.

"She *is* the earth!" I realized with a shock; "so of course I can only touch a small place on Her body. Ahhhhh," I groaned, so tired of trying to make sense of something so far beyond my understanding. I shook my head in frustration, and then felt Her hand on me, a hand of normal size. "What?" I said, wondering how this gargantuan Mother could have such a small hand. Then I said, "Oh, of course *She* can do that. She can be any size She wants," and I dropped into a light sleep. The Mother stroked me as I slept, doing this to comfort and communicate her loving care.

"This work in Lithuania is complete," I said to myself when I sat up, "the trip will simply formalize and recognize it." Then the Mother spoke. **"Great blessings will descend through all the earth,"** She said. **"Mother is awakening."**

At this point the Grandmothers came in, surrounded me, and with their wings, blanketed and enfolded me. Then they lifted me up and we began our journey back. As we flew into the night sky, I looked down for a moment and saw Lithuania waving good-bye to us. The earth lights in Lithuania were blowing kisses, sending blessings and waving and tenderly I waved back to them. "There is such love now," I said to myself. And on the way back home it felt as if I was riding in a very comfortable plane, except that it was the Grandmothers who carried me through the sky.

Our visit to Lithuania in ordinary reality turned out to be almost as magical as the one in non-ordinary reality. The charm of the old cities of Vilnius and Kaunus was of another time; strolling down those streets was like walking through a fairy tale. And the people met us with open hearts and arms—especially after I told them what I had learned about the presence of the Great Mother in their land. But the most thrilling thing of all was to speak heart to heart about the Grandmothers and the Great Mother to people from an entirely different culture and have them understand what I was talking about. I believe the people of Lithuania took to the message of the Grandmothers so quickly because within their culture the Great Mother has always been revered. Whether as pre-Christian goddess or as the Virgin of the Dawn Gate of the city of Vilnius, She is very much alive in their land.

Lithuania is a country of forests and rivers, a place where farmers walk with a bucket over their arms to the field nearby to milk their cows, where storks often fly right over your car on their way to nest on the roof of a barn nearby. Jane and I were taken to sacred sites throughout the countryside, feted with unending supplies of chocolate, hugged and held in long embraces, invited to dinners in people's homes and almost loved to death. We were aware that we had been greatly blessed to have had this opportunity to carry the Grandmothers' message to this country and we hated to leave, but knew we would always carry the love of that land in our hearts.

"Practical Guidance for these Times"

I returned from Lithuania jetlagged, but my heart was singing. Now there was a group of people I knew and loved and who were working with the Grandmothers on the other side of the world. I shared my Lithuanian pictures with the women in California, just as I had shared our California pictures with our new family in Lithuania. Family, that is exactly what it felt like. The Grandmothers' family was growing. I glowed from the thrill and love I experienced on this trip and the glow lasted for quite a while, but glow or no glow, I soon discovered there was more work to be done.

All I had to do was be around the political situation in America a few days to realize that those of us who work with the Grandmothers had plenty to do. As soon as I read the morning paper and saw the horrors taking place in Iraq, the African genocide, and the political lying and cheating in the government, I knew it was time to return to my wise teachers.

I entered the upper world and when I came upon them, they were standing on a dais in a half circle formation. "Grandmothers, I ask this question in utmost sincerity," I said as tears spilled down my cheeks. "I wish to serve," I said, "and there are so many like me who wish to serve, but we feel so overwhelmed by evil." (I hesitated before using that word but I couldn't think of how else to label the cause of all the suffering I was seeing.) **"We know,"** they said. "Grandmothers," I continued, "please show us how to help infuse the energy of yin back into the earth. And please speak in clear, easy to understand language," I said. "I need you to be very practical. **"We understand your question."**

As I waited I became aware of a golden flame glimmering in the space between us. And as I watched it, the flame fanned out, glowing brighter and larger. It was growing. **"This is the fire of transmutation. Transmutation is going on right now."**

I didn't want to hear this. 'Transmutation' sounded like vague, spiritual jargon to me, and at this point the last thing I wanted was theoretical explanations for what was going on in the world; I wanted to know what could be done. "I ask you, Grandmothers," I said again, trying to be respectful, "I ask you to speak to me in practical language." Then I took in a breath and asked again. "What can we do at this time to help infuse the energy of yin back into the earth? We are *sick* of seeing this suffering," I said, my frustration building. "What can we do?" Reading the newspaper had made me feel desperate and now it was showing.

"**Do not be sick at heart,**" the Grandmothers said. And as they regarded me with concern, I got even angrier. "Easy for you to say," I replied. "*You* are divine, and have the larger view. You aren't stuck in the middle of the mud like we are. There is so much mud piled on us right now, Grandmothers, that we can't see through it," I said, my voice charged with passion. "You've got to help us. Please! Please!" I pleaded, and burst into tears.

Again I saw that golden light but now I was crying so hard I couldn't speak to ask what it was. "**There are many working with the light now,**" they said. "**Light shows the truth. It shows the way. It peels back darkness and burns away whatever stands in its way. This is happening now, taking place around you as well as inside your body. Many of you are aware of this. Old states of consciousness are coming up within your bodies, and as this happens they reveal themselves as pain, pain that has become locked into physical memory patterns. Much is also coming up in your relationships with one another. Transmutation is taking place there too. It is occurring in every facet of life, all over the earth. Transmutation is both a macrocosmic and microcosmic event. It is at work now, burning away obstacles on every level of life.**

"**Although this is taking place all over the world, it looks different in different places. This worldwide and at the same time cellular event is social, political, spiritual and personal. It is all pervasive. The light is relentless,**" they said. "**Re-lent-less,**" they drew the word out, to make their point. "**It is time for everything to come to light, and it will! You see,**" they reassured me, "**there is purpose in the madness you are witnessing. There is more taking place than you know.**

"**There has been so much suffering on earth for so many eons that suffering is now encoded into your DNA, coded into the soil particles of the earth. It permeates everything and must come to light in order to be transmuted. This is the time of transmutation,**" they repeated, "**and because it is, you will see all matter of filth rising to the surface. It must,**" they said, "**because that which remains buried only festers and causes disease, pain and imbalance. We cannot have that, not any more,**" they said and emphatically shook their heads.

"**There is a lifting taking place now,**" they said, and I sighed as I felt it. "**You are being lifted. Whenever you work with the Net of Light you are lifted, and you help lift the world. We know it's hard for you to hold onto this thought,**" they said. "**The tragedies and barbaric acts you see claim your attention and you forget about the Net of Light. These acts must also come to light, and they will. Get used to it,**" they said and wagged their fingers. "**Those who cannot stand the fire of transmutation will be taken out.**" "Ohhhhh," I shuddered, "they're not letting up." "**Yes,**" they nodded, "**We are telling you the truth.**

"**If you truly wish to be part of this work and wish to be trans-formed, you must get used to witnessing evil in the world. This *is* the Kali Yuga,**" they said, hands on hips as they stared me down. "**This *is* the age of destruction. This is the age when evil *will be* destroyed and *is being* destroyed. And in order to be destroyed,**" they said, "**it has to first be revealed and identified. The greed and lying that are so prevalent in your country are coming to the surface,**" they said "**while other states of consciousness are coming to the surface at different points on the globe.**

"**Stay with us. We promise we won't let you go through this by yourself. We will not abandon you,**" they said and gazed at me with love. "**Call on us and we will hold on to you through every trauma that arises. And there *will* be more,**" they said. "**These things must arise. You know that. You know what happens when evil goes underground,**" they said. **It lies there and waits for another time to pop out again. So,**" they gestured, spreading their arms wide, "**everything must come to light.**

"**You will see more scandals,**" they said, "**more monstrous behavior. You will see it all. It will happen. You will also see things within yourself that you don't want to see. These also need to come to light,**" they explained. "**Everything that has been buried and suppressed *will* and *must* come to light.**

"**You are part of the Net of Light,**" they said, "**so let the Net hold you now while you affirm your place in it. This is who you are. All these states that rise up within you are simply old. Let them come. What do you care? Stay identified with the truth. You are light,**" they said, holding me with their gaze. "**You are part of the Net of Light that holds this world. Do not defend or even attempt to defend against the states of consciousness rising up within and around you. Let them!**" they cried. "**Now is the time for everything to be revealed.**

"**Sometimes we repeat ourselves because you need to hear it,**" they explained. "**Now is the time for everything to come to light. No more secrets!**" they announced. "**No more lies. There is no time** to waste in equivocating, face-saving and defending ones' 'self,'" they said, laughing at the absurdity of the idea. **"What is that 'self' anyway?"** they asked. **"You aren't some little thing that needs to be defended. You are great! You are light! Hold to the truth, and affirm the Net of Light of which you are a part. This is what will hold the earth steady while the pain and lies come to the surface."** Then they placed their hands on their hips and nodding their heads, said, **"Welcome** *everything* **that arises.**

"We know it is hard for you to see the suffering of others. It is hard for us also, but these things are passing," they assured me. **"Let them go. Love everyone and bless everyone. The wrong doers and the ones who have been done wrong—bless each one.** As the poisons come to the surface to be purified by light, pray that everyone in all the worlds be happy. This is a blessing prayer," they said, "so let it rise to your mind and lips. Then they threw their arms wide and cried, "Bless them all.

"Should you catch yourself condemning a 'wrong doer,' stop yourself and quickly bless them. Do this as soon as you become conscious of your mistake. All of you have done terrible things in the many lives you have lived so do not condemn another now. Especially at this time," they said, **"all the hidden garbage that has been denied and overlooked, must rise up into the light. Let it."** Then standing tall, they threw back their heads and sang, **"May everyone in all the worlds be happy."** Looking at me, they smiled and said, **"That includes you! You are light. That is your true nature. Be happy in that knowledge, and love your own dear self,"** they said as they took my hand. **"Love the lighted one you are, and love the dear selves of everyone else too. Love the lighted ones that they are.**

"We bless you," they said, **"and we will always hold you in the reality of who you are. You are the light we showed you today,"** they said, pointing to the glowing flame they had initially held before me. **"You are this flame that burns true and bright. That grows bigger every moment. Rejoice in this,"** they said, **"This is your true identity."**

They hugged me then and waved goodbye and I blew them a few kisses and then focused on coming back. I felt a stronger sense of mission now. What they had shared was so important, even life-saving in a way, that I wanted to share it with everyone. I would write it down and send it out.

CHAPTER 14

Strengthening the Net of Light

"Satsang, Communion of the Good"

Most of the time I simply went along with the Grandmothers work, letting myself be guided by the next thing that showed up. If someone wanted to start a Grandmothers' group, I helped. When people said they'd like CDs of the Grandmothers' lessons, I made CDs. When a woman in Holland offered to translate *A Call to Power: the Grandmothers Speak* into Dutch, I said, "Sure, go ahead." I had no plans of my own for the work; I had learned that the Grandmothers were in charge, so I simply followed wherever they led.

This way of operating worked well most of the time, but now and then if I got upset by what was happening in the world (I had inevitably been reading the paper or listening to the news), I would catch myself thinking I should be doing more to spread the Grandmothers' message. Then I'd begin to wonder if maybe there was something else I could be doing, or if perhaps I hadn't been listening well enough for their guidance.

I was going through a bout of this when I next approached the Grandmothers. I remember that as I began this journey, even though I knew that at this point I could reach them immediately, I insisted on going through all the steps anyway, using the traditional method of journeying. It was like I wanted to have some control over this work and though I was aware of what I was doing at the time, I felt uncomfortable and a bit curious about my choice.

"Grandmothers," I asked as I finally stepped before them, "how can we spread your love and message so more can have hope? I don't think enough people are learning about you," I said and as I stood before them, they cocked their eagle heads, took a look at my furrowed brow and, regarded me with compassion. Then they smoothed the lines from my forehead. "Oh, Grandmothers," I repeated, "Your message is one of such hope and beauty. How can we pass it on so other people can have hope too? More need to know about you."

They eyed me for a minute or more, then took in a breath and puffed out their feathers. **"We will show you something,"** they said, and took me by the hand. Together we lifted off, flying for what seemed only a little way before we began to circle downward again, lighting on a rocky formation that stood just above the sea. The words that came to my mind as we landed were 'Mount Olympus,' and as I looked over the sea to a group of distant islands, darkened by low-lying clouds, the Grandmothers said, **"This darkness that you see on earth today has occurred before. This is not its first time in all the ages of the earth."** I listened to their words as I watched the scene before me and held onto my question. "How can we spread your message so others can have the hope and love we have experienced?" I asked again and noticed that now the Grandmothers were looking at me strangely. I didn't like that look.

"You will break your hearts over this," they said. Their words stopped me cold and I was conscious of their use of the word, 'hearts' (plural), signaling that what they were saying wasn't just for me, but for everyone. I looked up and they said, **"Don't try so hard."** Again they were gazing at me with compassion. **"Let us do everything,"** they said. "Oh," I replied, "I realize what you mean," and suddenly I did. "You're right, Grandmothers," I said. "I was slipping into doer-ship again, thinking that spreading your message was my responsibility. I'm so prone to that," I admitted. They began to chuckle then, delighted that I had caught myself at my old tricks. We had a good laugh together and as we stood looking at each other, I noticed how much lighter I felt. Thinking I must do everything had created a heavy burden on me, a phony burden. It was an old habit of mine; one I was sick of.

"Okay, Grandmothers, I can tell you're right about this because I feel so relieved," I said, "and I'm ready to relax about it now and let you lead. That's that," I said, hoping this really was the last time I would get caught in the 'ultra responsible' game. We grinned at each other but suddenly I remembered that there was a Grandmothers meeting coming up on Saturday. "Uh, Grandmothers," I asked, "people are coming to a meeting Saturday. Is there anything you'd like me to say to *them*?"

"Tell them how beautiful they are," they said and I stared at them. "Tell them what?" **"And how loved they are, tell them how much we love them. Encourage them to feel the joy they get from loving us and from loving one another. These gatherings,"** they pointed out, **"are a safe place for them to practice experiencing our loving presence."**

"Grandmothers," I asked, "how can I communicate this so they really get it?" They nodded their understanding and then showed me what looked like a web of light. **"You weave this web,"** they said, **"whenever you affirm your connection to the Net of Light and one another,"** and as I looked at it, I saw that the Net of Light had thickened in places and become a web. **"Wherever people with high, loving hearts meet and call on the Divine, this weaving takes place,"** they said, and as they spoke they pointed to Grandmothers' groups scattered all over the world. **"These meetings create a light weave. *This*,"** they said, **"is called 'satsang' or 'communion of the good.'"**

"Whenever you gather to affirm your love for the Divine and for one another, you expand and become more fully yourself, more fully awake. And *this* is how others are reached. Your light and happiness draw them." Turning their heads, they gave me a sly look and said, **"You become irresistible, and draw them to you."** The idea of being irresistible, coupled with their mischievous looks tickled me and I laughed out loud. The Grandmothers then smiled, leaned over and whispered, **"You become *totally* irresistible,"** wiggling back and forth to emphasize their point. **"Who, after all,"** they asked, **"can resist someone who loves them, someone who sees them as they are and then goes ahead and loves them?"**

"Yes," I said, "you're right." **"So when you next meet, share how being with us has affected your ability to love. Share what's easy and difficult for you about loving. Share situations where loving takes an effort, when it feels impossible. Then share how you've dealt with this. Perhaps something that happened that made you come more alive so you could love more. Maybe a stuck state that had been denying the truth of who you were dropped off,"** they said. Then they interwove their wings, and swaying back and forth, launched into an old pop song. 'How deep is your love,' they sang, and I rolled my eyes, groaning in mock horror as I watched them, though of course I loved every minute of it.

When they finished their performance they said, **"You live inside a nimbus of light,"** and I looked at them in surprise. **"Remember the fairy godmother in Cinderella?"** they asked, **"how she was encased in a glow of light? Well, so are you,"** they said and this made me laugh again. For years I had harbored the desire to be a fairy godmother and had even dressed up like one for parties, outrageous costume and all. The Grandmothers of course knew about this and were playing with me.

After a moment they became quiet again and said, **"Call on us and experience this nimbus of light."** I saw their look and knew that I was to do this *now*, so I closed my eyes and turned within myself and as I did, tears came to my eyes. There was a quiet, glowing vibration inside and around me that seemed to tremble with beauty and a loving feeling. When I later played back the recording of this journey, at this point I heard myself murmuring, "Beauty…beauty…oh, wo-o-o-ow…such beauty."

When I opened my eyes again, they were standing around me, happy and so proud of their fledgling. I bowed to them in gratitude and after a pause while I collected my thoughts, I said, "And so the real purpose of this meeting, Grandmothers, is satsang, the communion of the good." **"Yes,"** they nodded. "And because of this communion, there will be a thickening of the web of light you showed me earlier, the one that strengthens the Net of Light." **"Yes,"** they said. "Oh, and expansion too," I added, "An on-going expansion." **"Yes, the web provides a focal point for the Net of Light, and because of these places on earth that create a thick web with the Net, the entire Net of Light is strengthened."**

The drumbeat changed at this point, signaling the time to return to ordinary reality. "Thank you, Grandmothers," I said, "thank you so very much." I turned to go then and as they waved good-bye, they called out, **"All of this is much easier than you think."**

Their parting words stayed with me a long time, playing over and over in my mind. I had gone to them in full doer mode ("what can we 'do' to spread your message, Grandmothers?") and they had showed me yet again there was *nothing* I needed to do, that this work was theirs and they were in charge of it. I could be along on the ride if I wished and share the joy of the ride with others. That was my part if I wanted to play it. "Easier than you think…. "Hummmmm," I muttered, "I wondered if *I'm* the one who's making this voyage with the Grandmothers more difficult than it needs to be with my constant need to feel in control…of something."

"A Purer Channel"

I wanted to operate more on faith and less on fear. Theses days I was no longer as overtly fearful as I had been in the past, but the desire to control life in some way, to think I had value because I was "doing" something was surely based in fear. What, I wondered, did I need to learn at this point to be entirely free of this habit? Actually, I could take that question even farther. What did all of us involved in spreading this message need to learn at about this? This would be my next question for the Grandmothers.

I made my way to them, and after I asked my question, without a moment's hesitation they replied, **"How to be a purer channel."** I blinked and stared for a second or two, and they stared right back. **"This is the answer to your question. This is what you have been wanting for yourself and for those involved in this work,"** they said, **"to be a purer channel, to be a greater force for truth and good in the world. There is only one way to do that. You must align with the Divine. This,"** they explained, giving me school teacher-ish looks, **"is why *we* have come.**

"We know that many today have a fear of the Divine, that it's hard for some of you to hear even the word 'god' or 'goddess' without cringing. When we tell you to 'align with the Divine,' you give us that blank stare," they said and I had to hold back my laughter because this so perfectly described me.

"This is because of religion," they said, shrugging and flicking a hand in dismissal. **"Religions have taught people to be afraid of the Divine. Over the years religion has become so manipulated that today, at its worst, it is a series of power systems and pecking orders. Religious systems are often run by fear tactics and worse. What a mess!"** they cried and threw up their hands. **"But manipulating is something the human mind does. Unfortunately, whenever the ego/ mind grabs hold of a pure concept, it lessens and taints it. Although there is still beauty and truth in the world's religions,"** they said, **"so much has been lost and manipulated over the years that the original purity has suffered.**

"This is why, from time to time, the Divine shows up in a new form—to once again show the clear path. The clear path is very simple," the Grandmothers laughed, **"and at their inception all the religions of the world show this path until it becomes so distorted by man-made rules and regulations, (do this, not that, our way is the *only* way)…the simple truth is no longer recognizable. After this layering has gone on for a while you can no longer see the path.**

"Now that the world is once more in grievous peril, the Divine has come again. It has come in the form of some of the world's great teachers. Many way-showers are present on earth now," the Grand-mothers said, nodding firmly. **"The Dahli Lama, Sathya Sai Baba, Ammachi, and scores you have never heard of are here. We have also come at this time,"** they said, **"and there are many who will reso-nate to the form that we have taken, that of the Great Council of the**

Grandmothers. All who have come now have done so to remind you of the way home," they said, "and the way home is to constantly think of and call on the Divine.

"Let yourself become so soaked in the presence of the Divine that you yourself become divinity," they said. "That, after all, is what you are. In truth, you are divine, but all the overlays in your mind as well as the mass-mind conditioning of your culture have cut you off from who you are. We have come," they said, nodding and giving me a fierce grin, "to plug you back into your source.

"To become a force of light on earth, not fodder for the mass mind bullying that pushes things around to suit itself," they said, zeroing in on me with their eyes, "the only thing you need do to is call on us constantly. We ask you to stand in truth and radiate love from the core of your being. If you do this, your life will change so much," they laughed; "it will become almost unrecognizable to you."

"You will have peace and happiness within. Steadiness," they said and slowly ground a fist into the palm of their hands. "What we urge you to do is simple, not complex. But…" they paused, "it's not easy *because* of the mind. Your mind wants to convince you of how important it is, to fascinate you with diversions of every sort in order to keep you away from that steady place within. This is how it controls you," they said. "So we will remind you to always turn your thoughts to us.

"Think of us now," they said and held up their hands before me to help me focus. "Take this moment to call on us or any form of the Divine you love. Think of us. F e e l us," they urged, drawing out the word, "and as soon as you call on us, we will surround you." Standing tall, like the queens they are, the Grandmothers said, "We will flank, protect, and hold you within our love. Always.

"Let yourself be held like this," they said, and I closed my eyes and relaxed into their care. I felt supported and complete, like I was in my perfect place. It gave me an unshakable sense of belonging. "Feel us at your back and in the center of your chest. We will fill your core and awaken you to who you are," they said and then tenderly added, "you are one with us.

"You walk around inside a body and perform specific roles in life. This fools you into thinking that this is what you are. No, no, no," they said, shaking their heads. "These roles are only parts you are playing. The truth is, you are one with us. Not only we, but you have the long view of life, the great view. When you turn within as you are at this moment," they said, "you fill with wisdom. We have mentioned that the world is set up as a big distracting machine, one that constantly draws your attention outward. 'Oh, look at this!'" the Grandmothers pantomimed. "'You'd better start worrying about that. Don't you feel bad about…? Oh, my…,'" they said, throwing up their hands in mock horror. "And so it goes.

"Distraction is constant, constant! But you have a still center point within that remains unaffected by all the drama and trauma of life. Remember it, feel it, and rest at this center point," they said. And as I listened, a line from an old hymn ran through my head, 'Restore us in our rightful minds,' it went. "This, what the Grandmothers are describing, *is* this rightful mind." "Yes," they agreed. "You are coming home now, turning within to the core of your being, turning to the changeless wisdom and love that you are. You are an embodiment of love," they said and gazed at me with such tenderness that tears rolled down my cheeks.

"When you are awake and aware of who you are and then step forward and greet one another," they said, "*this* is the one you greet. You greet the inviolate soul within each being. Namasté," they said, folding their hands and bowing. "I salute the divinity within you." "Namasté, Grandmothers," I said, bowing back.

"The mind likes to rush ahead and chatter. It is either in a hurry for 'more,'" they said, their expressions reflecting the futility of this eternal search, "or depressed about how 'awful' life is. But the steady place within you is real and changeless. The core of your being existed long before you were born into this life and will be with you long after this body dies. This is who you are.

"So when you come out of this quiet moment and open your eyes again, remain silent," they said. "And if you hold this silence for three or four minutes, you will become aware of how much your mind is accustomed to running your life. You will notice the contrast.

"We're not trying to change your mind. We just want you to be aware that this is what it does and recognize that you don't have to go along with it," they said, shaking their heads. "If you practice this in a group meditation, when you are finished and open your eyes, even if your mind is still chattering away, slowly look around the room at one another. And as you look, peer past the societal mask to the place at the center of each person. Then bow slightly and namasté. I salute the divinity within you," they said as they bowed. "You can do this physically as we have just done, or you can do it silently. **And you can do it at any time.**

"**You are beginning to learn how to settle into the home place where you belong. This place will effortlessly align you with the reality of who you are and step you into your power,**" they said, nodding wisely. "**Here is where you can live. Because of the present crisis on earth, you need to occupy this space within. Namasté,**" the Grandmothers said and bowed good-bye.

"The greatest use you can make of our message is to live it."

Around this time I was invited to be a guest on a radio show where the host asked a question that stayed with me a long time. He wanted to know how being involved with the Grandmothers had changed me as a person. I can't remember what I said to him, but after that show, I thought about his question again and again. The Grandmothers had told me, "**The greatest use you can make of our message is to live it,**" so now I wondered, "Am I living it? How am I living it?" His question plunged me into a period of self-examination where I stayed for quite a while.

As I thought this over it came to me that I was no longer self-conscious in the way I used to be. These days I seldom considered what people thought or didn't think of me, now and then showing a confidence in Self that amazed me. This was certainly new and I noticed that it occurred at moments when my little self got out of the way and the Big self, the 'I am' that I am, took over. Whenever this happened, words came out of my mouth and thoughts sprang forth—ideas I didn't know were there, and I understood things I had never understood before. It was clear the Grandmothers had indeed changed me.

Calling on the Grandmothers and receiving an immediate response taught me to rely on the presence of the Divine day and night. It was no longer possible to deceive myself into believing I was alone in the world. This was saying a lot, because I used to feel alone *all the time.* Now, no matter what I was doing, saying or thinking, at some level I was aware of these good-humored wise women with me. Their presence inspired me and reassured me that I was part of something much bigger than my little self.

I seldom experienced fear now and this is a monumental change as fear used to be my home base. I was afraid of *everything.* For instance, now when I give a talk on the Grandmothers, no matter what size the audience, I have no fear because I know if I keep my focus on them, I can open my mouth, stand back and they will speak through me. As I listen to what comes out at these times I know it's not Sharon McErlane who is wise; it's the Self the Grandmothers have awakened within me who is wise.

It's easier for me to love and forgive both others and myself than it used to be. Nothing feels better than loving, and the Grandmothers have increased my capacity for it. **"We love all,"** they say, **"we love the fathers, the mothers and the children. We seek the greatest good for the entire human family."** This is exactly what they do, and I've noticed that when you hang out with the Grandmothers, their qualities begin to rub off on you. I love and understand my husband more now than I did before. I feel the same way about the rest of my family, friends and even complete strangers. Feelings of love well up in me at the oddest moments. I don't know where they come from, but since the Grandmothers, I've become a woman in love with the world.

The Grandmothers encourage us to lift our vibration by loving them, everything, and ourselves. And they assure us that moving into a state of love is the highest service we can perform. **"As your vibration lifts,"** they said, **"it affects everyone and everything around you. Whenever you do this, you become a walking prayer. Then there is nothing you must do or say because your very being will say it all."**

"Honor yourselves. You are the light of the world."

In September of 2006 Roger and I were getting ready to visit some of the countries of old Yugoslavia. It had been ten years since the war in Kosovo and Bosnia and tourism there was booming. We would begin our trip in Slovenia, go on to Croatia, take a quick look at Bosnia and end up visiting a dear friend in Montenegro. Roger had again chosen our itinerary and he was especially looking forward to seeing the Croatian coast. As usual, I was along for the ride, except for visiting my friend Keka in Montenegro.

I had passed on the Grandmothers' Empowerment to a young Slovenian woman when she visited California, so when I realized we would be in her city, I let her know that we were coming. She quickly arranged a Grandmothers' gathering in Ljubljana and said she'd be at the airport to pick us up. This gave the trip added luster for me, and I was thrilled by the way it had fallen into place. Secretly I found myself hoping that this might turn out to be another 'working' vacation.

A few days before we left, I went to the Grandmothers to ask the purpose and significance of the gathering in Ljubljana, Slovenia. They were happy that we were going to this area and welcomed me with smiles and hugs. "Slovenia occupies an area central to and surrounded by many cultures—Germanic peoples, Croats, Italians, Serbs, Muslims and more. It sits in the midst of the mountains, near the sea, holding a position similar to that of a button on a coat. Slovenia connects and holds things together." Later they showed me different influences or threads within this particular region and demonstrated how the country of Slovenia is a sort of place keeper or hub for them all.

"The consciousness in Slovenia is naturally one of spiritual elevation, although presently it is a bit foggy and shut down. There is some spiritual awakening taking place now, but the consciousness there has been asleep for a long time so it will take a while." To illustrate the numb state that hangs over this land, the Grandmothers showed me an image of an ostrich with its head in the sand and another of a person continually 'looking the other way.' Slovenians had witnessed so much negativity, bloodshed and war that over the years many of them had gone numb.

Then they spoke about the gathering in Ljubljana. "The women and men who will come to the Grandmothers' Empowerment there are pure of heart. They have already begun to awaken from the big sleep that has held their country in thrall for many years. They want to awaken even more, and are interested in being of service in the world. As with most Grandmothers' gatherings, this one will be comprised primarily of women."

Looking at me to be sure I got the import of what they were about to say, they continued. "After they receive the empowerment and cloak of comfort, these people will carry the Grandmothers' message of hope, power and universality throughout this region of the world. Take extra scarves/cauls with you when you go," they instructed me, "to give to women who will want to start Grandmothers' groups in their hometowns. Our message will filter through them to the countries surrounding Slovenia. The empowerment will also bless the city of Ljubljana and the country of Slovenia will be further strengthened by it. It will become affirmed as a spiritual center, a "button" that truly does its job of holding things together."

When I took the Grandmothers message to Lithuania, the work had been with the Lithuanian people, but to an even greater degree, with the spirits of the land. Lithuania was itself awakening and the spirits of that land wanted to work in partnership with the people there. In Slovenia the purpose of the Grandmothers' work would be different. Here it was not the land that was awakening, but the people themselves, many of whom were eager to reach out to one another through the Net of Light. The Grandmothers showed me that as Slovenians reached out to their neighbors and spread the Grandmothers' message in this area of the world, they would bring joy to the Great Mother who, after all, wants nothing more than to see her children happy and loving one another. This act of reaching out would be especially important in the Balkans where for so long there has been so much war, distrust and separation.

When they finished speaking about our trip, I asked if they had a message for those of us in other countries as well. In response, they showed me how those of us who work with them have come to resemble fully lit flames. We anchor light on earth and help light penetrate into the earth itself. Because we are fully lit, we stand out in the darkness that surrounds us. Those who hold the flame steady inevitably become beacons for others who are also seeking light. We stand out, and become aware of others who also stand out because light calls to light. **"The light you hold is the light that you are,"** they said. **"It is your nature."**

Then they showed me how this light reaches deep into the earth. After radiance infuses our being, it enters the earth through our feet so wherever we touch ground, light spreads downward and outward from there. Each of us is a contact point for light to shine through. The Grandmothers showed me what this looks like from the earth's perspective, and seen from underneath, our lights look like the glowing roots of trees that spread far and wide. As I observed I couldn't help but smile; from this vantage point each of us looked like an inverted Christmas tree.

On the surface of the earth our lights stretched out in every direction, each flame sticking up like a candle on the biggest birthday cake imaginable. It was thrilling to see these flames standing all over the earth, each one illuminating an area and at the same time anchoring light deep into the earth. What they showed me is yet another way of understanding the Net of Light. And when the Grandmothers had finished demonstrating the flames that we are, my heart caught in my throat when they said, **"Honor yourselves. You are the light of the world."**

Slovenia was dramatically and romantically beautiful—like a small, friendly Switzerland. And Ljubljana was a perfect jewel of a city. In the last century it was beautifully restored by the architect, Joze Plecnik, whose work followed the dictates of sacred geometry. Sophia, my young Slovenian friend, took Roger and me all over Ljubljana, showing us how Plecnik had followed the ancient power or ley lines when he refashioned the roads and monuments in the city. Together we also discovered a neglected Black Madonna site on a side street in the old quarter and worked to reactivate this power place. The Grandmothers' gathering in Ljublijana was a great success and after we'd been back home for several months I got a note from Sophia saying a woman was asking my permission to translate *"A Call to Power: the Grandmothers Speak"* into Slovenian.

"Each of you is better, greater by far than you know."

After we returned from our Balkan trip I journeyed to the Grandmothers to thank them for giving us such wonderful experiences. We made some good friends in Croatia and had fallen in love with Keka and her family in Montenegro. I had searched out Black Madonnas wherever we went, lighting candles before them and calling on the Grandmothers and the ancient Mother of those ancient sites to come forward in full force to help humanity at this time. We explored an enormous cave in Slovenia where the presence of the Mother was palpable, found a Black Madonna on the island of Hvar and another in the ancient former capital of Montenegro. The trip had been full of opportunities for work and that of course had added to my pleasure.

When I next journeyed to the Grandmothers, they showed themselves as great birds with human faces and after they enfolded me in an embrace, they said, **"Experience our wings as we cover you. We have covered you like this from the beginning, and we always will,"** they said. **"When we first began to teach you, we showed you the power of the wings, how these wings nurture, enfold and lift."** As they spoke I remembered how loved I felt the first day they enfolded me with their wings and how thrilling it was when they showed me the span of my own wings. **"Yes,"** they said, nodding in understanding, **"you have always known how the wings—ours, yours and others—lift and comfort.**

"From the power of the wings, the Net of Light came forth. They nodded, and as they fanned their wings and puffed their feathers, understanding dawned on me. The Net of Light had been brought back to life by the loving, nurturing power of the wings; it had been activated by love. "Grandmothers," I said, "In a way the Net of Light *is* the universal wings, isn't it? It covers, nurtures and lifts everything, just the way your wings do." **"Yes,"** they said, **"and as each of you claims your power, you will magnify the Net.**

"You have been casting the Net of Light for many years now," they said as they looked me up and down, **"and this has made it very strong. Today the Net of Light covers the entire earth. On your recent**

trip through the countries of old Yugoslavia, wherever you went, you anchored the Net." I looked up in wonder. I hadn't thought of this. I had wondered why Roger and I had been drawn to take three weeks in this part of the world but hadn't realized it had anything to do with the Net of Light.

"You were anchoring the Net. Share this information. Everyone needs to hear it because each person who calls on us is doing the same thing. They too are anchoring the Net of Light and they need to recognize it. We tell you that no matter where you are, at home or abroad, the moment you call on the Divine, feel our love for you and/or feel this love pouring from you to others, you anchor the Net of Light. At that very moment you bless the earth," they said, smiling at me as only they can. "Know this truth and honor yourself. Honor your work with the Divine. Too often you underestimate yourself and are unaware of the good you do." I held my hand over my mouth as I listened to them, my chin trembling while tears welled up.

"Everywhere you traveled you saw and felt places of power and you saw and felt places of wounding." "Yes," I nodded mutely. "You felt the presence of the Great Mother in the cave outside Ljubjiana, and you felt the left-over sickness of violence in Bosnia and Croatia. You are becoming a fine-tuned instrument," they nodded, "one aware of the state of people and places you encounter.

"This is true for many who are working with us, and we wish to remind you to trust in this inner knowing. The more each of you calls on the Divine, then listens to and asks for guidance, the more clear your awareness will become. The work you do with the Divine is cumulative and many of you have come a long way on the path to inner wisdom," the Grandmothers said. "We ask you to honor the place where you stand today."

As they said this, my mind went to Keka, the wonderful woman we visited in Montenegro. "Yes," the Grandmothers said, interrupting my reverie, "you are correct in surmising that she is a saint. But take a moment now and remember her words to you; the words that shocked you."

I remembered. We were driving through the countryside near Macedonia where we had visited the burial site of a great Muslim holy man. We were talking about holy people, and I had said I wasn't sure we had any saints living in America. In my country no one ever spoke about living saints. When I said this, Keka looked at me out of the corner of her eye and asked, "Is there any way you can know you are not a saint?" This was what the Grandmothers were referring to.

"Each of you is better, greater by far than you know," the Grandmothers stated. "We are telling you the truth. You carry within yourself the source of wisdom and whenever this wisdom speaks, you 'know' the truth. This is the place for you to live," they nodded fiercely, "especially at this time. The source of power/beauty within you never lies, so whenever you follow it you will experience joy and peace.

"Now," they laughed, "we will give you a little tip to help you live more from the core of who you are. You will recognize the voice of inner wisdom, the place of beauty/power within you by its relative silence. This voice does not argue, it will not manipulate or try to convince you of anything. It simply shows the truth, gives you an idea, points you in a direction and then is silent.

"Whenever wisdom speaks, your body will feel good. Wisdom will never make you feel agitated, angry or afraid. It is the mind that agitates, argues and manipulates, not wisdom," they said, "so when you live from this place of inner wisdom, you are living as what you call a saint. This is what your friend wanted you to know.

"Each of you is far greater than you think you are. Entertain this thought for a while," they said, lifting their eyebrows as they peered at me, "and begin to be willing to accept your intrinsic goodness and greatness. Why not?" they asked. "It is time to accept your own beauty/power. This is what is needed now," they said, their heads rocking up and down. "This is a sacred time. Use it well and take joy in our work together. This," they laughed, "as we have told you, is part of the joy of being on the ride with us."

On the way back to ordinary reality I thought about what they had said—that when wisdom speaks, my body will feel good. This, I knew, was true. If I could just remember it, I thought, I could let my body be my guide. "If it doesn't feel good, it isn't good," I said to myself. I wanted to remember.

CHAPTER 15

Gratitude for the World that Loves and Holds You Dear

"Place of rest"

Up to this point I had done most of the Grandmothers' work myself and now I was beginning to feel it. I was tired of being 'out there' by myself. Now I realized rather than doing everything by myself, I wanted others to share the work *with* me. Not only being concerned about how *I* could live their message, I wanted to know how *we* could live their message. This shift occurred over time and finally became clear the day I heard myself say, "No more Lone Ranger for me, I want to be part of a team." And as soon as the words were out of my mouth, I set aside time to go to the Grandmothers.

I saw how truly ready I was for this change as I watched myself take off for the upper world. "Wow!" I exclaimed as I leaped onto Eagle's back, hugging and embracing him with playful abandon. I had always been reserved with Eagle; he had such a fierce dignity about him that he intimidated me and so I had kept some distance. Not today however, and as I observed how I was behaving with him, I remember thinking, "If Eagle could smile, well he'd be smiling now."

I had my arms around him, I was singing to him, petting him, and telling him how wonderful he was. He seemed to enjoy every bit of it. When at last we came to the Grandmothers' valley I looked like a cowgirl from the 1940s, as I raised my hat above my head and rode into the midst of the Grandmothers on my bucking eagle-bronco—except of course that Eagle wasn't bucking. In other words, once I made the decision to share the Grandmothers workload with others, I was absolutely giddy with joy. "Grandmothers," I said as I slid from his back, "I want this group to really *be* the mother ship. Please show us how to do that."

"We are *pleased* with your question," they said, and when I mentioned that I would also like help with the aching sensation in my right leg, they said, **"Let that be part of today's work too."** I was to turn everything over to them, let all of it be part of our work together.

"When you next meet we will walk among you, weave through the chairs and cushions you sit on, and touch each of you. We will bind this group—the group that meets at your home *is* the mother ship. Other people will look to you to see what our work means," they explained, and as they spoke my mind began to race ahead. It would be good, I thought, if someone would help me with the newsletter and the website. And it would be much more fun to get input from people rather than have to figure everything out by myself. As these thoughts came, I watched the Grandmothers weave their way through the meeting, whispering into an ear here, patting someone on the head there, touching shoulders and backs. I smiled as I watched; "Its love that's weaving its way through the group," I said.

"Tell all the group members to be at home whenever they gather." The Grandmothers would create this sense of home for us. **"Many of you have been searching a long time to fill an emptiness inside, to find a place that fits. Well, this is it,"** they said, and as they spoke, I saw puzzle pieces settling in to their spaces. **"Feel what it's like to have found your place. "**

Now I watched the puzzle sink into the ground, first becoming a bowl, and then forming what looked like a kiva. **"A place of renewal, restoration and growing power,"** they explained. **"When you share with one another, meditate and sing together you create a home place, a deep home place, and we will hold this place for you. We have made it available and will hold it for all who come to be with us. Wherever you go we will be with you and wherever you gather, we will deepen a place for you. Each time you meet you will experience this resting point, this still point.**

"If you have a worry, something on your mind that won't leave you alone, let it sit in this space with you. Don't try to make it go away, fight it or explain it away, but let it sit. We ask you to let it be, and don't focus all your attention on it. Stay in the place we have created for you and let it sit with you. Everything and everyone is included in this place," they said. **"All are embraced here.**

"If there is pain or distraction in your body, let that also rest with you, welcome and included. This is a place of deep rest, restoration and integration. Sink into it now while we hold you and magnify its power. It will support you and draw away everything that wears you out, everything that is not you. This is the still point, your point of being," they explained.

"When you come to this place it is time to rest. And you have no idea how much goes on during this so-called time of rest," they laughed. "Because of your culture, you think of rest as a cessation of activity. As passive. Passive!" they looked incredulous and laughed again. "As opposed to active, which in your culture is *god.*" Here they slapped one another on the back and dissolved in hilarity. When they finally quieted down again, they said, "You have no idea of the great work that takes place at the still point.

"Begin to inquire about what is happening during this time of rest," they nodded as they spoke. "There are worlds within the cell beds of your body, and whenever you truly rest, you open and explore these worlds. Observe your body as you turn within, the vibration within and the movement of your breath. However," they said, "when your mind is agitated, we will not give you this experience. If we tried to work with you at such a time, your mind would then be off to the races and you would learn nothing.

"We are deepening yin now and deepening your connection to it. You will benefit from this, and all life will benefit. The threads of creation, some of which have become frayed and broken, are being mended now as this sinking in and deepening takes place. Whenever you lie down to rest, recall our words and remember this. Ah," they sighed, "yes, it is time for integration.

"Let your body lead while your follow and begin to explore. It's only the arrogance of your mind after all, that prevents you from having this experience. The mind that tells you, 'I think, therefore I am,'" they laughed. "Although many have enshrined this maxim as 'truth,' it is only the mind talking. Your being is far greater than mere conscious thought. Conscious thought is only one aspect of thought. You are deepening into wisdom now, and wisdom goes far beyond conscious thought. Let yourself deepen."

They remained silent and in the quiet I reflected on what they'd said. There was so much here. What they termed "the threads of creation which have been frayed and broken" have an opportunity to mend whenever we truly rest. This sounded like the Hermetic principle at work ("As above, so below, As below, so above.) As I understood it, if we made a change within the microcosm (our self), we would affect the macrocosm (the world.) So deep and mindful rest like the kind they were advocating was good for the planet!

The business of conscious thought being only one aspect of thought I understood. My experience with the Grandmothers had taught me that my most valuable insights *never* came from my conscious mind but instead showed up from some other level, taking me by surprise each time.

They watched as the wheels turned in my head and smiled indulgently. "Thank you, Grandmothers," I said, "thank you. It may take me a while to integrate everything you've said today, but thank you for giving me such a good start."

They smiled broadly and nodded. **"When you come together to study our messages and pass on our empowerment, it's a joyous time for you, a time to receive. Have fun with this work. Each time you join together for this purpose, you deepen your connection with the Divine,"** they paused as they looked at me thoughtfully. **"And at last there will be a melting away of any ideas of separation from the Divine. Then you will recognize, 'Oh, I am the Grandmothers and the Grandmothers are me. This will happen."**

I looked at them, my eyes wide. "I am and Grandmothers and the Grandmothers are me?" I said, not believing what they were saying. I waited for them to explain more, but when they smiled knowingly and remained silent, I understood that our time together was over. I thanked them and prepared to go, but when I turned back for one more look, they were laughing. Giving me a playful look they fluttered their fingers in good-bye and shooting me that knowing look, said, **"Pretty good, huh?"**

Their parting words, "Pretty good, huh?" haunted me. Their look said, "Isn't it time for you to accept your own divinity?" I didn't know what to do with that. Right from the start they had told me they didn't want my/our worship but instead wanted us to be at one with them. I knew they were right and it was what I wanted too, but somehow I was still holding myself back. I figured it had to be my early conditioning. Taught to worship God *up there*, I still battled with accepting my own divinity. "It's a good thing," I said, "that the Grandmothers are so patient. This is taking me a while."

A few days later I asked myself, "What is it going to take for me to finally let go of my religious conditioning and embrace the truth?" While mulling this over, I walked onto the back porch and a humming bird dove at me and almost hit me. She came at me on purpose. I gasped and jumped back and when for a few seconds she stood whirring in front of my face, I remembered that hummingbird is the totem for joy. There was the answer to my question. The joy I was finding with the Grandmothers would move me out of the past and into the present.

"You are our message"

I had begun to think about what I could do to create a stronger Grandmothers' team, how to encourage women to take on more responsibility for the Grandmothers' work. This was an entirely new way to operate because everyone, including myself, was accustomed to me carrying the load. It had been that way from the start and this way of working had made sense when only a few of us were involved in spreading this message. But now that we had grown into the thousands and groups were meeting all over the world, we needed another system. In the previous journey the Grandmothers showed me how they had begun to bind this group together, but how, I wondered, could we speed up this evolution? Guidance. I needed more guidance.

When I went to them next, I found them standing together, wearing long skirts and colorful shawls, and as soon as I stepped before them, they spoke. **"We wondered what you were waiting for."** Startled by their comment, I blinked and shook my head. When I heard a sound, I looked up and saw a flock of geese forming an enormous v as they winged their way across the sky. Their pattern was so perfect that they looked like an arrow in flight. Wings beating in concert, they flew on and on and when the leader grew tired from breaking the wind for the group, she dropped back and another seamlessly moved to the front. Their honks grew fainter as they winged over the horizon.

When the birds had passed and all was quiet again I looked at the Grandmothers with a question. They pursed their lips and nodded firmly. "Are you showing me how it needs to be in the Grandmothers' group?" I asked, "working together and spelling one another?" Again they nodded and said, **"There is no time to hesitate. Now is the hour for each to step forward and ask what she/he can do,"** they explained, **"time to ask, 'How can I live this message?'"** Then they turned to me and said, **"Ask that now."**

"Yes, Grandmothers, okay," I stammered and quickly shut my eyes. And as soon as I asked the question, I heard, **"Trust and go forward. And once you have done that, then trust and go forward again."** The Grandmothers were all smiles. **"Each of you needs to ask the question. 'How can I live the Grandmothers' message? How can my life reflect this message?' And as soon as you have asked this one, the next question is, 'what prevents me from living the message right now?'"**

Again I turned within myself and asked what prevented me from living their message now. Fear was the answer that came, and I felt its chill as it hovered over my back like a hooded cobra. The Grandmothers nodded, **"Then ask, 'how do I feel about allowing this impediment to prevent me from living this message?"** "Tired of it," I answered, "fed up and impatient to move on," and as I spoke the words I could swear I heard cheering inside me.

"Ask us to show you what your life would be like without this impediment," they said as they tilted their heads, eyeing me from the side. I perked up when I heard this; I loved thinking of fear as an impediment. The word cut it down to size. "Okay," I said, and as I took a breath, I asked, "what would my life be like without the impediment of fear?"

Immediately I saw myself skating—flying over the ice, jumping, whirling and gliding for joy. As I raced across a frozen expanse, I was skating from joy to joy. **"Brave,"** the Grandmothers said, and threw their heads back, **"perhaps even audacious. Generous and joyful,"** they said, **"gliding forward with the flow that only moves forward."** As I listened and watched this skating self, I heard myself take in a breath, thrilled to the core of my being.

"It's time now. What are you waiting for? Step up. Be seen, be heard, be counted, be noticed. *Be loved,*" they said as they took my hands in theirs. **"Let your light shine."** And as they looked into my eyes, they said, **"Tell the world that we are here. If people remark on your confidence, if they admire you and want to know what gives you strength, tell them about us. We are here for all.**

"Let this be the topic of a workshop. It is time for each of you to step up and live our message. *You are our message,*" they said, and when they said this, I knew they were speaking to everyone engaged in this work. **"We are, as they say, taking off the gloves now, so step up and be counted."** "Grandmothers," I cried, my voice vibrating with joy, "this is Great!" They laughed then and holding me with their eyes, said, **"*You* are great."**

"You will spread the energy of shakti, the feminine principle."

I felt as though I had received my marching orders. I was full of enthusiasm, and thoughts of a Grandmothers' gathering kept coming to my mind. Wouldn't it be wonderful if women running groups could get together and share with one another? We could probably squeeze forty or so of them into my studio so we wouldn't have to rent a hall.

We could spend a few days together, get to know each other, share ideas, and talk about the effect the Grandmothers were having on our lives. Grandmothers group leaders were scattered across the country and most of us had never seen each other, so a gathering like this would give everyone an opportunity to bond as well as strengthen our ability to live the Grandmothers' message.

Once the idea came I could hardly wait to go to the Grandmothers about it. "Grandmothers, I want to ask you about having a summit meeting here," I said as I stepped before them and I hadn't gotten the words out of my mouth before I saw them jumping up and down with excitement. And of course their excitement blew my own wide open. "Grandmothers," I finally said, struggling to remain rational, "it's a long way for some of these women to travel. Will they come?" **Many will come,** they assured me, **"and it will be an enriching time for all of you."**

"Tell me about it, Grandmothers. What good will come from this gathering?" **"Kinship,"** they answered, **"bonding, joy, enthusiasm, and commitment. You will spread the energy of shakti (the feminine principle); your coming together will reactivate the spark. You will also amplify the Net of Light. After this gathering there will be more power and light in the Net."**

I took the idea to the study circle in Laguna Beach and they were also enthusiastic. Many volunteered to put out-of-towners up in their homes, help with transportation, housekeeping and whatever else needed to be done. We were working as a team. Kate volunteered to cook for us and we passed a jar at each study circle meeting and began to grow our funds. Just before the Gathering of the Grandmothers we counted up what we had amassed ($1046) and took it to her so she could buy food for the event. She hadn't told us how much she needed, but this was what we had. And before we could tell her how much we had gathered, she said, "Gosh, I hope you have enough. I need $1046." You could have heard a pin drop. She couldn't understand why we were standing there with our mouths open, but when we told her that this was *exactly* the amount we had, she too gasped. "It's the Grandmothers," she said, and we nodded in agreement.

We held the first Gathering of the Grandmothers in May of 2007 and women from as far away as England came. My studio just barely held forty-six of us and we spent three glorious days together, deepening our connection to one another and most of all, to the Grandmothers. On our last afternoon as we sat meditating, God the Mother made Herself known to us, appearing in the center of our circle. Some of us saw Her and all of us felt the earth shaking power of Her presence. She laid her blessing on us and with our hearts full of joy we set our plans to meet again the following year.

"Something good is coming."

After the Gathering of the Grandmothers, life returned to normal and for a while everything ran smoothly. I was painting, working in clay, seeing clients, and spending time with my husband and friends. I had nothing to complain about, but even though my personal world was a happy place, I was painfully aware of the suffering around me. I had once heard a great spiritual teacher say, "People and animals are suffering, starving and dying—how can you sleep?" And now I understood what he meant. For whatever reason, while there was suffering in the world, I could not lock myself in my private life and escape its pain.

Once again I journeyed to the Grandmothers, to ask them to clarify our/my purpose at this point in history, while so much upheaval was taking place. "There are many difficulties now, Grandmothers," I said, speaking in understatement. "I really do have a hard time sleeping when others cannot. Please talk to us about these times so we can take heart," I pleaded. **"Yes,"** they said, and nodded. They liked this question, especially the part about taking heart.

Immediately they showed me what looked like boxes or building blocks stacked one upon another. As I watched, I noticed some of them swaying as they rubbed against each other, while others bumped with more force so that some blocks fell over. **"You think that once something exists, it is permanent,"** the Grandmothers said, pointing to the stacked blocks. **"A business, a bank, a country, a home. Because it's there, you think it will last. Buildings, institutions and schools of thought are no more permanent than those boxes you just watched fall. What is permanent is what lies beneath all of them, what lies beneath the buildings, institutions, political parties, financial and religious establishments on earth. What is permanent is what lies beneath,"** they repeated. **"Other things are ephemeral and will come and go. They have always come and gone.**

"We know this period of change frightens you." "Yes, Grandmothers," I said, "it does. And it frightens a lot of people." **"We understand,"** they said. **"You don't know what to hold onto or what to believe in now that there is so much upheaval in the world. But your heart connection with us and with one another is permanent. The loving connections you have made—caring, understanding, hold-**

ing one another, and your love for us—these are forever," they said, spreading their hands wide. **"These spring from love and are therefore real.**

"These times of change that are now upon you have been foretold. You know this, but you forget," they said, their heads rocking up and down. **"The distractions of the world lull you into forgetting that everything in life *is* change. You are not the same as you were when you were a baby, or the same as you will be twenty years from now. Always you are borne along on the river of life,"** they said, and the timeless poetry of their words formed a lump in my throat. **"A river flows,"** they said; **"it is not a stagnant pond. In order for something new to arise, the old must give way. Old institutions and ways of thinking are falling so that what is real and unchanging can take center stage."**

"Grandmothers," I asked, "given what you've said, how can we weather the storms of these times?" They looked hard at me and said, **"Although these are difficult times, you will be carried along by the river of life, nudged and moved to where you need to be.**

"Something greater is coming soon; greater and better by far than anything you have ever known. A new way of being," they said and stood tall. **"The old clinging, greediness, fearfulness and rushing from sensation to sensation are going. These are too brittle to withstand the flow of the river of life,"** they explained. **"Anything that cannot bend with and accommodate the flow of life has to go."**

"What can we do to cope with these changes?" I asked. "So much is in flux that it's hard to get a foothold anywhere." **"Turn to the love within your heart, and when things get difficult, we will be there inside you, holding you. Whenever fear shows its face, call on us. What is fear anyway except a desire to cling to artifacts from another time? So call on us and let us hold you. We will!"** they announced and laughed until at last I laughed with them. **"And while you're at it, every chance you get, give your love to one another.**

"*Something good is coming*," they repeated. **"All the change and upheaval you see is not for nothing. It is making way for the new. You may not remember this, but you chose to be born during these times. You chose to be part of this work with us. No matter how wild the weather, you will be able to ride these waves of change; you will actually ride them with ease,"** they said with a smile. **And we will hold and support you through it all.**

"Those of you who read our messages and gather to do our work were born for this time. We ask you to remember this now, to let go of fear, and instead get in touch with, and own your own greatness.

Own your expanded heart, your heart that is growing larger every day, that is loving more and more. *This,* we remind you, is how we love you.

"**Feel us holding you now in the Net that supports the earth and supports you,**" they said, and as I sighed I felt myself rocked in a great, lighted hammock. "It's the Net of Light," I said, my voice full of reverence as I felt it under me as well as surrounding me. The Grandmothers waved good-bye then and cradled by the Net, I swung my way back home. "Where is fear now?" I asked, parroting the Grandmothers. "Where indeed?" I giggled to myself.

"This is the Net of Light that will hold the earth though these times of change."

Although some call it by different names—net, web, grid, or network—many are now working with the Net of Light to support the earth. "**This is the Net of Light that will hold the earth through these times of change,**" the Grandmothers say, and since these are the times we are living in, I asked them how we could work to magnify the power within the Net of Light.

No sooner were the words out of my mouth than the Grandmothers said, "**Come with us,**" and taking my hand, together we rose high and sailed above the Earth, so high I could see the curvature of our planet, its oceans and major land masses. When I glanced down, I saw the Net of Light inset into the earth; it covered everything and penetrated the earth's body, spreading out both horizontally and vertically—like a grid. In some places it was faint and hard to make out, and I noticed that this was especially true in parts of the northern hemisphere.

I looked to the southern hemisphere to see if the same was true there, but in the south, it was different story. In Africa and the Middle East the Net had been torn and lay open like a wound. A soon as I saw this, grief rolled over me like a wave. "Grandmothers," I said, "I can't stop crying, I don't know why this is so devastating, but what I am seeing is terrible." I could feel the rips in the Net of Light as if they were in my own body and the pain was excruciating.

The Grandmothers wrapped me in their wings and said, "**We are teaching you through experience so you will know the value and essence of the Net of Light. We do not want you to suffer, but it is important that you understand the nature and purpose of the Net.**" "Yes, yes, Grandmothers," I said, "I agree. Teach me. I want to learn, I want to learn."

As they held me, they said, "**It was difficult for you to see the Net of Light at some places in the northern hemisphere, because the people who live in these areas have not recognized and honored it. They operate through their minds only and have not yet learned how to work with both their mind and heart. This is why the Net appeared faint there.**"

Then they explained why I had sobbed so hard when I'd seen the rips in the Net in Africa and the Middle East. "**All is one,**" they said, searching my face to see if I understood. "**Through the Net of Light, you see, feel and know another's pain and joy. You do not and *cannot* (no matter how hard you try), live as an island.**" Speaking with great seriousness, they said, "**You felt the pain of that land because it is your pain.**" I looked and looked at them, my eyes big, hanging on their every word.

"**Return to your heart now,**" they said, "**and unify with all who work with the Net of Light—no matter what they call it.**" I did and immediately saw that these were simply different names for the same thing. The Net of Light is a pattern/network/fabric or grid of love. It *is* love. It anchors, supports and penetrates everyone and everything on earth. For several minutes I stayed focused in my heart and let the Net of Light do its work and, as I did, my breathing slowed and the presence of yin within me swelled until all I felt was peace.

Now I became aware of the presence of Net within every cell of my body. A dense pattern of light glowed inside me. As I focused on this internal Net of Light, I became aware that it was thickening, not only in me, but in other places as well. I shot a puzzled look at the Grandmothers who laughed at my surprise. "**It is the old saying, as above, so below, as within, so without.**" Mute, I marveled as the work of the Net of Light within my body began to activate the mending of the Net's tears in Africa. And now I cried again, but this time from happiness.

The Grandmothers showed me how everything within my home is also infused with the Net of Light. "**It is easiest for you to observe this in the living things in your home—the animals, plants and wood pieces, for instance. But as you live with, handle and love everything in your home, the plastics and other man made things will also awaken to the presence of the Net of Light.**

"**This is true for everything—for high-rise buildings, for freeways, terminals, subways, factories and other man made structures. These too are held by the Net of Light. Rather,**" they corrected themselves, "**the Net of Light is waiting within them, ready to embrace and infuse them. So whenever you see or think of these places, rec-**

ognize that they are also held by and infused with the Net of Light. Reclaim the sacredness of your earth!" they cried. *"Reclaim everyone and everything on earth."*

They then looked thoughtful. **"People who appear to be cruel, deranged or mentally ill need you to recognize that the Net of Light is also within them. Do them this favor. Politicians and people of influence on your planet are also penetrated and held by the Net of Light."** They began to giggle and jostle one another. **"Do them and your world a favor,"** they said, **"by honoring the Net of Light within them too.**

"Call on the Net of Light within every ugly, blighted and destroyed place on earth. It is lying there, waiting to be recognized. The Net of Light covers and permeates your world. Recognize and honor it wherever you go. Remember the Net of Light and think of it everywhere. It is waiting to be recognized.

"This is how you can magnify the work of the Net of Light. This is how you can help the earth. And this is the answer to your question," the Grandmothers said and "Oh!" I replied. I had been so absorbed by what they were telling me that I had forgotten that this was the question I had asked them.

"There is more love now."

It was now almost summertime and I would soon be going to Lithuania for the second time, traveling from city to city, and then on to Holland for a Grandmothers' meeting in the Hague. Roger would be with me this time and together we would visit friends in Delft and then travel with a Dutch group to see Mother Meera, the great Indian saint at her ashram in Germany. As our departing date drew near I decided to journey to the Grandmothers to ask about this trip.

"I'm leaving in two weeks to take your message to Lithuania and the Netherlands, Grandmothers," I said. "Please guide and teach me about the highest good for this trip." They were in human form this time and smiled broadly when I asked my question. **"For the women who have been working with us in the Netherlands it will be a great joy to have you there. Your presence will ground them in the work they have been doing with us and they will provide the center, or beginning point for our message to spread in this area of the world. This gathering will help them grow in confidence and personal connection with us. They have already formed a good foundation; your visit will simply give them more to build with. It is good,"** they smiled, **"it is very good."**

Then they pointed to the Netherlands and I saw the Grandmothers work spreading outward from Delft, moving at what appeared to be right angles and as I watched, I noticed that the pattern it made was almost architectural. It formed a tree shape, but not a natural looking tree. This tree's branches grew at right angles, ran parallel to the ground and then sharply turned upward. The pattern I was seeing had to do with the way this part of the world is connected. It's patterned at angles and so the work will spread that way. This is the way information and commerce has always spread there—along the dykes and after the dykes, the roads. "It's very orderly," I said as I watched it spread." "It's very Dutch," the Grandmothers laughed happily and I could see how much they loved these Dutch women.

I observed as the Grandmothers message reached throughout the lowland countries—Belgium and beyond, moving through a network bordered by roads and dykes. And as I watched it flow, turn sharply and then flow again I felt a sense of contentment. This was how it was in this part of the world and how it should be. "Grandmothers," I asked, "is there any more you want to tell me about taking your message to the Netherlands?" Smiling, with a knowing look in their eyes, they said, **"They will bloom."** Immediately tulips popped into my mind. I saw them giggling and said, "Grandmothers, Grandmothers," as I shook my head in amusement. They never lose an opportunity for laughter and play.

Next I asked about Lithuania. This would be my second trip to this country. **"Ahhh, Lithuania,"** the Grandmothers said, the word rolling off their tongues and immediately I felt how different the energy was there. The landscape was one of curvaceous lines, and there was a cupping, lifting movement in the earth. **"The work in Lithuania will be easy for you this time because the groundwork has already been laid. Many pathways of love were opened when you were there last year. Now these will widen so more love can rush in, soaking the land in love."**

They then showed me the Great Mother sitting in the land there, holding the space, and I noticed that She looked very happy. **"The visits to the Netherlands and Lithuania will be a blessing for you and for many,"** the Grandmothers said. **"Our message will bring more joy and peace to these areas, seeding joy and peace in Grandmothers' groups everywhere.**

"Love is building. The Gathering of the Grandmothers in California this spring increased the capacity for love within you and within the earth. Gaia is now able to hold more love; she is also able to give forth more love and now the same is also true for you.

"This is what the word 'blessing' means," they said, "**being filled with and receiving love. The Gathering of the Grandmothers was a blessing for each one who participated as well as for everyone on earth. Let yourself be carried along on this blessing. There *is* more love now,**" they said, "**so it will be easier to feel and access it. All you need is to ask for it. Ask for love and we will give it. In any situation, wherever you are, we will give the blessing of love.**"

As they spoke, I felt myself soaked in the love they were talking about, wrapped in and penetrated by it, so engulfed that I no longer wanted to speak, but only to *be* this love that I was recognizing as myself. "**What you are experiencing is present within each woman who participated in this gathering. You share it, and as you share such experiences you wordlessly pass them on to others. Love is contagious, and because you strongly hold it now, everyone you come across will also have the opportunity to hold it. This state of consciousness is one of mergence with the Great Mother,**" they said, smiling and nodding wisely. "**That is why you feel so good. The Mother *is* love.**"

I was so filled with love, so thick and swollen with it, that not only could I not speak, I could barely think. Still, I was able to hear the truth, that whenever I moved into the state of mergence with the Mother, so did others. This is inevitable because at the core of our being we are interlinked. As I observed the world around me from this place of mergence I saw that I was being held within the body of the Mother and at the same time, *I was* the body of the Mother. It was that limitless feeling again. I was both lover and beloved. When I looked up at the Grandmothers with a question in my eyes, all they said to me was, "**This will never end.**"

It took me a long time to return from this journey. I couldn't and didn't want to move. Why would I? I was floating in a bathtub of love. But after I had spent some time there, I asked the Grandmothers to show me how to come out of this state. I couldn't muster the will to do it myself. And as soon as I asked for their help, the phone rang, popping me back into ordinary reality. But now it didn't seem so ordinary.

"You will become a blessing upon the earth."

I returned from Lithuania and the Netherlands to a flood of Internet newsletters and emails focusing in some way on the Divine Feminine or God the Mother. Before I had left home I had rarely seen stuff like this, but it was certainly appearing now. There were announcements of classes on reawakening the Goddess, tours to Goddess sites around the world and lectures on who She was and is. Why this sudden upsurge, I wondered, and what part were the Grandmothers supposed to play in it? Since I couldn't answer these questions myself, I journeyed to the Grandmothers to find out.

"Grandmothers," I said as I came before them, "teach me the role your work is to play at this time. People are offering workshops and lectures on the Divine Feminine and a few are even mentioning the Grandmothers. Should I get in touch with these people? Is there something I should be doing?" They regarded me patiently as I blundered on. "You know everything," I said, "and after all, you are the ones who called this work into being. So now, as people become more aware of the Mother, what would you like me to do? Should I be doing more to get your message out into the world?"

Silently they circled around and enfolded me in their embrace. **"Turn to us,"** they said, and as I felt their arms around me, I did. I felt their embrace and focused on them, only them. **"It is confusing out there in the world,"** they said as they patted my back. "It really is, Grandmothers," I whispered with feeling. **"Turn to us,"** they said again. **"We told you long ago that the greatest use you can make of our message is to live it. And what we said then is just as true now.**

"Open to us and do not reach for the fruits of your actions. Do not worry about advertising and promoting our message. Much of what you see in the so-called New Age community is the same salesmanship, the same yang-driven commerce, although with a spiritual bent, that you see anywhere. We have not come for that. Your world has had more than enough of buying, selling, advertising and promotion.

"We work through the hearts of those we call, and through them we strengthen the Net of Light. There are some who come to us only fleetingly. They come seeking a new sensation. flitting from teacher to teacher, from message to message. We cannot work with them. This work is only for certain ones," they smiled, and patted me to reassure me.

"Go slow," they said, **"go deep. You will find us there in the depths of your being. We have come to awaken you to the presence of the Great Mother. She lies within you. Her nature is your nature. And as you awaken to this greatness, to the presence of the Great Feminine within yourself, your presence will bless, hold and comfort everything that lives. Your vibration will change,"** they promised and quickly added, **"it *has* changed. Your very being is deepening and awakening.**

"We have also told you that our work is not for everyone," they repeated. "Numbers are not important to us. What is important is intention; intention underlies everything," they said, their looks serious. "It is the purity of your intention that calls us to you in the first place, and it is the purity of your intention that holds us captive. We cannot resist the purity of your intention," they said, shaking their heads, bemused. "We then become yours and you become ours." The Grandmothers stood tall and with great dignity, spoke as one. "Our mission is a selfless one, so only those who have this quality within themselves and wish to serve others will come to us.

"We say again," they said as they fastened their eyes on mine, "it is not about numbers. Those who have come to our call are already doing more good than they will ever know," they said. "They are working on multidimensional levels to anchor the Net of Light. And they are accessing the Mother's presence for many."

After a few moments of silence they intoned, "Invite us in," their voices so powerful that I responded instantly and as I thought of opening to them I began to plunge downward, surprised to note that, although I was diving, I was diving very slowly. It was slow motion; my descent so gradual that I remarked in surprise, "What a serious movement this is! Thorough," I added, as down, down, down, through the layers of the earth I plunged.

What a feeling! I was in my element here and swam through the layers of earth like a subterranean jellyfish, fully immersed in the flow. I was both in the earth and of it. Steady and present, I was a force to contend with as I ploughed downward, ever downward. At last I reached the Grandmothers who stood waiting for me, and reaching out my arms, I merged into their embrace and into them.

I was complete. This was bliss. I was so thrilled, so grateful for the depth and breadth of this experience I was literally oozing joy. And when I gazed at the Grandmothers, they smiled and said, "We will do this for anyone who asks for it. We will give this same experience of depth, unshakablity and presence to she or he who desires it. We are waiting for them."

Then they explained, "We cannot hold you the way we are holding you now, when you are caught up in the surface activities of life. We may initially call you to us while you are living on the surface, while you are going about your 'normal' life," they said. "We have done this with many of you," they explained and I nodded in agreement. They had certainly done this with me. The first time they came, I was simply going about my 'normal' life walking the dog.

"But now," they said, and pointed at me, "**we are calling you to dive to the depths of your being. When you do, we will hold you in these deep places until you learn that the one who dwells in the deepest place is who you are. You are wise beyond imagining, you are great and fathomless,**" they said, fixing me with a look that brooked no dissent. "**You are Not this body,**" they said, fierceness in their tone, "**you are Not this personality. What** *you* **are,**" they emphasized, "**is eternal and unshakable. You are a wellspring of understanding and compassion.**

"**If depth is what you want,**" they said, giving me an appraising look, "**we will give it to you.**" "Yes, Grandmothers," I gulped, nodding up and down. "Please, it's what I want." "**Go slow then, go deep, and we will lead you.** *This* **is your part to play,**" they said as they studied me. "**Not running here and there, seeking to promote us, but standing steady and anchoring the presence of the Mother. Living our message. This is, who you are. After all,**" they said and broke into laughter, "**aren't you tired of pretending you are less than this?**" I looked at them in surprise but as their words sank in I too began to laugh—at myself and at the game of life that often led me to ignore my own divinity.

"**When you are ready to own who you are, call us,**" they said and peered at me over the tops of their noses. "**You will then hold the vibration of the Great Mother. And whenever you open to and hold that place, thousands upon thousands will benefit. You will become a blessing upon the earth. As we say,**" they smiled, "**a walking prayer.**

"**You are not here to simply talk about the Great Mother, or share ideas about the Great Mother and the return of the Feminine,**" they said, their hands on their hips. "**You are here to** *live it,* **to live as you were born to live. You ARE the great yin,**" they said and drawing themselves to their full height, twelve queenly Grandmothers chorused, "**Own it! Live it! Call on us, and we will hold you, teach you and make your lives joyful. It is time.**" "Yes, Grandmothers. Yes," I answered.

"Gratitude, gratitude for the world that loves and holds you dear."

The next time I went to the Grandmothers I didn't have a clear question for them, but had felt them pulling on me for several days and was going because of that pull. And when I came before them, twelve majestic eagles greeted me.

With their great heads nodding, and before I even had a chance to speak, they said, **"We are making the turn."** I looked at them, squinting my eyes, wondered what they were talking about. "What? I asked, but they said no more and as I continued to stare at them, suddenly I saw what looked like a narrow dirt road trailing off into the distance. And just before it faded from site, it made a turn to the right. I hunched my shoulders, leaned forward as far as I could and as I peered down the road, somewhere near the end I glimpsed light glistening on water. I had no idea what this was, but I wanted to find out, so I followed the road, and the Grandmother eagles walked with me. When we rounded the turn, there were birds skimming over a great expanse of water. Not too far from shore, a dolphin leaped, splashing down and sending concentric circles far into the bay. Softly the Grandmothers spoke. **"Nature will out,"** they said.

Again I wasn't sure what they were talking about. What lay before me looked and felt wonderful—a paradise—but I needed them to say more. **"This is a good time to nurture and give loving attention to something in the natural world. Do this however you like, in a large or in a small way. As you do this, you will affirm your loving connection with the natural world, the world that holds you, supports you and infuses your very body."**

Then they showed me the entire human family, each one of us cupped and held by the earth, the sky, the waters, the animals and plants. **"Make a point to do something loving and giving at this time. Give back to the natural world. Now is a good time for this. And when you perform this action, think also of the Net of Light. As you reaffirm your connection to the natural world, honor the Net that holds and upholds *all* life.**

"Recognize a tree for instance," they laughed as they lovingly placed their hands on the trunk of a tree. **"Give thanks for the breeze,"** they said. **"Go out of your way to affirm a loving connection to the natural world. It is especially important to do this now when there is so much destruction on earth. You know all about this,"** they said, speaking specifically to me, **"we need not tabulate it for you."** "Yes, Grandmothers," I replied. Indeed I knew what they were talking about. Not a day went by that I didn't think about and grieve the destruction of the natural world taking place on earth.

"This particular message is for those who are working together to reactivate the energy of the Mother here on earth. She is asking you to demonstrate your love for Her by reaching out to something of the natural world. From time to time, let this be your prayerful

focus," they said and nodded their heads sympathetically. **"Gratitude, gratitude"** they said, **"for the world that loves and holds you dear."** Then they bowed their heads, softly folded their wings/arms and said, **"We bless you."**

The Grandmothers' words touched me deeply and after this journey I began to look for opportunities to show my gratitude to the natural world. I spent a few days working in my garden, talking to my plants and giving thanks to the grass I walked on in my bare feet. I decided to forgo the dryer for a while and dry my clothes in the sun and most rewarding of all, I spent extra time with my wonderful dog, McBear. These were not particularly new activities, but thanks to the Grandmothers, I was now doing them with more heart.

CHAPTER 16

Go Big and Then Go Bigger

"The source has been hidden by the fog of illusion"

Spending time walking and playing with my dog reminded me that it had been a long time since I had journeyed to the compassionate animal spirits. I missed them. At this point I didn't need to go to them for healing, I just missed hanging out with my friends. "Well," I said to myself, "there's no law that says I can't just go and see them," and after that I set aside time to visit Wolf. Strangely, when I picked up the newspaper the next morning, there was an article about a wolf refuge and people traveling there to interact with them. "Hummmm..." I wondered, "Is this a coincidence?"

I began to drum and when I called on Wolf, he came immediately. "Wolf," I said, "you are the teacher. Please teach me and also teach through me. After I said this he gazed into my eyes, gave me a big lick and then breathed on me. In response, my heartbeat slowed, my shoulders fell a good two inches and I felt all the muscles in my face relax.

"Follow me," he said. "Yes, Wolf," I replied, and placing a hand on his back, I walked beside him. We went a little ways like this and then sped up the pace, trotting then walking, trotting then walking through a forest where we crossed a stream and followed a pathway upward through a field of coarse brush. And when the path became too narrow to walk abreast, Wolf took the lead.

Now we pulled ourselves upward, Wolf leaping over rocks and me clambering after him until at last we reached a summit. He sat down at the edge of a precipice and with his nose pointing upward, he sniffed the air. I sat beside him, my legs dangling over the edge of the rock face. **"Look!"** he said, his nose now jutting forward as he surveyed the land that lay below us.

I looked too, but my view was muted by a thick mist. A blue-ish light bathed the valley floor and everything appeared indistinct, as if painted by a messy paintbrush. Tree-like forms rose out of the valley and clouds of fog blew across it. **"Look!"** Wolf said again, and I did.

Now I was able to make out packs of wolves running together, racing toward a river and somehow I understood that this was the River of Life. The wolves were racing toward this source that drew them like a magnet.

"The Source," Wolf said, **"has been hidden by the fog of illusion."** "What?" I said, and when I realized I had heard him right, that he had said exactly what I thought he had, my stomach clutched in rebellion. Was Wolf going to start speaking new age jargon, just like everyone else? I hoped not, because if he was, I was going to have a hard time believing him. "Wolf," I said, "please speak plainly. Don't go theoretical on me. I've heard so much of this kind of talk," I said, "that it actually makes me sick."

Wolf threw back his head at this and howled with delight. Then he smacked a paw against the ground and panting and howling, rolled around until he wore himself out. Something I said had tickled him silly, but now I was bewildered. What in the world had set him off? I stared at him, mystified. "What are you doing, Wolf?" I asked.

"I am teaching you," he replied, drawing himself tall, his dignity restored, **"I am doing as you asked."** "I'm sorry, Wolf," I said, shaking my head. Now I felt bad. The last thing I wanted to do was hurt his feelings. "It's just that I've heard stuff like 'fog of illusion' so many times that it sort of makes my skin crawl," I explained. "People use clichés like that too often that they've come to mean nothing," I said. **"I understand,"** he replied. **"I will try another way.**

"Stay with me now," he said. "Yes, Wolf," I agreed, blowing out my breath, and hopefully my resistance with it. **"The wolves running toward the life-giving waters of the river were showing good sense. Even though, as you saw, their view of the river was obscured by fog, they followed their instincts and went toward it. *Everything* is now obscured by, excuse the expression,"** he eyed me from the side, **"the fog of illusion. You must trust your instincts, your inner knowing,"** he emphasized, **"in order to find the Source. At this time there is no clear view of the Source, yet you can still find it. The wolves were showing you how."** "Oh!" I said, chastened, "*That* was what they were doing." **"Wolf,"** he reminded me, sitting even straighter, **"is teacher."**

"Thank you," I murmured, shaking my head over my behavior. "I think I get what you're saying, but how can I/we apply this lesson in life? Our world today is in a mess and you're right about not being able to see things clearly. People say they're something they aren't," I said, "in fact, almost everyone seems to be occupied in twisting the 'truth' to their advantage. Everyone is a salesman, pushing something," I said, "and we don't know who or what to believe. Nothing is as it seems," I said in dismay; "what can we do? How can we find this River of Life you are talking about?"

Laying a paw on my shoulder, Wolf leaned in and again breathed on me and again my shoulders dropped. I hadn't realized how tense I'd become as I tried to explain myself to him. Silently he stared into my eyes and continued to breathe on me. Mesmerized, I watched his nostrils gently flare as he inhaled, and relax as he exhaled and as I watched, I fell into a deeply relaxed zone. **"Receive,"** he said and I did. We breathed together like this for only a few seconds, but the change in me in that time was profound. **"Now you are ready,"** he said and my eyes flew open and fastened on him. Ready? **"The River of Life is flowing within you. Open to the flow."** I dropped into myself then, and with the thought of opening to the flow, quickly felt myself *as* the flow. At that moment, I *was* this river. I recognized there was nothing for me to seek because I was already there. *I was it.*

Wolf smiled his lupine smile and gently swayed back and forth and as I watched him, I relaxed further, going deeper into myself. Soon I too was smiling that smile and together we swayed back and forth as peace permeated the space around us. **"This is it,"** he said. **"There is no need to run and seek after anything, and there is nothing to fear. This is it."**

I chuckled and my heart was so full of love at that moment that tears welled in my eyes. We took in a breath together, and with our arms intertwined, fell back onto the ground. As he licked and nuzzled me, I burrowed into his fur. "Oh Wolf," I said, "what a teacher you are!" **"Yes,"** he said, **"I am.**

"Now take this lesson and share it with others. Those with the ability to hear it, will hear. It is only for them anyway." Thank you, Wolf," I bowed. "I thank you for myself and I thank you for everyone. **"You're welcome,"** he replied, and bounding to his feet, he started back down the trail. I got up and walked behind him. "Thank you, Wolf," I murmured under my breath, "thank you." He turned then and looked back over his shoulder, to make sure I was following.

"Go big and then go bigger."

After this lesson from Wolf, I began to think about Bear. But although he was much on my mind, I didn't feel I had time to visit him. That is, until I took a break from working on the Grandmothers' next book to check my e-mail. Instantly the most hideous expose of people 'farming' (read 'torturing') bears popped up on my screen. I gasped and was sick. Now I had to see Bear.

Pushing away from the computer, I grabbed my drum and began to call to him. I felt so desperate to reach him that before I had even entered the lower world I was crying out, "Come to me! Bear! Please come to me! I am heartsick. I cannot bear it." When I heard what I'd just said I remembered how much Bear loves to play with words. "And that's not a pun," I said. By this time I was sobbing so hard I could barely speak his name and when he finally appeared in front of me, I threw my arms around him. "Oh my beloved Bear," I sobbed, "What can I do to help? This is terrible, so terrible."

"**Call on me,**" he said, "**and let me merge with you.**" "Yes, Bear," I stammered, struggling to take a breath and calm myself. I slowed my breathing then and purposefully held back my tears while I waited for him to make himself known in me.

"**I am here,**" he said at last, "**I am with you, I am in you.**" And I could tell he was, because suddenly I was calm. "**This,**" he said, his voice heavy with disgust, "**Is part of the filth of this age. The cruelty and unthinking greed that control so much of life on earth now. This is part of it,**" he said and then he roared, "**Go big! Go big and then go bigger! You must expand,**" he said, "**not contract. Let your heart expand so fully that you can embrace even the perpetrators of this suffering. Embrace the bears *and* their torturers. Embrace them all!**" he roared.

"**Do not fear evil,**" he said. "**Embrace all of it.**" "I will, Bear," I answered, my eyes glued to his face. "I will hold my arms and heart open for all of them. I'll do it. Somehow I'll do it," I said, shuddering at the thought. "But help me, please," I said. "Help me not to be overcome by despair." "**I will,**" he grunted. "**I will help you,**" and taking me by the hand he began to lead me down a pathway.

"**Look here,**" he said, and I glanced to where he was pointing. Just to the right of the pathway the land dropped off into a gully, and far down in the bottom I saw bears of all sizes. Some were dead and some were dying. When I realized what I was seeing, my heart caved in and I began to sob. "**Watch!**" Bear commanded and so I did, trying with all the strength I could muster to calm myself.

As I watched, the bears began to leave their bodies, exiting through the tops of their heads. And as soon as they did this, they were happy. Happier than they had ever been. "We are free!" I heard them cry as they rose upward. "We are free!"

"Bear," I asked, "what does this mean?" I could see and feel the happiness of the now liberated bears, but didn't understand what I was seeing. Was this happiness after leaving their bodies supposed to atone for the suffering they had undergone? If so, I wasn't buying it. That kind of thought smacked of Sunday school teachings, of suffering here on earth in order to have life everlasting in heaven. "Bull shit!" I said.

Bear smiled, an expression of tolerance and understanding on his face. "I don't get it, Bear," I said when I had calmed down a little. Please help me understand." **"Hummmmph,"** he grunted as he nodded his massive head. Then he turned to face me and said, **"Listen to me. I will explain.**

"What you are seeing now is the death of an era, the death of a flawed and destructive way of life. This old way has to die," he said and shook his great head. "But all the suffering!" I cried. "All the suffering of the innocents! How can that be, Bear? How can that be right?"

"It is neither right, nor wrong. It *is*," he growled deep in his throat. **"There is purpose even in this suffering. Mankind has sunk as low as it can sink. Cruelty and immorality have become so commonplace that today evil has free reign. Those bears are happy to die. They have been tortured beyond imagining, and are happy to be freed by death."**

"Oh God, oh God, oh God," I cried, dissolving in tears. "Forgive the horrible, horrible things we have done," I said, praying for forgiveness for the perpetrators, for myself, for all humanity. **"*You* have not done this,"** he said, bringing me up short. **"*You* are not creating suffering for others. Do not include yourself in these evil acts,"** he said. **"This is important."** I looked at him and held my breath, waiting for him to say more, to help me understand what he meant.

"I still don't get it, Bear," I said at last. "What can I do to help?" **"Expand your heart,"** he answered, and I recalled that this was what he had told me earlier. "Okay," I said, "I'll do everything I can to expand my heart—no matter what. I will hold the victims and the perpetrators in love," I promised. "I will, I will."

Bear took me into his huge arms then and as he stroked me with his paws, he rumbled to himself. **"This will pass, finally this too will pass."** I clung to him and burrowed my face into the ruff at his neck, hoping with all my heart that he was right and that 'finally' wouldn't be too far off.

"Expand your heart," he growled and held me with his gaze. **"I will hold you while you do."** "Thank you, Bear," I whispered. "Thank you. I will need you to hold me.

I meant that. I would need his help. Here was my Achilles heel, the place where equanimity deserted me. The abuse of children and animals, the harming of any helpless creature caused me soul pain I could hardly bear. And as the world dove to the pit of the Kali Yuga, the age of destruction, I would many times need to rely on Bear's strength and wisdom. "Please help me to develop these qualities of strength and wisdom myself," I prayed.

"All negativity has its origin in the mind"

Life is for learning; that, after all, is the point of our time here on earth. I knew this was true, at least my brain 'knew' it, but the rest of me sometimes lagged behind. I hadn't been born with a naturally sanguine temperament—easy going I was not. I felt things emotionally and felt them deeply. And each time a new horror struck, it hit me square in the heart. No sooner had Wolf told me to go within my heart and Bear asked me to expand my heart than another catastrophe appeared on the scene.

Wild fires were raging all over Southern California and even though our city was many miles from the nearest conflagration it was difficult for us to breathe because of smoke. Hot air pressed in on us both inside our houses and out. Our homes and cars were covered with ash and the smell of smoke hung on everything. In the grand scheme of things these, of course, were minor inconveniences. Whole communities to the east of us were going up in flames and the mountain town where my friend Mahri lived was surrounded by fire.

I was praying non-stop for the people, animals and plants in the endangered zones, but I decided to go to the Grandmothers to see if there was something else that could be done. "Grandmothers," I said as I entered their circle, "how can we help? Please teach us a practical way to quell these fires.

I figured I might as well speak my mind. "Why beat around the bush?" I said to myself, "the fires are out of control and something has to be done to stop them." The Grandmothers turned to me with a knowing look and said; **"We will show you how to accomplish this with the Net of Light."** Clearly they weren't going to beat around the bush either. **"And the method we will show you,"** they added, **"will work with all manner of disasters."**

"Grandmothers," I said, "I'd also like to know why we're having these fires. So many people and animals are suffering, not to mention the trees, and the entire atmosphere is affected. Why is this happening? I know," I added, "I'm supposed to ask you only one question each time I come to you, but if you can tell me this too, I'd be very grateful."

"We will teach you a bit of this, but we don't want you to focus long on the subject. It is not truly helpful." "Okay, Grandmothers," I nodded. Obviously the 'why' was not as important as the 'how.' Had we not been in the midst of an emergency, I might have begged them to tell me why these things were happening, but because I was eager to get down to business and do some good, I agreed.

"To restore balance to the places where the fires are raging, work with the Net of Light," they said. "First call on us or on any form of the Divine. If you do this before you do anything else," they said, "we will be able to work through you, and you won't become depleted by trying to do this work on your own.

"There is a large concentration of negative energy in the vicinity of the fires, and because of this, the Net of Light's connection to these areas has been weakened. Sometimes negative energy accumulates in a place, and when it does, such spots are prone to disaster of one sort or another. All negativity has its origin in the mind. That is why we always remind you to banish bad thoughts and turn your minds to something good. Right now there is a concentration of negative energy in the vicinity of the fires. This is all we wish to say about 'why' they have occurred.

"To work with the fires or with any disaster, call on us and then invoke the Net of Light. After you have done that, move to the lighted center of your heart, and from there ask us to pour light into the Net. We will use the Net of Light to transmit light to the areas you are thinking of and inundate them with radiance. Each time you do this, we will broadcast light through the Net of Light to assist the afflicted areas."

Smiling sweetly, they studied me and said, "You will perform great service each time you do this. The Net of Light will become fully strengthened in these places and thousands of beings will benefit. The fires will ease," they said and dusted their palms together as if to say, "that is all there is to it." "Thank you, Grandmothers," I said; " I'll communicate what you've said to everyone who wants to help." They smiled again and tipping their heads in what looked like a bow, they said, "We thank you for coming forward to be of service at this time."

I was so taken aback by their thanking *me* for being of service that my hand went up over my mouth. They chuckled at my response and waved me off. Our interview was over. We would talk no more of this now. I had work to do.

As soon as I opened my eyes, I thanked them again and went to the computer where I wrote what they had asked, urging everyone to begin working with the Net of Light to quell the fires. It was gratifying to later hear that the Grandmothers' message had helped people stand steady in the midst of the trauma of the blazes. Others wrote saying the Grandmothers' message helped them not to feel helpless as they watched the news, but rather of service.

E-mails poured in from Australia, Germany, Canada, Switzerland, and from across the United States. This human outpouring touched me greatly, and all I could do was thank those who had so willingly come forward to work with the Net of Light.

"We know your heart."

By the next time I journeyed to the Grandmothers, the days had grown short and we were in the autumn of the year. It had been a while since I'd come to them, not for a message to pass on to others, but just for myself. Perhaps it was the interior feeling that comes over me every autumn or maybe it was just because I missed them. In any case I decided that this time I would go to them just for the pleasure of see-ing them again.

As I rose on my way to the upper world, I found myself flying next to eagle—very close. Our wings overlapped and I said to him, "Oh! It's beautiful," but Eagle, as was his custom, said nothing. We flew on in silence until at last he called out, **"Come!"** and then we began to dive. I happened to glance over my shoulder as we plummeted toward the Grandmothers' valley and saw that I was trailing ribbons behind me, long, silky ribbons of many colors. Laughing delightedly at my tail of beauty, I landed and quickly sat down in front of the Grandmothers.

I flexed my pinions, then really stretched them and said, "Oh, Grandmothers, I'm getting old." I had recognized what a treat it was to be able to fly alongside Eagle, to land with aplomb, and stretch like this. "Here, in this reality," I said to them, "I can fly, I can sit cross-legged, I can dive and do everything, but on earth, inside my body…ugh!" I gri-maced. "It's a different story."

"But anyway, here I am," I said at last, grinning as I realized how happy I was to be with them. We sat smiling at each other until I said, "What would you have me do with your message at this time—for the greatest good of myself and others?" I hadn't consciously thought of this question. I hadn't even come *with* a question—it just popped out of my mouth. After I asked it, I bowed low to them, leaning over so far that my forehead rested on the ground, and then I sat back on my knees and waited for them to speak.

"**Rise up,**" they cried, and lifted their arms in emphasis. I did as they said, and when I came to standing, first I saw, then felt my human self and then saw and felt my eagle head appear. I was a human and a raptor, all at the same time. When I got over my surprise, I said, "Well, here I stand, Grandmothers, however I am. I have come to you and I wait for you to guide me."

They reached over and quickly marked my third eye. "**This is how it should be,**" they said, meaning I *should* wait for their guidance. As I stood quietly, the thought came to tell them of the difficulties I'd been having with people wanting to make money from their work and urging me to make money from it too. But when I looked up at them, I realized that none of this mattered. While I was with the Grandmothers the topic held no charge for me. I would simply let things progress the way they progressed—not hold an opinion or try to determine an outcome of any sort. And when this thought became clear, I watched the issue of money and the Grandmothers' work rise and float out the top of my head, wafting up to heaven like a cloud. There it merged into an army of clouds and I watched them all float past, layer upon layer. And as they floated by, I remembered that all the drama on earth is just this, passing clouds.

While this was going through my mind, the Grandmothers came in close and placed their hands on my heart. As they held me, they said, "**We know your heart.**" "Hummmm," I murmured, and shook my head in wonder. "I'm so glad you do, Grandmothers," I finally replied, "because I don't always know it. Sometimes I become confused by other people's demands and criticisms and when I become unsure of myself, I don't know what to do." "**We know,**" they said, while they patiently continued to hold my heart.

Next they sat down in a circle and pulled me in with them, making me part of it. There we sat, smiling at each other, happy just to be together until at last they said, "**It is beautiful when you have no ambition for our work.**" I looked up and they nodded. They were letting me know they weren't interested in me promoting their work or making money from it and as they held my eyes I saw that they hoped I didn't have this interest either. I was to let go of all ambition for this work. "Yes, Grandmothers," I said, "I agree."

They pointed out that writing more books would be a good thing to do. "**There is more to be shared.**" "Yes, Grandmothers," I replied, "Just guide me as to how to do it." "**Consider this work an enjoyment, a pleasure,**" they said and I sighed in relief. It felt so good to think about writing in this way. I was usually so deadly serious. "It feels so free, Grandmothers," I said, "to entertain the notion of no ambition, none at all."

They smiled and before long we began the 'Oh Grandmothers' song, our heads and upper bodies swaying left and right, left and right, in rhythm while our hands clapped the meter. When we sang the word 'Power,' our hands gestured straight out. The Grandmothers were showing me how to use my hands to evoke power. "Wow! Grandmothers," I exclaimed, "this is fun!"

Next we sang, 'I am one with the heart of the Mother' and they taught me to begin this song with my palms open in my lap in order to receive this gift—that we *are* one with the heart of the Mother. "I am one with the heart of the Mother," I sang, "I am one with the heart of love." **"As you receive in this way and let this truth go deep into yourself,"** they said, **"the truth of this song will also go deep into the earth."**

When we sang the second part, 'I am one with the heart of the Father," the Grandmothers made a circular motion with their hands and then when we sang, 'I am one with God,' we let our hands and arms float upward. After that it was back again to the receptive posture with our hands in our laps for 'I am one with the heart of the Mother.'

"We will send you more songs," they said. **"The peace song is good because it shows what happens as you begin to live our message. Peace, peace peace,"** they sang, **"peace in me, brings peace, peace, peace—peace in my family,"** and as I recalled the rest of the words—"peace in my community, peace in my country, peace on earth…." I said, "Aren't you just beautiful, Grandmothers?" Turning to me, they replied, **"Aren't *you* beautiful? How lovely it is to come together for joy. To visit with one another and come together simply for joy."** I looked up then and understood that they were talking about my being there with them and also talking about those of us on earth coming together to share our love for the Divine.

"In this season of giving, give us the gift of your loving devotion to truth."

Fall passed by quickly, and when it was nearly Christmas I realized I had never spoken with the Grandmothers about the true significance of the holiday season. Most of the time I was so offended by the commercialization of this time of year, I didn't even want to think about it. But for some reason as the holidays approached this time, I began to wonder if there might be another way to deal with them. "Grandmothers," I said, "Forgetting about all the commercialization of this season, what is the actual significance of this time of year?" I was asking, not just for those who celebrate Christmas, but for people of all religions as well.

"**Listen to us,**" they said and quickly I sat down and gave them my attention. "**We will show you.**"

They flew me upward and showed me our planet spinning in space and as I looked down, I saw all the continents, countries, and cultures on earth. And everywhere I looked I noticed that this was a time for people to come together. Gathering together at this time of year was as prevalent in Afghanistan as in England, as true in Columbia as in Canada. No matter what the culture, at this time of year people turned to their loved ones and gave thanks. The holiday might be Christmas, Hanukah, Ramadan, Thanksgiving, Sangranthi or another, but over the next few months, people would come together to celebrate their loving connection to one another and to the Divine. As I stood back and observed these special times, they seemed not so much part of a holiday, as a series of holy days.

"**This *is* a holy time,**" the Grandmothers said, interrupting my thoughts. "**This time of year calls forth love.**" Then they broke into smiles and added, "**Celebrate that. One purpose of this time of year is to share love.**"

Turning to me, they said, "**We know you are distressed by the greed that surfaces at this season. People have always used love as a hook for sales purposes, and in this way the times you're living in are not different from any other. Greed, however, has become more obvious today because the ease of global communication has made it a worldwide phenomena.**

"**But don't worry about that; it is not your job to change the world. It is your job to be yourself and let the love inside your heart shine out. This time of year needs to be held sacred, and you can do that. But you will need to turn to the presence of the Divine within you even more than you usually do.**

"**We say this,**" they explained, "**because as the holidays approach, the energy of buying and selling escalates. Many go into a frenzy of excess, worry, and stress, so it is important to stay awake and not be drawn into those states. If you let yourself be fooled by the siren song of your culture, you will spend another holiday season confused and frustrated. Please don't do that. We promise to hold you** steady throughout the hullabaloo that bombards you during the winter months.

"There are greater things you are called to do now than fall into the trap of buying and selling. Listen to us and turn within, call on us and use this time to re-sanctify your life. In this season of giving, we ask you to give us the gift of loving devotion to truth. If you give this," they raised their heads and held my gaze, "**you will bless your life and the entire earth.**

"This is the only gift we want from you. We ask that you give the gift of loving dedication to the Great Self that you are. Do not let the world talk you into anything less than this," they said. "This gift is needed now."

Their words were just what I needed to hear. Again and again I returned to "This is the only gift we want from you," and the Grandmothers' words held me steady throughout the holiday season. Focusing on their message proved to be surprisingly easy because as it turned out, the gift of truth was the only one I wanted too.

"You are going where you have not gone before."

Soon after this, the New Year came around and I decided to mark the holiday by going to the Grandmothers. I wasn't interested in New Year's resolutions, but I hoped they could give me some guidance for the coming year. As I stepped into their presence, I said, "Grandmothers, we are about to turn to the New Year, but my question is about more than that. Many of us are longing and waiting for the Golden Age," I said, "but we aren't seeing much gold. In fact, now things seem more frightful and frightening than ever. We have been waiting such a long time for the turn to the light, but lately the hope of that seems far away. There are so many tragedies and so much ugliness on our planet today," I said, my voice trailing into sadness. "Grandmothers," I sighed as I pulled myself together, "in spite of all this, I want to know the truth. What should we be prepared for as we move into 2008? What is coming?"

No sooner did I ask the question than there was a whooshing sound as my wings expanded, readying themselves to fly. "**It's coming,**" the Grandmothers said; "**the golden age is coming sooner than you think. The turn is happening now!**" they cried, and I was too overcome to respond. "I've wanted this so much," I said, and as I turned to them they responded by wrapping their wings around me.

"**When you fly,**" they said, "**look straight ahead.**" "What?" I asked, but when I looked down, I was startled to discover that I *was* flying. I hadn't realized I had even taken off, but I was air-born, and now I was looking straight ahead. **"You are moving forward,"** they said, **"not backward. In fact, you seldom even glance down. The impetus of flight carries you forward. Forward,"** they repeated, **"always forward."** And high in the clear air where the colors are piercingly true I repeated to myself, "Forward."

"You are going where you have not gone before," they said. **"We cannot describe what this is like,"** they chuckled, **"because there's nothing to compare it to."** They shook their heads at the human tendency to attempt to explain the inexplicable and said, **"Feel the sensation in your chest and body as you move forward. As you *fly* forward,"** they corrected themselves. **"Move,"** they said, **"is not the right word for to this. It doesn't have enough speed or power. You are racing forward,"** they said and nodded happily, pleased to have found the correct one.

"Enjoy the ride—don't turn back to hang onto things," they said. **"Everything is new now—new. In the past you worried about what people thought of you— if you were accepted, if you fit in. Worried whether or not you had a place in the world,"** they said. **"All of that is going now, and the world is not and will not be the same as it was before. What you may have had in the past, or wanted to have, is now going, gone. You are on your way to somewhere else."** They smiled at my look of bewilderment. **"Enjoy the flight,"** they said, still smiling. **"Enjoy the process, the moment, the now!**

"History," they interjected, **"whether personal or cultural, is nothing but stories. Stories,"** they repeated, **"that is all. But you are here now. Come with us. Come forward."**

They beckoned me and as they did, suddenly I became aware of the speed at which we were traveling. I was a rocket in a brilliant sky, and as I shot through the rarefied air, I realized that history, literature and the old tales I had loved all my life were just that—stories. Some of them contained a nugget of truth and some didn't. They had been formulated by human beings, and compared to what I was experiencing at this moment they were dark and closed. As I soared through the air, I took a good look at these tales and saw all sorts of attachments hanging onto them. Certain cultures were attached to certain stories and each of these was reciprocated by other stories that influenced them and overlapped with them. From my vantage point I now saw them as they were—a mass of repetitive tales, piled in a great heap.

"The movement is forward, it is now!" I said, thrilled by my discovery. "It's in the joy of becoming, of exploring something new," I said and exhaled a big "Ahhh!" As I looked down at the the earth I was able to see the world as it is. This was a new way of being for me and as I glided through the rarified air I was thrilled as one by one the old attachments I had once thought of as 'myself' dropped off me.

"Even asking the question, 'What does the future hold?'" I said, "is thinking in the old way. Implicit in that question is an attachment to what life used to be, to some identity in the past. There's fear in it too," I said. "We worry, 'Am I going to lose that?' and 'What is this going to be like?' We're trying to compare the unknown to something that is no more."

The Grandmothers nodded approval and I broke into laugher. "So the question I asked you, Grandmothers, about what we could expect in the new year can't be answered because we're going now where we've never gone before." **"Yes,"** they said, and opened their wings/arms and took me in. "Then yes, Grandmothers, yes!" I said. "This is what I want too. No more looking back. I am flying forward."

"There is nowhere that God is not."

As thrilled as I was about this forward momentum, I had a hard time staying in it in everyday life. I found I was still affected by other people's pain and confusion. I had always been this way—able to read people and situations—and this 'gift' was not always a blessing. Basically, whether I liked it or not, I was a psychic barometer, and this skill/gift/curse was nothing I had consciously chosen. It was the way I was made.

I had also become a psychic garbage collector—picking up feelings, attitudes and ideas everywhere I went and all this stuff was starting to make me sick; certainly it was getting in the way of joy and freedom. If people were angry, I felt it, if they were sad, my heart ached. Whatever it was, I took it in. One of my dear friends now had cancer and, not only was the disease extremely challenging to her, I was also being challenged. We were trying to build our faith through her experience, but she was doing a better job of it than I. "Sponging up everything around me can't be right," I said to myself. "How helpful can I be to her if I am always 'feeling her pain?' I didn't want to, but I fell into the habit automatically. I decided to go to the Grandmothers for help.

This time as I approached, I saw them standing together beside a lake, and as I came near, they opened their circle so I could step into their midst. "Grandmothers," I said, "I don't think I know how to be in right relationship to others—to animals and people. I'm too affected by their pain and it wears me out," I explained. "Please teach me how to live in right relationship."

Immediately their hands went to my heart and I stood still while they held and nourished me with their touch. Everything in me began to calm, quiet and fill with peace and as this happened we smiled at each other. "Thank you," I whispered and they motioned for me to look at myself and compare the way I looked now to the way I had looked a moment earlier.

In my minds eye I 'saw' both images of myself and noticed that I looked fuller, calmer and softer now. My energy had initially appeared frayed and ragged, a result, the Grandmothers said, of too much reaching out to others. As I thought this over I happened to look down, and lying on the ground beside my feet was what appeared to be tail ends of that energy. Frail and ragged fragments were being blown about by a wind that eventually picked them up and carried them off.

Turning to me the Grandmothers said, **"No more horizontal."** They fixed me with a fierce look then and said, **"Vertical."** "What?" I gasped. But before I could say another word, suddenly my friend Mahri appeared before me and as I studied her, I saw that the Grandmothers were with her and in her. I blinked, looked again, and the Grandmothers *were* her! There she stood, cancer and all, and it was the Grandmothers who gazed at me out of her eyes. I stared at her in amazement. I had been told to "see God in everyone," and had tried to do that, but the idea of God being present in others remained only that to me—an idea. But now I was seeing the truth of this. God was not to be sought in some far off place; God was right here—right now. And here was God, gazing at me out of my friends' eyes.

I had been trying to be helpful to Mahri, trying to fulfill her needs myself and with the combination of her distress and mine, I hadn't been able to see who she really was. "How ridiculous of me!" I laughed, astounded by my own blindness. Mahri's suffering had fooled me into thinking this person with this particular disease was who she was. I had been mesmerized by the drama of the disease and missed who she *really* was.

"Yes," the Grandmothers said, patting my hands and stroking my shoulders. **"You didn't see us in her. You were caught up. playing along with the myth of separation from God. Whenever you were physically with her, you prayed and called on us as if we were far away and needed to ride in from far away to her rescue. As if we weren't already in her and of her,"** they said, good-naturedly slapping me on the back. **"In thinking we were far away, you held your breath,** did everything you could for her and then called on us as if we were off in the distance. No wonder you are tired," they said, shaking their heads. "We were already there," they said as they gazed at me with compassion. "We are there now.

"Don't be so easily fooled by pain and distress," they said and shook their heads again. "It is dramatic, we are aware of that, but we are present in *every* part of life. Don't forget that. We are not only present in the so-called 'good,' they said, emphasizing the word. "We are also present in what you call 'the bad.' We are within everyone at every moment. We are there in the most distressing of human acts. It is a pity that no one remembers this because, if you did, such events would change. Call us forth!" they said with feeling, "call us forth. Don't act as if we are coming from afar. We are right there with you, just waiting to be summoned.

"We recognize what we are asking you to do is difficult for you because for thousands of years you have been conditioned to believe that God is far off somewhere. Moreover, you have been taught that God is good and will therefore only be found where goodness is present, and that pain, suffering and evil actions denote the absence of God. But this is not true," the Grandmothers said, riveting me with a fierce look. "God is good and God is everywhere. There is nowhere God is not. God is never absent," they said, "it is just that God is not always remembered. We are at one with God and as such, we hold and love *all* life at every moment. We are present in the best of times and we are there in the worst of times," they said, firmly nodding. "Call us forth.

"Life is not some sort of macabre mistake," they said, "not a series of random events. *Everything* has its purpose—even cancer, and *We Are There*. Call on us and recognize our presence."

This lesson touched upon the most complex issue of life, one that human beings have wrestled with for years. I wasn't sure I fully understood what the Grandmothers were teaching, but they had given me a small glimpse of the truth. Inside me now a dim bulb glowed. The Grandmothers were urging me to let go of my conditioning, to let go of my dualistic view of life—good and evil, black and white, right and wrong—and embrace *ALL* of life. "There is nowhere God is not," I told myself, "nowhere." And when I spoke those words I realized that when I really *knew* this, I would be free from suffering.

CHAPTER 17

The time has come when together we shall do great things.

"The message drawing you together is an unselfish one."

I had been working hard on the Grandmothers' book and between writing, seeing clients and doing every day tasks, I hadn't had much time for myself. I'd probably been working a little too hard, and now all I could think of was getting into a nice hot tub. On this particular day I'd looked forward to floating in those bubbles for an hour or more, telling myself that as soon as I finished one more section I could climb into the water.

"Ahhhh," I moaned, as I sank beneath the foam, "nothing could feel better than this." And no sooner were the words out of my mouth than the Grandmothers began to talk to me. First I heard them and then I felt their presence, and in the steamy air that filled the bath I was almost able to make out their figures. There was something they wanted to say and they wanted to say it now. "Yes, Grandmothers, yes," I replied, "just let me soak a little," but no matter how I tried to put them off, they wouldn't be denied. They wanted to talk about the Gathering of the Grandmothers coming up in March, and wanted me to hear what they had to say. Finally when I realized their showing up like this was an opportunity that didn't occur every minute, I climbed out of the tub and gave them my full attention.

"Okay, Grandmothers, I'm all yours," I said. "Please tell me, what is the potential for this second Gathering?" I didn't bother asking about the purpose of the event because I knew it was a good one. It was its potential that interested me.

"There is great potential in gatherings like this," they answered, **"great potential. When you come together like this, you come for a good purpose."** Smiling, they added, **"The Divine always supports you when you have a pure and purposeful intention.**

"In the case of the March Gathering, many who are truly dedicated to serving Mother Earth and helping one another are com-

ing with this purpose in mind. The purity of their intention and the energy of your shared commitment will rise far above the facility where you will meet."

"What?" I asked and nodding sagely, they said, "**It will be seen for thousands of miles.**" They pointed behind me and when I turned around, I saw a mountain of light floating above the inn where the Gathering was scheduled to take place. This was what they were referring to.

"**The message drawing you together is an unselfish one, and the quality of unselfishness is rare on earth today,**" they said, shaking their heads. "**Whenever you gather to serve the greater good, the entire universe stands up in support of you.**" Their words thrilled me and when I glanced at them and saw their fierce expressions, tears started in my eyes.

"**Women from around the world who lead Grandmothers groups do so from a pure motive. They want to help,**" they gestured, opening their arms wide. "**They are happy to give and receive love. We rejoice when we see a purpose like this!**" and as they spoke, each Grandmother raised her fist in triumph. "**You have no idea of the happiness in heaven when such a one steps forward and offers herself/himself in service. We are happy to see you come together like this. We are very, very happy,**" they grinned and by this time tears were running down my cheeks.

"**There will be more and more gatherings like this one—both large and small. The time has come for the loving, holding force of the Feminine Principle to step forward and be recognized. To be recognized and honored,**" they emphasized.

"**Life on earth needs its Mother, and at last She has come. The work you are doing is ushering Her in. We rejoice in you and with you.**

"**We ask you to feel our presence whenever you gather like this,**" and I understood that they were speaking through me to everyone. "**We love you deeply,**" they continued, "**and take joy in working with and through you. We ask you to take this same joy in yourselves, to own this joy and live in it.**" Then turning to me, their faces wreathed in smiles, they said, "**The time has come when together we shall do great things.**

"**We are delighted that so many of you have decided to come along on the ride with us,**" they laughed. "**The time is now.**" Then each Grandmother crooked a finger, threw back her head and together they cried, "**Let's go!**

Eighty women and two men came to the second Gathering of the

Grandmothers, arriving from across the United States and from as far away as the Netherlands and the Gathering was as the Grandmothers had said it would be. We shared Grandmothers' stories, learned how to call on them instantaneously, and grew our commitment to spreading their message. We danced, sang, and plumbed the depth of our beings. There was joy, tears, fun, and a deep bonding with one another and with the Grandmothers. And when it was all over, we didn't want to go home.

"You will not find unselfish behavior. Stop looking for it."

After the Gathering was over I realized how much I missed having like-minded people around me. It had been wonderful to be with those who understood and fully supported this work and after they left I was again on my own. "I need to get into the world more," I said to myself, "I'm by myself too much. I'm so isolated by my focus on the Grandmothers' message and working on the book all the time, I probably need to mix more in the 'real' world. It's not the same as being with people who are engaged in the same work or purpose," I grudgingly admitted, "but getting out into the world more might do me good."

Around this time I began to be barraged by people offering to promote, advertise or in some way expose the Grandmothers' work to a larger public. For some reason this stuff was flooding my e-mail and I didn't know what to make of it. Having been raised with the dictum "There is no free lunch," I tended to observe offers like these with a jaundiced eye. However, one person who contacted me didn't sound like a salesperson but actually seemed sincere. She knew about the Grandmothers' work, had been receiving their newsletter for a while, and was offering to help get their message into the world.

She introduced herself as a founder of an organization formed to connect humanitarian groups to one another and sent me to their website. I took a look at it, but wasn't clear on what they did, or how one worked with them. However, her group was holding a conference in Los Angeles in a few weeks, lots of famous people were going to speak, and she invited me to come and be her guest. I figured, why not? Just by listening to the speakers I would learn something and I could also get a better understanding of her organization. Three or four of the speakers were stars in the new thought movement and just hearing them would be worth the trip. Besides, this would get me into the world and out of my isolation.

I drove to the conference and was greeted with a great deal of enthusiasm. Several hundred participants were there and the first thing I noticed was that a lot of them looked like aging hippies. "Oh well," I said to myself, "this is L.A. after all," and sat down to listen. The main leaders of the movement were introduced next but I noticed the woman who had invited me wasn't one of them. They were all men and each man was addressed by his first and last name, while the women who ran the conference were introduced with one name only—and what names they were: "Sparkle, Elfin" and a few others. I started to squirm.

I made myself sit still, however, to listen to the founder of the organization because by now I *really* wanted to know what this group was about. Besides, I reminded myself, I had decided to get out into the world and this was my first foray. I would be patient.

The founder began to wax eloquent about the humanitarian "vibes" of his organization, and, in line with this, he hugged everyone who came onstage. But something about him didn't feel right to me. There was dissonance with his words and body language. I was puzzling this over when I noticed my stomach tensing up. "What?" I wondered was this? and then I called on the Grandmothers and the holy man, asking them to surround me. By this time I was so uncomfortable that I called on Bear and Wolf too and as soon as I felt the presence of my teachers, I felt safer and not so squirmy. But I still couldn't figure out what it was that was 'off' about this presentation. Finally I asked my teachers to let me view the speaker through their eyes.

No sooner did I make my request than I saw him surrounded by swirling, dizzying energy. Clouds veiled, unveiled, and then veiled him again while his energy swirled erratically. It seemed to converge on itself and then spin outward and ricochet off the walls of the room. Nothing was steady and nothing was smooth. In fact the experience was so jarring that *I* started to get dizzy.

After he hugged a few more people, he let slip a few words that made my jaw drop. Quickly I nudged a young man in front of me who had come with his father and asked him if he knew anything about the conference. He obligingly told me the purpose of the conference was to earn money for the participants, by inviting folks (like me) who would pay a small monthly fee to have their businesses promoted by this organization. People like me would then 'invite' others to join the organization so everyone 'up the line' would make money. The woman who invited me to the conference knew that the Grandmothers wasn't a business, but she surmised that I was in contact with large numbers of women and hoped I would pull them all in. This had made me attractive to her.

My mind reeled as I took this in and then it came to me that the big name speakers who were appearing here were basically hired guns—put on the program to give it legitimacy and attract people like me. I could hardly believe what I was seeing, but as I sat in the midst of these new age charlatans, my stomach did a few flip-flops and as soon as I got my bearings I said a hurried goodbye and flew out the door.

Later that evening as I was re-running the day's happenings over in my mind, I walked into a door jam and broke my toe. I hadn't been looking where I was going. "Hummm," I mused, "not looking where I am going...." And that night I dreamed of Bear—an illusive, disturbing dream. When I woke up all I could remember was that he had wanted to tell me something.

I wasted no time in journeying to him that morning and asking why he had come. **"To wake you,"** he said. **"To wake you once and for all."** "Okay, Bear," I said as I studied his dear face, so full of concern. "I'm willing to awaken, but I'm sorry to tell you I didn't even know I was asleep."

He began to growl, growing more and more fierce until he began to fling his head from side to side. His roars were frightening, growing ever more wild, and in his rage I watched him snap his jaws at things I couldn't see. "Bear," I gasped, shaken by his performance, "why did you come to me? Please tell me." **"Wake up and be alert,"** he growled as he continued to scan the area around us. "Okay, Bear, okay. I agree," I said, "but awake to what? What is going on?"

"You do not understand the way things work on earth," he said and narrowed his eyes. **"You are innocent, and now you must be awake, not innocently asleep. People have their own agendas,"** he said as he angrily paced up and down, **"and you are always surprised by this—even shocked by it. Don't be. They seek their own ends. They want things to be comfortable for them. They are not unselfish. Just know that,"** he grunted. **"It is true for almost everyone. You will not find unselfish behavior,"** he said and stomped the ground for emphasis. **"Stop looking for it."**

I was concerned that he was so upset—and so adamant. "Bear," I said as I studied his form that had over the years become precious to me, "this is also true for me. I seek my own needs too. I'm no different from anyone else." **"Yes,"** he said, **"Yes, you do, but there is a difference. Not a great difference."** He made a rumbling noise in his throat (was he laughing?), **"but a *medium* difference,"** he nodded, pleased with himself for finding the word he sought.

"You have a certain confidence in your connection with the

Divine and you count on that. You know you were born to teach what you have been given and that the teachings will be provided to you to pass on to others. Trust the things you know and keep your eyes there. The more you do that, the less you will find yourself seeking after your own needs," he said, and as he spoke, he swayed his great body from side to side. **"You won't have to seek your own needs,"** he grunted, **"they will be provided for you. Stay tuned to what you know is true. That,"** he dipped his great head, **"is a good way to avoid selfishness.**

"As to what you experienced yesterday at that conference, observe and take heed. Watch out for such people, and trust your instincts. People like this are everywhere. They will approach you over and over again. You don't have to respond to them," he shook his head and grunted. **"Unless you see value in what they're offering, let them pass you by.**

"Go forward with the Grandmothers' work. Learn more and take a new road. Come with me, come with the Grandmothers, and we will teach you. Didn't we teach you yesterday at that abominable meeting?" he growled. "Yes, yes," I nodded, "you sure did. As soon as I asked to see through your eyes I saw the clouds and veils floating around that speaker and immediately understood that not only was he confused, he was confusing everybody else." **"We will teach you like this all the time,"** he said. **"Just ask."** "I will, Bear," I said. And I meant it. Now I understood that the so-called "isolation" brought on by my absorption in the Grandmothers' work was not something to be avoided, but embraced. My experience at that conference cured me of any desire "to get out into the world."

"Let the river of time flow by while you watch."

In the next few days I thought of Bear's words many times. Suddenly and seemingly from out of nowhere I began to encounter strange and hurtful behavior where I had least expected it. People I had thought of as friends and had worked with for months suddenly became angry with me and withdrew their friendship and support. When I realized something was off and asked what was wrong, no one would tell me. They made a few cutting remarks, withdrew, and that was that. It turned out to be quite a week—a broken toe, deception in the world 'out there' and anger and jealousy from those I had trusted. I kept seeing that image of Bear raging and snapping at invisible (to me) things around him, things I had not seen, but he did.

Being flooded by so much drama in such a short time was making me aware that, no matter what we call them or how we dress them up, most of us are still run by our baser instincts. The ego still holds sway, even in so-called 'evolved" persons. And as I thought about this I of course began to wonder about myself. Are my motives pure? I asked myself. Am I also controlled by jealousy and competition? I wasn't aware of it, but I bet the people who were trying to use and control me weren't aware of it in themselves either. Clearly it was time for me to go back to the Grandmothers.

The next morning I journeyed to them and as I stood before them they gazed at me with infinite patience. "Grandmothers," I said, "our world is in peril and quite possibly our souls too. We are trying to lift up, expand and elevate in order to be proper vehicles for the Golden Age. There's lots of talk about transformation and awakening to our higher selves, about moving to a new level of consciousness, but I'm not seeing it happening. How?" I asked. "How can we (me too) get beyond the pull of our egos? How can we go beyond our not-so-lovely human qualities?"

"You are born of love," they responded. **"You are born in love. You come from the Divine and the Divine is *only* love. This is who you are. Anything less than this is a lie,"** they stated. **"Stand back and watch,"** they said and I looked at them in surprise. **"When you become confused, when you find yourself bombarded by others needs and demands or by your own ego's needs and demands, simply step back and watch.**

"Do nothing at a time like that. Let the river of time flow by while you watch. Simply watch," they repeated, nodding slowly. **"The ego wants to engage. It wants to do, do, do! Be wary of this hurried desire to 'do.' Most of the time it is coming from the ego. There is a certain agitation in the desire to 'do' that is one of its trademarks."**

"The Divine moves from within you and it moves with great purpose. When the desire to 'do' comes from the Divine, you will be *drawn* to something. You may experience this as 'being guided," they said. **"When the Divine is 'at the wheel' as you say, there will be no effort involved.**

"We are watching agitation swirl about you now," the Grand-mothers said, **"as individual egos try to have their way with you. They seek to feed only themselves and in their greed, they push against you and push against others. Expect this sort of behavior. This is where the world lives.**

"You are involved in our mission," they said and gave me a serious look. **"You are working with us to reach beyond this way of living, to bring heaven to earth as you say. This is a worthy goal and together we will reach it, but never be deluded that heaven is here already. It isn't,"** they said and stood with their arms folded across their breasts. **"Don't be fooled by sweet words and new age jargon. Don't pay attention to psychic 'interpretations' and modern day prophecies. Knowingly or unknowingly almost everyone is still controlled by his or her ego.**

"Trust your radar," they said. I had heard this so many times, from them and from Bear that it made me wonder. I thought I had trusted my radar, but hearing them say it again made me ask myself, "Do I?" I looked up then and they shook their heads 'no'. "Well, that's it then," I said. "I guess I don't. Okay, Grandmothers, then why *don't* I trust it?"

"Pooh!" they answered in disgust. **"Why, why, why?"** they waved their hands in dismissal. **"Forget the why. We are telling you to trust your instincts, so pay attention to what we are saying, and then *do* it."** "Okay, Grandmothers," I gulped, "I will."

"You must never delude yourself that a particular culture, a specific group of friends, or an individual is truly 'good,' and free from ego because it isn't and they aren't. Heaven is still to come, so expect jealousy, confusion and devious behavior. These will occur. You are too naïve." "Yes, Grandmothers," I replied, "I know it." I was naïve. After all the years and disappointments I'd lived through, I still looked for and expected the good from everyone. In some ways I was like a child.

"Each time you have encountered difficulties with people it is because you believed they were more than they were." "Yes, Grandmothers," I repeated, determined to hear them out. **"Continue to spread our message, continue to love everyone, but face and accept life the way it is. For someone like you, earth can be a lonely place. You are ever ready to love, but most people are not like that. Their hearts are not yet open.**

"Continue to teach, they repeated. **"Do this in person and do it through writing. This is your part to play in turning the dark on earth to light. Do your part in this way, but don't look to others for support. Most people have *no* understanding of what you are doing,"** they said, and as I listened, I shook my head and sighed—an enormous sigh.

They were telling me the truth. Sometimes even I didn't understand why I continued to do this work with the Grandmothers. I often felt that I was moving blindly through life, being led along to somewhere.

I simply followed wherever the Grandmothers and the teaching spirits led me. "So," I mumbled to myself, "if *I* don't always understand where they are taking me and why, is it any wonder others don't either?"

I was aware that many of the women involved in the Grandmothers' work were struggling just as I was to hold to a consistent position of love. Like young trees, not yet sturdy oaks, we stood tall and taller as time went on, but we still bent with the winds that blew over us at times. All I could do at difficult times like these was to look to my own roots, deepen and expand them; then no gale, or storm of criticism could knock me over.

I didn't realize how engrossed I'd become in my own thoughts until the Grandmothers interrupted my reverie. **"This 'transformation' of the world we are telling you about will take time, and everyone is in a big hurry for it to happen *NOW*. Many times we stand back and watch all of you rushing about,"** they said and shook their heads in bewilderment. **"It is almost funny. Such tearing around is fueled by the ego,"** they said. **"Everyone is hurrying to get this group together, to pray or meditate together at a certain hour, visualize this, or chant that. Many of these activities, although well intentioned, are merely attempts to manipulate the cosmos in some way. This is utter nonsense,"** they said and wrinkled their noses in disgust. **"The cosmos cannot be manipulated by humanity's puny efforts. When you pray and meditate, let your own agenda go and open your heart to the Divine. The cosmos runs on and responds to love—pure love and nothing else,"** they said. **"And when you go into a frenzy of activity, where is the smooth and steady river of love then?**

"Slow down," they said, peering at me over the tips of their noses. **"Go slow and go deep. Instead of chasing after an experience or trying so hard to 'make a difference,'"** they shook their heads in disbelief, **"stop all that and delve deeply into yourself. When you move into the reservoir of yin energy within yourself, everything in your life will change. You will know when you have reached this reservoir by its calm, steady feel.**

"Drop into yourself and drop in deep. Dive into the wellspring of wisdom and peace inside you. If only one of you did this, the world would change. You want to know how to bring heaven to earth?" they asked, as they arched their brows and placed their fisted hands on their hips. **"Well,"** they said, **"this is how."**

This visit to the Grandmothers had a sobering affect on me, making me realize that even after my years of experience with them, I still had a tendency to yield to the energy of yang. Although these days I seldom wound myself into a frenzy of activity, I wasn't quiet and still either. "It's yang," I told myself, "the yang conditioning of my life and the genetic tendency toward quick movement that comes from my family." Nonetheless, I needed to slow down more, dive to the depths the Grandmothers were urging me to visit, and now I was motivated to do it. I made a vow to 'go slow and go deep' and for a time, I set aside time each day to visit the Grandmothers, sit with them and drop deep into myself. And of course they were right. It helped.

"Our message is universal and unlimited."

Around this time I asked the Grandmothers for a simple way people could use to access them. For the past two years I had taught the shamanic method, but had found shamanic journeying to be too difficult for some. When I asked the Grandmothers for an easy way to reach them, they quickly agreed and directed me to include it in the new book. **"This method will help many, allowing them to form a stronger relationship with us. The Shamanic journeying method is fine for those who wish to use it, but it is not for everyone,"** they said and gave me a meaningful look. "Yes, Grandmothers, I know what you mean. Shamanism is too far 'out there' for some," I said, "and frightens them."

"To reach us, you no longer need to use that method," they said, **"unless of course you want to. By this time so many people have come to the Grandmothers that the road to us is well paved. You no longer need to chop your way through the jungle with a machete,"** they laughed. **"The road has become a super highway."**

For over twelve years I had shared their message and passed the Grandmothers' Empowerment on to others. I'd also and written *A Call to Power: the Grandmothers Speak* and by now so many people had been drawn to these wise women that there were thousands around the world with a personal relationship with them. When the Grandmothers first appeared they told me they were "very accessible." They were again demonstrating how true this was.

"Grandmothers," I asked, "how would you like me to describe this simpler way of reaching you?" **"Pass on what we will show you now; use the Circle of Stones."** As soon as they pronounce "Circle of Stones" they took their places on the ground, each Grandmother sitting with an opalescent stone before her. The stone, perfectly smooth and ovoid, was imbedded in the earth, rising gently, until at its highest point it stood eight to ten inches above ground. Eighteen to twenty inches in length, about twelve inches across, each stone glowed with a pinkish-grey color.

The Grandmothers sat quietly for a moment, then they nodded to me and said, **"This circle is a sacred space, an opening to the great below and the great above."** As I thought about what they were saying, they added, **"From this space let *us* call the spirits that you need to you. We will do that."** Then they motioned me to enter their circle.

As I took my place in the center I became aware that this point did in fact open both upward and downward. From here I could easily enter both the lower and the upper world, exploring everything in non-ordinary reality. I eyed the Grandmothers questioningly and they said, **"There is no need to go through the barriers between the levels of the upper world or lower world now. We read your heart,"** they said, **"and if your intention is pure, we will speed your journey.**

"This way of working will be easier for many people, because they will not have to perform the work alone. They can journey to different levels of reality by themselves if they so desire, but when they use the method we are giving you, they will journey under our guidance and protection. We will show them the way and help them get to where they want to go.

"The old way of journeying was about being a warrior and proving yourself worthy. This way of working is not like that. For this method, you work *with* us and let yourself be guided. You will find that there are fewer ego entanglements in this way of working."

"I see that, Grandmothers. I can already see that. By working like this we'll be automatically working with the Divine. Ummm…" I mused, "I get it. With this method we will work both *with* and *for* the Divine.

"Once you have given your heart to us or to any form of the Divine, committing yourself to love and service, we will protect and guide you. Always," they said. **"In this world and in *every* world,"** they emphasized. **"There is no need to go off on your own now and slay dragons. It's not necessary to work in that way, not when you are with us."**

Then, turning the full power of their gazes on me, they said, **"Feel your place as you stand in this circle with us. We will work with you; you will work with us. And remember,"** they said, **"that present as we work together are all forms of the Divine."** I looked up when they said this and as I gazed at them I saw figures hovering over the Grandmothers, enormous energy structures seemed to tower over the circle.

The figures were vague, so I wasn't able to recognize any of them, but they emanated tremendous power and love.

"**You are an integral part of this circle,**" the Grandmothers said and when I looked at them, they said, "**teach others about this. The fact that you are *part* of this circle, not separate from it, is important,**" they said. "**There must be no more separation now, no more worship of the Divine, but instead, mergence. Mergence,**" they repeated. "**You are one with us. You are one with the Divine. This is true for each one who chooses to work with us. Teach this.**

"**The moment you step into our circle you will begin an adventure, an experience, a direct teaching,**" they said. "**Once you step into the circle, you will become the focus of the entire circle and your questions will be answered.**"

I nodded, realizing that though much of what I would do when I used this method would be similar to classic shamanism (one question per journey, for instance), in this case, right from the start, I would be working with the Grandmothers. "**Yes,**" they said, reading my mind, "**ask only one question when you step into our circle. And just as in shamanism, after you ask your question, everything you hear, see and experience will be in response to what you asked. Pay attention to what happens to you after you ask and do not stray from your question.**" "Yes, Grandmothers," I said, "I understand." This would be a much faster and easier way of working. "**Yes,**" they nodded, again responding to my unspoken thought.

"Okay, I'll try it," I thought, and stepping carefully between two of the Grandmothers, I walked into the middle of their circle. Twelve expectant women waited, their attention trained on me. I took a deep breath then and said, "Grandmothers, you have brought us a long way on this journey with you. Your message is spreading everywhere and there are many who are eager to work with you. As we go forward at this moment in time," I asked, "what would you like to tell us?"

"**Our message is universal and unlimited. It is not confined to any one arena, religion or culture, so of course it is spreading over the earth. We are present everywhere,**" they said, holding their heads high. "**We love and embrace all people, animals, and forms of life. We have told you many times that now is the time for the return of the Great Mother.**" Then they nodded and with great dignity pronounced, "**We, the Grand Mothers, have come to usher her in.**

"**Do not waste time dilly-dallying along the edges of life. You have done that for far too long.**" I looked up in surprise. "Dilly-dallying? Me?" I wouldn't have described myself that way. What did they mean? But they waved their hands in dismissal and said, **"We are not speaking only to you, but to everyone."** But from the look in their eyes I could tell that this statement was as much for me as for everyone.

"It is time to plunge into life," they said, gesturing emphatically, **"to commit yourself once and for all to love, and to one another. You are one family after all,"** they said, smiling happily, **"and since we are the Grand Mothers of this family, we want to see our family happy."**

Then they rose to their full height and, swaying first to the left and then to the right, they loomed over me. **"We have told you that your potential is great. Humanity's potential for happiness is also great,"** they added, **"and the two are connected. To reach a high level of happiness yourself, you must fulfill the potential you were born for,"** they said. **"Each person who does this,"** they added, **"increases the pool of happiness for the family of life.**

"All you need to accomplish this feat (living up to your potential) is to begin to think like a family member—like a member of *our* **family. For instance, ask us, what can I do for my family? We will tell you,"** they nodded, their eyebrows arched, their hands on their hips. **"Simply ask and once you have, sit quietly and listen. Listen to what we communicate at that moment, observe whatever we show you, and most of all,"** they said, **"listen to the way things happen.**

"As the Council of the Grandmothers we are not separate from the world," they explained. **"We infuse the world. And because we are present within everyone and everything, we communicate with you through the life around you. We are in the trees in your garden, we are present in the food you grow, and we look out at you from the eyes of your cat or dog. We infuse** *everything*," they said, smiling with satisfaction.

"Listen to the wind," they said, **"pay attention to who telephones and when they call, notice the birds that appear before you, observe whomever or whatever crosses your path, and be open to the messages of so-called strangers. We, the Grandmothers,"** they said, drawing themselves to their full height, **"make up the pattern of life on earth. We are within and around everything in this pattern and you too are part of the pattern."** They regarded me in silence for a minute or more and then repeated, **"Listen to the way things happen."**

Their words echoed in my mind. They had said them before. "Listen to the way things happen," meant pay attention to events as they occur—to the events themselves and to their sequence. They were again confirming that ours is not a random universe, nor is anything in our lives random. Purpose and meaning underlie everything. I was certainly more aware of this truth today than I had been in the past, but whenever I got caught up in the daily dramas of life, I forgot it.

"We promise if you ask us for help, we will give it. We will guide you. If you let us help you and begin to give your life over to love, you will know a joy you never thought possible. It is your birthright to live in joy," they said and gave me a fierce look. Then they slowly shook their heads, chuckled to themselves and said, **"Isn't it time you claimed your birthright?"** And gazing at me with eyes full of love they said, **"We are waiting for you."**

"Thank you, Grandmothers," I said and bowed. Then I turned and quickly stepped out of their circle. "Oh my gosh!" I whispered to myself, "they were right about this work. That really was easy."

"Cast the Net of Light to those who want to serve and don't know how."

Many times in the next few weeks I reflected on the Grandmothers saying, **"We are waiting for you."** I recalled the look they had given me when they said this and realized they hadn't been speaking in a general manner. They were waiting for me. There was something they wanted to give or teach me. By this time I knew I would be learning from the Grandmothers for the rest of my life, but after that look I began to wonder what they had in mind for me *now*.

The next time I went to them I again used the Stone Circle, and when I came into their midst, I asked, "Grandmothers, is there something you would like to teach me? Something you want me to know at this time?" And as soon as I asked, before me appeared the Net of Light. **"Yes,"** they said. **"Listen to us. This is important."** I leaned forward—not wanting to miss a word.

"There are those on earth at this time who long to serve the highest good, but don't know how. Many of them don't have a way of connecting with the Divine. They have become alienated by the strictures of one religion or another and, cut off, they haven't been able to find their way to the Divine. They are full of compassion," they said, shaking *their* heads in compassion, **"they see the suffering of Mother Earth, the suffering of life on this planet, and they want to help.**

"We ask you to begin now to cast the Net of Light to those who want to serve and don't know how," they said, **"so they too can take part in lifting and blessing the planet. At this point they cannot find their way to the Divine,"** they said and for a moment they looked terribly distressed. Then they shook their heads, took in a breath, and said,

"The Net of Light will take them to the pathway that is appropriate for them."

"Yes, Grandmothers," I responded. I was well aware of the pain carried by people who longed for God. For years I had been one of them. And now, much later, when I looked back on my life, I saw how the Divine had held me at every stage of my journey. I had been pulled along on what had seemed to me at the time to be a painfully circuitous route, but blind as I had been then, I had still been led to the Source. However, I had never before thought of the Net of Light as a vehicle for helping others find that same Source.

Early on the Grandmothers asked that each time we held a Grandmothers' meeting, we cast the Net of Light to those who didn't know of the divine connection we all share. And for the past twelve years everyone involved with the Grandmothers had followed their guidance, casting the Net to those who were suffering whether physically, emotionally, mentally and/or spiritually. We also cast to the animal, plant and mineral kingdoms and finished this meditation by praying, "*May everyone in all the worlds be happy.*"

Now they were asking us to broaden our reach. **"Give everyone the opportunity to come along on the ride with us,"** they said and chuckled, **"It's time for reinforcements."** Many were now seeking access to the Divine, and the Net of light would illumine their path.

Shortly after the Grandmothers gave me this guidance, they showed up in the middle of the night. I'd awakened around two a.m. and, tossing and turning, unable to get back to sleep, I decided I would lie there and work with the Net of Light—casting especially to those who longed for a way to reach the Divine. As I lay there I was following the Grandmothers' directions, casting to those who were suffering and those who longed to serve, but didn't know how when suddenly they appeared.

"This is all well and good," they said as they hovered above me, **"but what about you?"** "What about me?" I asked, perplexed. "What do you mean, Grandmothers?" **"Humph,"** they grunted, and pointed, showing me that the Net of Light was also inside my body. The Net was penetrating everything and everyone on the planet, including me. Oh," I gasped, thrilled by the sight. **"Let the Net of Light support you too. Go ahead,"** they urged, **"move inside your body and experience the Net. It's right there within your organs."**

I hesitated a moment, but then did as they asked. First I felt myself holding and being held by the Net of Light and then the Net began to rock me until soon I was floating in its expanse. It was the strangest thing. On one level it was I who was doing the rocking and yet I was the one being rocked. I was held and supported by the Net of Light and at the same time I *was* the Net of Light. "How is this possible?" I asked, shaking my head in wonder, but at that moment my body effervesced and suddenly I was as aware of the pattern of beauty that was flowing within my own bloodstream as I was of the pattern of starlight in the sky above my head. Rocked and rocking, held and holding—I was the Net of Light and the Net of Light was *me*!

For what seemed a long time, I was carried by a wave out into the cosmos and then drawn back into my body—pulled out and pushed back in by a surging sea of light. Out and in again, out and in, until at last the vibrating sensation created by this movement wore off and I lay there, glowing in my bed. Before I knew it I was sound asleep, but when I awoke in morning I could still feel that rocking, surging motion.

This experience showed me a greater depth to the Net of Light than I had previously known. The Grandmothers had many times said, **"You have no idea of the greatness of the Net of Light."** That night I glimpsed it.

Since then I have many times invited the Net of Light to reveal itself within my body, consciously moving into it and seeking the rocking, blissful movement I felt that night. Several times I sensed the rhythm of it and twice I felt it a bit, but never like that first time. I know the Net of Light is lying within the cell beds of my body, waiting for me, but I'm not able to summon it with my will alone. Some day I may again experience its bliss or I may not, but I will never forget what it was like to be so intimately at one with it. Now I know what it means to have every cell in my body held in love. *We are the Net of Light.*

"Call your tribe."

A few weeks after this I had a dream of being chased by a wolf. Frantically I ran into a house and slammed the door before he could enter, but as I did that, I also slammed it on my golden retriever. Was my dog safe? If I opened the door would I be safe? Would the dog come in or the wolf? Then I got confused between which animal was the wolf and which was my dog. Feeling torn between loving the dog and fearing the wolf created so much tension in me that I woke up and as soon as I opened my eyes, I realized, "Ah, Wolf, Wolf has come."

Lying in bed in an almost, but not quite dream state, I asked him why he had come. "Wolf, what do you want?" I asked, but he only smiled his lazy smile and said nothing. I would have to make a special effort to go to him to find out. So the first thing in the morning I did that and, to show him the seriousness of my intention, I even denied myself breakfast.

"Wolf," I said as soon as I saw his face, "you came in my dream last night and I barred the door to you. I'm not going to do that now. I just want to know why you came." He remained silent, looking me over, studying me, so I asked again, "Wolf, why did you come?" **"I miss you,"** he said and I stood dumbfounded. I didn't know what to say to that. Now and then I missed him too, but I couldn't truthfully say I had been longing for him. I sighed as I took in his words and replied, "That's wonderful, Wolf," and after a pause asked, "Did you come for any other reason, besides missing me?"

He caught my eye then and we both broke into laughter. He had been teasing, saying he'd come because he missed me. We leaned our heads together, chortling over his joke, and sat that way for a while, enjoying our camaraderie. "We've put our heads together," I said to him but when he didn't respond, again I asked, "Wolf, why did you come?"

Now he began to growl low in his throat. But instead of being frightened by his growl, for some reason I liked it and found myself falling into harmony with him and the growling—my body naturally entraining with his. I loved that rumbling vibration, relished the way it felt inside me. Then with no warning he tilted his head back and began to howl. Surprisingly I liked this even more than the growling, and my response to both of his actions took me by surprise.

As he continued to howl, I realized he was calling other wolves and in a moment, they raced in to join us. A pack loped in, gathered round, sniffed at both of us, and sat down on their haunches and waited. I surveyed them as they hunkered there, and observed myself too. As I watched these enormous, dog-like creatures, I began to recall terrifying stories I'd read of roaming wolf packs—attacking travelers in Siberia, attacking farms in Iraq. To still my wayward mind and prevent myself from going into panic, I reminded myself that this, after all, was non-ordinary reality and at last I heard one of the wolves say, **"council of wolves."**

"We have come to counsel you," they announced in one voice and when I heard this, I sat up very straight. "Thank you, thank you," I said, "I want to hear your counsel," and in my words I heard a depth of feeling. I *did* want to hear their counsel. The wolves nodded in understanding, kept their eyes on me and silently communicated that because I was now no longer so tightly wound, not trying so hard to control everything in my life, they could speak to me like this. Their communication somehow made sense to me and again I said, "Thank you, thank you. I'm ready," and leaned forward expectantly, eager to hear what they had to say.

When nothing happened and several minutes had gone by, I began to wonder if perhaps I'd misunderstood them. Maybe they hadn't meant they were going to talk to me *now*. Maybe they were going to make an appointment for later. My mind began to race in circles until one of them looked directly into my eyes and said, **"Call your tribe."** I was so taken aback by this that it took me a minute to respond. Finally I stammered, "Uh…uh, please explain. What does this mean—call my tribe?" And while I waited for an answer, for some reason I recalled what had taken place in our Grandmothers' study circle the day before.

We had committed to working with the Net of Light as the Grandmothers had asked us to do, casting the Net to people who were disturbed by the suffering on earth and wanted to be of service, but didn't know how. As soon as I remembered this, the wolves said, **"Call them."** They were confirming what the group had decided. "Yes, yes," I replied to the pack, "we have decided to focus on this."

"*You* call them," Wolf said, giving me a stern look and I realized that not only was the group to do this work, but I was to do something too. "I will," I said, and wondered what he had in mind. But he continued to hold my eyes with that fierce look until I finally got so nervous that I said, "I'll call them. Okay," I said as he continued to stare, "I'll call them right now."

I stood up and said, "Come, my tribe. Come," and as I spoke I heard the tone of my voice and was surprised to hear so little power in it. "What's this?" I thought. "Come," I said, again wondering why I sounded so weak. "Wait no longer," I said. "Come now," I tried again. "You are needed…. Now!" I stated at last and this time I heard power. When the thought came that these people were *needed* to do this work and needed to do it now, I gained strength and so did my voice. "Hold the Net of Light for the earth," I called to my tribe, "and let it hold you."

Later, when I played back this part of the session, I heard all hell break loose. The dogs began to bark, a garbage truck clanked and rumbled on the street, and I heard the front door slam. "I forgot my wallet," my husband shouted up the stairs and I laughed out loud on the tape. But after a few seconds everything subsided and again all I heard was my steady breathing as I refocused on being with Wolf and the pack. And all the while this was taking place my listening self was thinking, "Wow, look at that. I can be in two places at once. I can be with Wolf in non-ordinary reality and with the every day things too. One foot in each reality at the same time."

After a brief silence I heard myself speak to my tribe again, saying, "You are sorely, sorely needed. Come now!" I commanded. There was a pause after that and then I said, "Wolf, how shall I do this? Please give me practical guidance. How shall I call them?" **"Let the call go forth,"** the wolves cried in unison and for some reason their response irritated me. (I think it was the association I held with the prophetic language they used. It seemed to always set me off.) "Yes, yes, yes," I replied, "but get real. Get specific," I said. "How?" I asked. "How?" I repeated.

"Newsletter," they answered. "Yes," I replied, "I'll put it in the next Grandmothers' newsletter, but what else?" **"Article about the Net of Light,"** they answered, **"time to hold it, being called to hold it."** I took in a breath and released it with a huff. This was *not* something I looked forward to; I didn't like writing articles. **"Send it to all the contacts you have,"** they said, **"and notify the Grandmothers' group leaders."** "Yes," I said at last and sighed in resignation, "I'll do it," letting out a hiss and, at the same time, letting go of my resistance to taking on this project.

"What do I tell them when I call them?" I asked. **"Tell them the time is NOW!"** Wolf answered, baring his teeth. "Okay, okay," I meekly replied and after this there was only silence. Finally he spoke again. **"More are needed to do this work of holding the Net of Light. If they feel a resonance to it, if there is a longing within them, then they are needed to serve. Tell them to call on the Net of Light and take their place on it. Ask them to hold it, to hold their place on the Net and from this place, cast it farther. Wherever there is suffering,"** he said, **"and wherever there are people who long to serve and don't know how—cast to them,"**

"Oh,..." I exclaimed. When he said **"Cast to them,"** Jesus' words, "I will make you fishers of men," came to me. Wolf too was asking us to become fishers of men and women. **"When you go into despair about the daily news,"** he said, **"like the recent tragedies in Africa, then cast, cast, cast. To all!"** he said and then he turned away from me and sauntered over to sit with his pack.

I took a step backwards and as I surveyed the gathered wolves I felt the presence of the aggregate wolf heart—the power of it and the power *in* it. The bravery and extraordinary nobility of the wolf tribe. And then it came to me that as I call people to this work I will be honoring these same qualities within them—calling these qualities forward, the extraordinary bravery and nobility that lie within each of them. To take a stand like this in a world such as ours that denies the reality of this sort of inner work is a brave thing to do.

"I honor you," I said to all these as yet unmet friends, "for having the courage to take a stand. Tell others about the Net of Light," I said, "use it, use it every day and together we will strengthen it. This is the great Net of Light the Grandmothers have said will hold the earth steady during these times of change that are upon us."

"Whoosh," I exclaimed as I let my breath go with force. I had just realized how this message had come about. It had started as an inner prompting to do service of some kind, which I had brought to the Grandmothers' group. We discussed how we might do some sort of service and decided to act on the Grandmothers request to use the Net of Light to call people to their own lighted path. After that meeting Wolf appeared in my dream and after that, in a journey. One thing had led to another, with no idea of where it was heading. "It's true that the Divine works in mysterious ways," I said to myself. "And here I am now, as I've been so many other times before—stumbling along toward paradise."

I did as Wolf asked—sent his message to as many sources as I could think of and the responses that came back to me were almost overwhelming. People from every corner of the globe wrote, saying they would work with the Net of Light. Some of them even decided to start Grandmothers' groups. Clearly Wolf knew what he was doing when he told me to "Call your tribe."

"These are the times of change. They are upon you now and they will continue."

Shortly after this, I journeyed to the Grandmothers. Again I was in distress. "Grandmothers," I said, "I've come to ask you what to do. They are burning people alive in South Africa. A friend who lives there asked if the Grandmothers would please help. And while this and other horrors are taking place in Africa, people in our country are losing their jobs and homes, there are devastating earthquakes and floods in Asia, and the war in the Middle East goes on and on. "The times of change" you've been telling us about have definitely arrived. Grandmothers," I said, "you've given us the Net of Light and we're grateful to be able to work with it to support the earth, but can you tell us something to help us understand these changes that are happening so quickly and dramatically?"

As I stood before them, I became aware of the power of their circle. The Grandmothers were sitting on the ground, a familiar stone from the Stone Circle fronted each one and when I stepped into their midst, spherical waves began to spin round me, drawing me into closer and closer union with them. Someone began the song, "Where I stand is holy; holy is the ground." The Grandmothers sang it, and then they spoke. **"Anchor yourself,"** they said; **"this circle will anchor you."** "Yes, Grandmothers," I replied, and as I spoke, I felt the gyrations of the spinning waves drawing me into further union with them and the earth. Out of the corner of my eye I glimpsed what looked like a wine opener that turned clockwise, as it screwed itself into the earth and as I watched it turn, I realized that I was this corkscrew, that I was becoming more deeply fastened to the Mother.

"Anchored like this, you will be immune from the panic gripping much of the world. There is economic fear in your country and in others too. Instability everywhere. Like the fire you mentioned in South Africa, billowing fear is growing. Blazing across the cultures and continents of the world," they said; **"it will not affect you as long as you stay anchored to us. Screw yourself deeply into Mother Earth and watch from there."**

"This way you won't be swept away or react to the changes sweeping across the world," they nodded encouragement, **"and neither will you lull yourself into a false sense of security and ignore the obvious. You will be able to stay tuned to 'reality,' move and act in a real way, but not be overburdened by seriousness. You will be able to enjoy your life, stay awake at the switch, and be of service to others. Now doesn't that sound good?"** they asked and gave me a big smile. Clearly they were not as upset about the changes on earth as I was.

"These *are* the times of change. They are upon you now and they will continue. No matter how much you long for the past, there will be no returning to the old ways." And no sooner were these words out of their mouths than wind and water blew fiercely, whirling and scouring the earth. It was a deluge and I watched palm trees bend parallel to the ground as a hurricane-force wind blasted them.

Indeed, this was a time to move deep into the earth. This was where the only source of peace and safety would be. "Grandmothers," I asked as I watched the wildness of the weather, "is what I'm seeing here figurative or literal? I mean," I continued, my voice shaking with fright, "is the earth going to be blasted like this, or is this a demonstration of what will occur in our consciousness?" The Grandmothers gave a faint smile, but shook their heads and didn't say anything.

At last they spoke. **"Do not try to save yourself."** They had read my mind; I was about to ask if there was a safe haven somewhere. **"Do not separate yourself from life by trying to make yourself special and separate. You are not separate. All of you are one; you don't yet understand what this means, but you will.**

"Work with the Net of Light that holds and upholds your planet. Send light and give love to one another, and then give more of it. Affirm your communion with everything that lives and where there is an opportunity to assist life, take it!" they said with feeling. "This will fill you with joy and increase your life force.

"As these times of change arrive, people will begin to search for how they can save themselves, what they need to hoard, where they can hide, how they can prepare, etc, etc," they said, shrugging at the futility of such actions. "We tell you," they said, and they looked so stern that I sat up straighter; "you cannot save yourself. It is not within your power to do so, so give it up," they said, throwing their hands in the air. "Such thinking is foolishness. It is nonsense. How does a thread remove itself from the tapestry of which it is a part, in order to 'save' itself? Nonsense," they repeated.

"Send love," they said, nodding emphatically, "give love. Dive into life and serve wherever you can. You will never be able to figure out what is happening now on your planet, no matter how long you live or how hard you try. What is transpiring is beyond your comprehension. And," they said, appraising me from under raised brows, "the pace of change is accelerating so quickly that your mind cannot follow it." Shaking their heads, they said, "Keep it simple. Love and serve, love and serve.

"We have given you the Net of Light," they said. "Use it! Hold the Net steady while it holds you and cast it wherever there is need. As you do this your sense of union with the Divine will grow and grow, giving you the joy of your life." They stood back then, surveyed me, and smiled. "This is the joy you were born for. Cast the Net of Light!" they commanded. "You were born for these times. Do not back off now and huddle fearfully in the dark. Dive in!"

CHAPTER 18

The Grandmothers' Workbook

"These are tools for furthering individual empowerment."

"Knowing about' something, even 'knowing' it is not the same thing as living it. The Grandmothers' meditations are therefore designed to give a visceral understanding of the truths they have come to impart. Some of the meditations in this book have been gathered together here so the reader can easily access them.

These teachings contain layers of meaning and are **"tools for furthering individual empowerment."** Whether or not you have chosen to receive the Grandmothers' Empowerment, these tools will help you put their work into practice. **"These meditations anchor our teachings, allowing our lessons to go deeply into the viscera of your body/mind and be held there. Then they can become your own truth. When you have owned and taken in these truths, they will no longer be just thoughts that pass through your mind, but will be deeply known."**

The Grandmothers' meditations create change. Not intellectual exercises, they are opportunities to experience another way of being. This part of the book is a workbook for those who seek an active part in this work. Some meditations are simple, while others are more complex, but all of them are designed to help you heal, balance and expand your awareness and consciousness. And as this happens, you will by your very being, bless all life on earth. You can, if you like, record these meditations so you can listen directly to the power in the Grandmothers' words.

Preliminary Relaxation Exercise

If you are unfamiliar with meditating, this simple method will bring you to a point of relaxation, enabling you to work with the Grandmothers. Use it as needed to precede the following meditations.

To begin, find a place where you can be alone, take a seat and once you have, think of why you are doing this. What is it you want from this experience? You may be curious about these so-called Grandmothers, or you may want to open yourself to the presence of the Divine. Be clear about what you are seeking as you approach this work. Your clarity honors them and you. *This is your intention.*

Once you have taken your seat, let your body assume an open position. Uncross your hands and feet, unless you are sitting cross-legged on the floor, and take a moment to notice how perfectly the chair or the floor supports you. They support us at every moment, though we are seldom aware of it. Feel your contact with the chair or floor and notice how comfortable or uncomfortable you are.

How is your body occupying space? Where is its weight placed? Notice your entire body. Are your feet heavy on the floor? Do you feel your feet? Take the time you need to settle in and observe your total self with a somewhat disinterested air, like taking inventory. Is your heart beating fast or slowly? Is the rhythm of your breath regular or irregular? *Just notice.*

Take in a slow, deep breath and as you exhale, think of letting go of the old (old thoughts, old attitudes, old air) and when you inhale, think of taking in the new. Close your eyes and do this three or four times, feeling your breath moving in and out with a deep, slow rhythm. *Letting go of the old, opening to the new.*

Observe your heart beating and notice its rhythm. Is it slowing down? Speeding up? What is the temperature of your body? Your heart may beat fast or steadily. Your body may feel warm or cool. You may be tense or relaxed as you begin, but don't try to change anything about yourself. Don't force yourself to "try" to relax. Simply observe without judging yourself. *Observe and take your time.*

Notice where your body feels tight and where it feels softer, if you are holding your breath or breathing fast or slow ly. No judgment. No hurry. *Just keep observing* without evaluating yourself and when you are ready you can let the Grandmothers know you'd like to begin.

Meditation on living as the Container that You Are

Perhaps one of the strongest and most telling qualities of yin energy is its ability to hold, accept and nurture whatever presents itself. When we don't push against something, don't exclude or judge anything or anyone, but instead bring whatever comes onto our lap and hold it there so it can settle into itself and find its place, we allow yin to work through us. Not dramatizing the challenge of the moment, not being transfixed by the horror of the moment, but simply being *with* the moment. This quality of nurturing acceptance belongs to the Mother, and we ourselves can open like this to the Feminine Principle and deal with people, ideas, and situations—in short, with everything—in this way. Accepting, accepting. Initially this may seem a strange idea to you—a foreign idea but that is only because this concept has been missing from our world for a long time.

A position of openness and acceptance creates a force field of harmony. There is an undeniable greatness in what the Grandmothers call the *Container.* "She who holds" accepts what is, and this acceptance allows everyone and everything to relax and be who and what they are. Held by and at one with the Container, we become 'real.' And because this is so, this meditation creates a foundation for harmonious relationships. It harmonizes women and men, seeming opposites, yin and yang.

"It's time to experience the container that you are," the Grandmothers say. **"You are the container that holds love, that holds life, and supports everything that lives. Your capacity is enormous. Become aware of yourself."**

To experience yourself as this Container they speak of, begin by moving into a state of relaxation, sitting with your arms and legs uncrossed and your spine straight. Place your hands palms up on your lap and notice what it's like for you to sit in such an open posture. How does your body feel as you sit this way? How do you feel? As you do this, don't judge yourself or try to change anything about yourself—just notice. And as you sit, you will find yourself dropping into a deeply receptive state, the position of the Container. Open and receptive to whatever comes. This position evokes the presence of the Great Mother—She who accepts all life and holds everything. As you sit this way, you may become aware that She is with you, holding you and at the same moment, She is sitting inside you. Take a few minutes to enjoy your powerful connection with the Great Mother by being open and receptive.

As you sit, you may also become aware of the chair underneath you and the support you are being given by both the chair and the floor. At this very moment you are in your right place.

Now take a moment to invite in whatever comes onto the screen of your mind. Let it come up as it will, and when something appears, quietly hold it there. Simply hold whatever shows itself. Don't move toward it, and don't move away from it. Let it come to you and be with you for as long as it wants, and when it gets up and leaves, accept and hold whatever comes next.

You will find you are able do this because you are a container and this is what a container does. It holds. A container is not the least affected by what fills it. If you pour water into a pot, the pot is unchanged. If you pour milk into it, it is still unchanged. Become aware of how it feels to simply hold like this—just for this moment, unaffected by whatever comes to your mind. No judgment, no evaluation, and if judgment should appear, well, hold judgment in this nonjudgmental way too.

The Grandmothers are performing this action with you—holding you and holding with you so you can learn what it's like to be the container you actually are. **"In the vastness of your being, you can do this,"** they say. **"You are great enough to hold everything."** At this moment you may become aware of the truth in their words: that just for now you *can* accept and hold everything.

A succession of people, problems, and stories may parade through your mind. Let them come. You can sit there, and knowing that the Grandmothers are present with you, holding you, you can relax and watch the parade. Like me, you may discover it's a lot like being at the movies. Scenes come and go, rise up and fall away, and should a scene stay on for a while, hoping perhaps to become the main feature, let it. Simply hold. **"Hold, hold, hold,"** the Grandmothers say, for as long as is needed and while you're holding, be aware of your body too and notice how you're feeling. What is it like to be a container?

"As you go through life," the Grandmothers say, **"stay within the awareness of the container that you are and hold whatever comes to you. Hold it as a basin holds water or as a planter holds earth. Water does not change the shape or color of a basin. Earth does not alter the size or shape of a pot. A container is. It holds. *You* hold. You can encompass all this because *it is your nature to be the container. This,"* they say, **"is Yin."** Feel it.

Meditation on Blooming as the Flower that You Are

As with all of these meditations, first give yourself enough time to reach a relaxed state. Then as you begin, ask the Grandmothers to come to you so you know they are there, knowing that as soon as you make this request, the Grandmothers will swoop in and surround you.

They are all around you now. In front, behind, above, below, as well as to the sides of you—cradling you in their loving embrace. And among the Grandmothers are also all forms of the Divine. Kwan Yin, Jesus, Mary, Zoroaster. All forms of the Divine are with you in joyous numbers. Invite whatever form is dear to your heart to come close to you now and as you breathe, breathe *with the Divine* so the rhythm of your breath becomes a deepening into oneness with the Source. As you do this, love will permeate your body, penetrate your skin and the organs inside you.

"This is your natural state," the Grandmothers say. "You were born to love and be loved. Everything else is simply a diversion from this. Joyous, happy presence is your home and at a time of so much darkness and horror on earth, it is true joy to be at one with what is real.

"Here there is a joyous bloom of love. You are blooming. Each time you breathe with the Divine as you are now, you expand, soften, and become more of who you really are. Not that brittle, busy person the mind tells you, you are, but who you *really* are. The core of you that is limitless, the you that knows and feels the truth."

After you have breathed with the Divine for a few minutes, the Grandmothers will move inside your heart and take up residence there. You may see or sense them sitting inside your expanding heart. "We come into your heart," they say, "and as we do, your heart opens more fully. It blooms."

Notice what you are feeling at this point, and if you like, you can invite them to enter your heart more completely and if you say 'yes' to this, they will. As they anchor their energy inside you, you will feel a change begin. Any nonsensical stuff your mind may be jabbering about will quickly fall away. All the worries, fears, and labels the mind tries to give you will also disappear. The presence of the Grandmothers will create such a forcefield that there will no longer be room for that.

Breathe with them as they sit inside your heart. You breathe with them and they breathe with you, and with every breath you take, you draw them more deeply into yourself. Also, each time you breathe out, old blockages that may in the past have prevented you from receiving their presence, will leave effortlessly.

At this moment love is beginning to bloom inside your heart. Notice how you feel and what it's like to be centered here, observing while your heart continues to expand and deepen. This beautiful organ is beginning to form a pattern now, taking on the shape of a flower. Watch with a gentle curiosity and enjoy the transformation that is taking place inside you.

As your heart moves into the form of a flower, pay attention to the color it takes. This will be a hue that resonates with you. And as its petals form, also notice the movement, shape and direction they take.

As the flower of your heart expands, become aware of its softness and living quality—how big it is and how resonant. Soft and yet strong, it will begin to surge and swell and, as it expands, the hard and hurtful places inside you begin to fall off. Throughout our lifetime, most of us have taken a lot of things to heart and these have formed blockages that obstruct the flow of love inside us. As your heart opens more, these blocks begin to drop off—no need to hold on and no need to hold back. At every moment, your heart is becoming stronger and softer and from the center of your heart where they have taken up residence, the Grandmothers smile at you.

Again, notice how you feel. Warm? Cool? Soft? Tight? Sad? Peaceful? *Just notice,* and open to the freedom and joy now coursing though your heart. New energy is now lining the walls of your cells. So much old material is being removed, that new energy is flowing into places that haven't seen the light of day in a long time. You are filling with joy. In fact, even the room where you are sitting is filling with joy. How do you feel? Observe your body and the way you're breathing. Just notice.

You may also see and sense color as the flower that you are comes into full bloom. **"Each flower, each bloom is perfect,"** the Grandmothers say, so once you become aware of the flower at the center of your chest, place your hands over it to honor it—your heart—this beautiful organ. There is a great sweetness here, sweetness and depth.

Whenever you work like this you will become aware of painful places too. Little corners where energy has been blocked off begin to awaken. Don't worry about these pockets of pain, but let them be revealed and know that this is a normal occurrence, temporary, and a sign of your heart opening.

The capacity of your heart is growing. Now it can receive more love. Because you are enlarging the place where they live, your capacity for radiance and beauty is also increasing. These qualities live in your heart and spread throughout your body, throughout your mind and then into the world. Here is where the core of your beauty/power lies and as soon as you recognize it, you will feel it. Power/Beauty *is* one and *this* is what you are. In fact, this is all you are. Everything else is a passing show. The flower of your heart is perfect and at this moment you are beginning to experience it.

Turn your attention to the special beauty of the flower within you—its color, movement, shape, and petals. What is it like? Now take a moment to express gratitude to your heart for being the repository of such glory. And as you do, you'll feel how grateful your heart is for being recognized. It's been waiting a long time for this. Now there is a lovely flow of love and gratitude between you and your heart, between your heart and you.

The Grandmothers, say, **"As you focus in your heart, every breath you take in enables this organ to grow in beauty. The petals of your heart/flower will open wider while its color becomes deeper and more vivid. Each of you is unique in your beauty/power, unique in your expression of the Divine. In a garden every flower is unique, so with reverence for this divine unfolding within, experience the quality of that flower that you are."**

Stay with this experience long enough to register how you are feeling, and then see yourself standing tall and walking forward in your own distinctive beauty. As you step forward, notice how the glow of your radiant heart precedes you. A brightness goes before you, and after you pass, this brightness leaves an afterglow. This is your signature, the specific way that God expresses through you. Feel it and sense it, and as you walk forward be aware of the shimmering trace you leave behind. This is one way the flower you are expresses itself on earth.

Take a breath and as you exhale, reverently bow to your own preciousness. At this very moment you are in fact blooming as the flower that you have always been and always will be. How does it feel to recognize *yourself*? Notice your response, and *feel it*.

The Grandmothers say, **"We salute the beauty/power, the power/beauty that you are."**

Meditation on Holding a Sacred Space

"This is what each of you must do," the Grandmothers say. **"Tell all who work with us to hold a sacred space, to claim and hold it."** They ask us to do this always and wherever we are and, by so doing, re-sanctify not only our lives, but the very earth itself. **"There is no mundane world,"** they say. **"This world is sacred and the commitment to hold a sacred space is everything. This is primary."**

First we need the commitment to hold and claim sacred space, so to begin this meditation, give yourself permission to relax, and once you have, call on the Grandmothers. Sit tall, uncross your arms and legs and place your hands on your knees. As you take this posture, you convey your readiness to make this commitment. While you sit quietly, think of your desire to take this step and then let the Grandmothers know you're ready to live your life in sacred space, in touch with and at one with the Divine—not just some of the time, but all the time.

When the Grandmothers showed me how to claim sacred space they stood directly before me and stepped forward, first with their left foot and then with their right. As I watched I remembered that the left side of the body is the feminine or receptive side, so it made sense to initiate this movement on the left.

"The thought while stepping forward," the Grandmothers said, **"is to send energy downward through your foot so it sinks into the earth. Take only one step with each foot,"** they said, **"and as you do, think and say, 'Here I hold a sacred space.' You may also say, 'I hold a sacred space for the good of myself and all beings."**

It's time for you to do the same thing. After you have moved into a relaxed state, call on the Grandmothers and let them know you want to hold a sacred space, then stand up and when you feel firmly balanced, take a step forward with your left foot. As your weight transfers, think of energy pouring through the bottom of your foot into the earth, diving down through the subterranean layers of the planet and anchoring you deeply to Mother Earth. Down, down, down the energy plunges. You have begun the process of holding sacred space.

After you've taken this first step, turn your awareness inward and notice how you feel. How does this act register in your body? How do you feel and where do you feel it? Observe what's happening inside you and ask your brain to record the process.

It's time to do the same thing with your right foot, and after you have, stand quietly, and again notice how you feel. What is your body telling you? At this moment you are rooted in and rooted to the earth. This stance anchors power, and as you feel it you may be surprised to notice that all fear has left you. Fear cannot withstand the power of sacred space.

Breathe in deeply and own the space you have claimed. You are anchored to the Mother, steady and secure. Feel it and declare it. You may say, "Here I hold a sacred space," or "I do this for the good of myself and all beings." Let this be your vow, as you own the power of sacred connection.

"Do not forget to take this step," the Grandmothers say. **"In the times that are approaching, many will panic, but you need not. Simply choose to hold a sacred space, and then do it. Hold,"** they say, **"and tell others to do the same. Now is the time to step forward and claim sacred space. Once you consciously make this commitment, no matter what happens around you, no matter where you find yourself, you will not forget that you are holding sacred space."**

This exercise is what we call an active meditation—one that involves the body as well as the mind. You can, of course, perform it only in your mind, and not move your body, but most of us find that bringing our physical selves into the act makes for a stronger experience. Many say it also strengthens their commitment. And for this reason, holding and claiming sacred space is a potent exercise to perform in a group.

"**Taking the step to hold a sacred space, and doing it in a public way, will strengthen your resolve and make you conscious of having taken a stand,**" the Grandmothers say. "**It's a decision not to be caught in the ephemeral, willow-the-wisp activities of daily life, but to claim sacred space now and forevermore—for yourself and all beings. *This step* can be taken only in selfless love.**" Those of us who practice this meditation find that it strengthens us. It is also an offering.

"***This* is what it means to become a Grandmother,**" the Grandmothers say, "**and this is what is needed now.**"

Working with the Circle of Stones

When people began to tell me they were having difficulty using the shamanic method of journeying to the Grandmothers, I asked the Grandmothers for a simple, safe, and easy way that those who wanted to, could use to work with them. That was when they gave us the Circle of Stones.

To introduce to me the Circle of Stones the Grandmothers sat themselves down on the ground, forming a circle with a large, smooth stone facing each Grandmother. "**This circle is a sacred space, an opening to the great below and the great above,**" they said. "**You need no longer journey in the old way, unless it's something you enjoy doing,**" they said. "**Instead, you can let *us* call the spirits to you.**

"**This way of working will be easier for many people, because they won't have to perform the work alone, but can journey to different levels of non-ordinary reality under our guidance and protection. We will be there to show them the way and help them get to where it is they want to go. For this method,**" they explained, "**we will work with you and you will work with us.**" What follows here is not a meditation, nor is it a lesson in shamanic journeying. (That subject would require a book in itself.) What follows is a simple way of working, one you can use yourself in order to communicate with the Great Council of the Grandmothers.

To experience what it's like to journey with the Grandmothers, think of them sitting directly before you, in formation with the Circle of Stones described above. Then walk forward until you are standing in their midst.

"**Feel your place in this circle,**" the Grandmothers say, "**and remember that all forms of the Divine are with us as we work together. You are an integral part of this circle, and the fact that you are *part* of this circle, and not separate from it, is important. You are one with us,**" they say, "**one with the Divine, and this is true for everyone who chooses to work with us. Also, once you step into this circle, you will become the focus of the entire circle. Your questions will be answered here.**

"**Ask only one question each time you step into the circle and just as in shamanism,**" they say, "**everything you hear, see, and experience after your question will be in response to it. So pay attention to what happens after you ask, and do not stray from your question.**" In the years I've done this I've learned you can journey to the monotonous beat of a drum, to the swish/swish of your windshield wipers, or to any repetitive sound. And somewhere between ten and thirty minutes will give you enough time for a journey.

To form your question for the Grandmothers, ask about something you have already put some energy into and don't ask a 'yes' or 'no' question as a response to a yes/no question won't give you much information. We journey to non-ordinary reality to learn, so ask the Grandmothers something you *really* want to know. We could speak a long time about the importance of honing *the* question for them, but for now let me suggest that you begin your journey to the Grandmothers in humility, asking something that will help others in addition to yourself. The Divine *is* compassion and therefore operates on compassion. So if your question has to do with being of service in the world, it is much more likely to be answered.

You will be able to enter both the upper and the lower world from the middle of the Circle of Stones. But since journeying is not the subject of this book, I will not go into what working in these worlds is like. However, those of you who have some experience in the shamanic method may wish to try out the Grandmothers' route to see how you like it. The Circle of Stones is designed to make journeying simpler, safer, and easier and as I mentioned, everything in non-ordinary reality can be explored by starting from the center of their circle.

Once you have formulated your question, think of stepping between two Grandmothers seated on the ground near you and walk into the middle of their circle. Greet the Grandmothers, then humbly and sincerely ask your question. After you've done that, notice what comes to you. What do you see? Hear? Touch? Feel? Think? Smell? Taste? The Grandmothers may tell you something, show you something, or allow you to experience something. These journeys to and with the Grandmothers can be emotional events and surprising as well. The Grandmothers know how to circumvent the limitations of your mind and go directly to your heart. They know exactly what it will take to bring you to an understanding of the question you have asked, and that is what they will give you.

Once you've asked, open your mind wide and *observe*. Be curious about the process you're involved in and while you're noticing whatever it is you're noticing, remind yourself not to judge your experience, the Grandmothers, or yourself. *Just observe.* The Grandmothers are consummate teachers and know what they are doing so let the good student you are turn your awareness to whatever comes to you. You may find it helpful to speak your journey into a recorder so you won't have to struggle to remember everything that happens with the Grandmothers. Also, if you record it, you can go back later and listen to what transpires during your adventure.

When you make the decision to step into the Grandmothers' circle, you enter the realm of non-ordinary reality and when you step out of their circle, you make the decision to return to ordinary reality. So after your journey is over, thank the Grandmothers for having given you this time with them and then respectfully step out of the Circle of Stones.

When we journey to and with the Grandmothers, we do so to learn how to be of greater service in the world we live in. Working with the Grandmothers is not meant as an escape from the pain of the world but as a means of being of service *in* and *for* this world and all worlds. To be effective in the world, you must keep your feet on the ground so I suggest you journey to the Grandmothers no more than two or three times a week.

Meditation on the Power in the Wings

The power of yin energy is entirely different from the power of yang, which for most of us, is the only 'power' we have ever known. Because for several thousand years our world has been dominated by yang, it can be difficult for us to get beyond our conditioning and experience what the power of yin is. But by teaching us how to work with symbols, and thus with our subconscious minds, the Grandmothers show us new ways to experience yin. As they activate the power of our "wings," they awaken the power and dignity inherent within us.

To experience the power in these wings, begin this meditation as you would always do. Take time to get yourself to that relaxed state, and when you have, begin to think of the power of eagles and other raptors. What must it be like to rise into the air, to swoop and glide on mighty wings? Imagine it.

Allow yourself to think of possessing a pair of wings like these, wings that attach at your shoulders and back. Just think the thought, and then playfully and with a great deal of curiosity, open to the idea of having wings of your own. Focus on the area of your shoulder blades. **"As you focus on your wings,"** the Grandmothers say, **"you will feel *our* light shining and filtering through them. We will support you in the work you do, happy to see you explore your potential.**

"What we are doing now is play, but it is not idle play. Because our work is based on service," they explain, **"the power in these wings will serve the greater good. The wings we speak of are vehicles for power and care-giving on earth. We are happy to see you getting to know this aspect of yourself.**

"Few people have sensed this power within," they say. And if we were to talk about opening to the power of the wings with most people, you can imagine the reception we would receive. However, the Grandmothers declare that only certain ones will be drawn to their work, and since they have drawn us, we will go where they are leading us. To experience the power inherent in your wings, the Grandmothers ask you to be brave and for a minute or two, throw caution to the winds. Experiment. We will work together with the symbol of wings to experience them as a vehicle of power.

Think of a great raptor and when one comes to mind, stand up and stretch your arms out to the side, as wide as you can, making a 'T' with your body. Try this posture on for size and see how it feels to stand like this. Be sure to space your feet wide enough apart so you're balanced and comfortable as you hold the position.

When I first began to own the power of my wings, I extended my arms out and then flexed them in a waving motion, just as a bird would. And for me this movement was back and forth, rather than up and down. But either way is fine. I noticed that each time I flexed like this, the center of my back seemed to grow more supple, to open wider, while my neck rolled forward and backward, forming a graceful arc, and as all this took place I became aware of the grace and power in this movement. So now take a few minutes to play with *your* wings. Up and down, back and forth—play.

Breathe in rhythm with your flexing wings and as you breathe, a nimbus of light will begin to glow inside and around you. Your back will stretch wider until the reach of your arms begins to feel enormous. The Grandmothers tell us, **"There is power in the wings; this** work will stretch your idea of who you are. It will stretch you into greatness."

After you have expanded your wings and your idea of who you are for a minute or two, rest quietly and observe your body. How do you feel now? How are you breathing? If you were to describe what this is like for you, what would you say about the state you're in at this moment?

Once you have the feeling of these wings, try something else. Stand with your upper arms extended to the side, and bend your elbows so your hands face the sides of your head and point upward. Keep your spine straight and your head up. This commanding posture speaks of queenliness. You may have seen it. This is the posture of the ancient goddess of Crete, the one with snakes wound around her arms.

Feel the power in this stance. This position is another testament to the Grandmothers' statement, **"There is power in the wings."** It is difficult, perhaps even impossible, to disparage or demean yourself when you stand in this position. A posture like this challenges you to be the great one you were born to be.

Meditation on the Net of Light

We conclude this chapter and this book with a meditation on the Net of Light. The Grandmothers ask us to do this meditation often, in order to extend the grace of this lighted support system to everyone and everything on Earth.

"Begin to work with the Net of Light," they say, **"by thinking of a vast lighted fishing net spread over the earth and stretching into the distance, as far as your eyes can see. This is the great Net of Light that will support the earth and all life on this planet during the times of change that have come. The Net of Light covers the earth from above, it covers it from below, and it bisects the earth like a great grid—penetrating, holding, and touching everything. This is the Net of Light that will hold the earth while the energies of yin and yang shift. And they *will* shift,"** the Grandmothers say; **"the change has already begun.**

"Walk forward and take your place on the Net of Light. Somewhere where two of the strands come together forming an 'x' or a 't' is a place that will feel just right for you. Walk forward and take your place there. Here you can rest and allow the Net of Light to hold and support you while at the same time you support it.

"We have many times told you that the Net of Light is lit by

the jewel of the heart. This is true," the Grandmothers say. "Experience now as the radiant jewel of your own heart begins to open and broadcast its light along the strands of the Net. Every person who works with the Net of Light is linked in light with others who also work with it. Experience your union with people all over the globe who are now connected by the Net of Light. Some of them call it a Web of Light, some call it a lighted grid, some call it Indra's net, but whatever they call it, it is the same construct. This is the Net of Light that will hold the earth steady during these times of change that are upon you.

"As you call on the Net and find your place on it," they say, "think of receiving and sending light throughout this vast network. And as you think this thought, instantly your energy will follow it, and you will feel the Net of Light working in you and through you.

"Experience your union with us and with all those who work with us. There are thousands of you all over the earth. Also experience your union with the sacred and holy places on this planet and the sacred and holy beings that have come at this time to avert the catastrophe that looms over the earth—the great saints, sages and avatars that have come now and gladly give their lives in service. Experience your union also with those of good heart who seek the highest good for life on earth. Know and feel the power of this union and let your body experience this force of and for good.

"Once you have strongly felt this power, begin to cast the Net of Light to those who do not know about it. Cast wherever there is suffering on earth," they say, "to human beings, to animals, to conditions of every kind, to all forms of life, and to Mother Earth herself. Cast also to people who are longing to serve, but have not yet found a way to access the Divine and as you cast the Net of Light, many who have until this moment been asleep to the fundamental connection we all share, will begin to awaken and feel the spark of divinity within themselves coming to life. Now ask the radiant Net of Light to hold all life in its embrace and know that each time you work like this, you are adding to the reach and power of the great Net.

"Cast the Net to all women and men everywhere," they say. "Cast to the leaders of this world to remind them that they are a precious part of the Net of Light that holds and supports life. Cast to the animal kingdom, asking that every animal receive what it most needs. Cast to the plant kingdom and to the mineral kingdom as well. Cast to everything that lives," the Grandmothers say, "and when you have done this, ask, 'May everyone in all the worlds be happy.'

"This," they say, "is how to work with the Net of Light. There is no greater service you can perform. We ask that you give from your heart and work with the Net of Light every day. Do this for yourself, and do it for the sake of everything that lives.

"We bless you."

ABOUT THE AUTHOR

 SharonMcErlane has been a teacher and marriage and family therapist for more than three decades, teaching techniques for spiritual and emotional integration to guide people on their life's path. She is also an accomplished artist and gardener and has created an environment in her home and garden that many consider sacred space. She is married with two grown children and lives with her husband in Laguna Beach, California.

Closing Note from the Author

My work with the Grandmothers continues, and so whenever they give me a new lesson, I pass it on. Now people all over the world are sharing the Grandmothers' teachings, meeting to study their lessons and pass their empowerment on to others. As the holiness that lives at the core of these people awakens, they open to their loving connection to one another as well as to the Divine, and begin to live the Grandmothers' message. Many of them are active in passing on the Grandmothers' Empowerment, and a listing of empowerment groups can be found at grandmothersspeak.com.

I do not know where the Grandmothers' work will take me next, but the journey with them has been so enriching that I will go wherever they lead. As the Grandmothers say, **"There is great joy in being on the ride with us."**